TO WEAVE FOR THE SUN

Andean Textiles in the Museum of Fine Arts, Boston

REBECCA STONE-MILLER

With contributions by: ANNE PAUL SUSAN A. NILES MARGARET YOUNG-SÁNCHEZ

MUSEUM OF FINE ARTS, BOSTON

This catalogue is published in conjunction with the exhibition "To Weave for the Sun: Andean Textiles in the Museum of Fine Arts, Boston," August 7–November 15, 1992. The exhibition and catalogue have been made possible by grants from Malden Mills Industries, Inc., and the National Endowment for the Arts, a Federal agency. Additional support has been provided by Borden Manufacturing Co., Carolina Mills, Inc., Doran Textiles, Inc., E. I. du Pont de Nemours & Co., Lewistown Specialty Yarns, Inc., Monarch Knitting Machine Co., and Unifi, Inc.

Designed by Carl Zahn
Edited by Margaret Jupe
Typeset in Bitstream Candida on the Macintosh computer by Carl Zahn, Jane Dineen, and Acme Printing Co., Wilmington, Massachusetts
Printed by Acme Printing Co.
Bound by Acme Bookbinding Co., Charlestown, Massachusetts

All photographs except those listed below are by the Department of Photographic Services, Museum of Fine Arts, Boston: p. 37, fig. III.8, Museum Rietberg, Zurich; p. 58, fig. V.9, The Textile Museum, Washington, D.C.; p. 63, fig. V.17, Peabody Museum of Natural History, Yale University.

Cover: Mantle or shroud (detail, upper left corner rotated 90°). Early Colonial, Neo-Inca Culture, about A.D. 1550; interlocked tapestry, overstitched edging. Charles Potter Kling Fund. 1988.325

Frontispiece: Checkerboard tunic. Late Horizon, Inca Culture, A.D. 1476–1534; interlocked tapestry, embroidery. William Francis Warden Fund. 47.1097

TO WEAVE FOR THE SUN

for Doug, Dylan, Sunday, and Monster

◼◼ ACKNOWLEDGMENTS ◼◼

Many people have ably and generously assisted me with this important study of the collection of Andean textiles in the Museum of Fine Arts, Boston. First, I am grateful to Alan Shestack, director of the Museum, for providing me with the opportunity to undertake this challenging project and for his enthusiastic support. To the contributing authors of the catalogue, Anne Paul, Susan Niles, and Margaret Young-Sánchez, I express my profound thanks for sharing with me their impressive knowledge on all occasions, as well as for their promptness in meeting deadlines and patience with the slow procedures of an endeavor of this magnitude. Other scholars also unstintingly lent me their expert opinions: I gratefully acknowledge the help of Susan Bruce, Ann Pollard Rowe, Tom Cummins, and John P. O'Neill.

At the Museum of Fine Arts many departments and individuals worked tirelessly to bring the project to a successful conclusion. First and foremost, the Department of Textiles and Costumes dedicated themselves to this undertaking over a number of years. Deborah Kraak, former assistant curator, gracefully balanced all the demands of coordinating the research, the catalogue, and the exhibition with the rest of her many tasks. It was a privilege and a pleasure to work with her. Conservation played a large part in the final appearance of the Andean textiles featured in this volume. Deborah Bede, associate curator, and Jane K. Hutchins, former conservator, carefully evaluated, conserved, and then shepherded these fragile and often unwieldy masterpieces through the process of photography. They are to be commended for the beautiful results and for their insightful technical observations along the way. The able assistance of Katy Bishop, conservation assistant, Karin von Lerber, Getty Advanced-Level Intern, and Christine Giuntini, consultant, is also greatly appreciated. Other members of the Textiles Department contributed to various aspects of this lengthy endeavor: my thanks go to Marianne Carlano, curator of textiles, for her guidance in the later stages; to Nicola Shilliam, curatorial assistant, for her cheerful responses to my cries for help; to Deborah Abramson and Paula C. Cavaleri, department secretaries, for making endless arrangements; to Isabel Abbott, Ellen Averick,

Hildy Curran, and Moira Sutherland, volunteers, for lending their much needed organizational and clerical help along the way.

The Department of Photographic Services, under the direction of Janice Sorkow, deserves special mention for its part in this project: Nicole Luongo and Mary Lyons processed more than four hundred photographs; and Thomas P. Lang, Gary Ruuska, Marty Wolfand, and John Woolf produced the superb photographs that make the textiles come alive on the pages of the catalogue. Carl Zahn, director of publications, was a joy to work with, and the catalogue's handsome appearance is a testament to his considerable talents as designer. I also greatly appreciated the opportunity to learn from the gifted editor, Margaret Jupe, who so painstakingly labored over the manuscript with me. Jane Dineen, a freelance computer programmer and editor, was indispensable in helping to format the manuscript on the computer. Joan Harlowe and Gilian Wohlauer, of the Department of Education, helped to interpret the exhibition for the public through programs, text panels, and the exhibition brochure. Janet Spitz, former director of development, Jeffrey Wolfman, and Martha Reynolds were instrumental in obtaining grants that made the conservation, publication, and exhibition possible.

Since a major part of this project was completed in Atlanta, there are several people in this city to whom I am indebted for assistance. At Emory University, Valerie Watkins, a graduate student in art history, greatly aided me with the sometimes daunting amount of research necessary to present such a wide-ranging collection. Arlys Evans, Helen Thompson, and Angela Economy, administrative assistants, cheerfully accomplished a great deal of tedious clerical work that was fundamental to the endeavor. On the personal side, I appreciate the help provided by Belle Maddox and especially my cousin Charles Spencer, which allowed me time away from family responsibilities. Most of all, I am very grateful to my husband, Doug, for his understanding and encouragement and to my son, Dylan, for giving me a perspective.

R. S.-M.
June 1992

◖◗ CONTENTS ◖◗

The collection of pre-Columbian and Colonial Andean textiles is among the greatest hidden treasures in the Museum of Fine Arts, and is universally considered to be among the finest collections of these objects in the world. Although the Museum has regularly displayed selections of Andean textiles, a catalogue of sixty-seven objects published in 1932 has constituted the primary publication on the collection until now. The 1992 quincentennial of Columbus's voyage to the Americas presents a fitting opportunity for a thorough examination and publication of these masterpieces of a brilliant and creative indigenous culture, as well as a chance to focus on the extraordinary permanent collections of the Museum of Fine Arts.

When the Museum was incorporated in 1870, Boston was the center of the textile industry in the United States, and many of the Museum's trustees and patrons had a highly sophisticated understanding of the textile arts. Their desire to elevate the quality of industrially produced design in textile arts led to the formation of a collection of textiles, in part to give manufacturers access to well-selected historical examples of design. With the establishment in 1930 of a Department of Textiles, the Museum became the first general art museum in the United States to place textiles on an equal status with other art media in its collections; the textiles and costumes collection has continued to expand, and today comprises more than thirty-five thousand objects.

The history of Andean textiles at the Museum of Fine Arts began with gifts from Edmund Hooper in 1878. The Museum also received substantial gifts of Andean textiles from Denman Waldo Ross in 1916 and again in 1921, and made major purchases in 1931. There are currently approximately 325 Andean works of fiber art in the collection, spanning almost 2,500 years. Among the most intriguing are almost fifty textiles from the Paracas Peninsula, dating from about 200 B.C.–A.D.

200. The Paracas embroideries, along with the Colonial tapestries, are among the largest such collections outside Peru. Post-Paracas textiles include masterpieces of the Nasca, Wari, Late Intermediate, and Inca styles.

In our culture, mass-produced textiles are viewed essentially as functional or decorative articles. Pre-Columbian cultures, on the other hand, placed high value on textiles as ritual and symbolic works of art. Some were sacred objects, while others served as politically charged gifts; textiles which served as garments indicated the wearer's status and function in society, with particular fibers and designs reserved for distinct categories of individuals. Incredibly complex technically, their creation consumed the greatest percentage of human labor in the Andean world. These works of art are a striking testament to the sophisticated artists and civilizations that produced them, and to the important and valued role that textiles played within their societies. The Museum is proud to present *To Weave for the Sun: Andean Textiles in the Museum of Fine Arts, Boston*, in observation of the Columbian anniversary, and is especially grateful to Rebecca Stone-Miller, principal author of the catalogue and guest curator, for her critical role in making this project a reality.

We are also deeply grateful to the National Endowment for the Arts, a Federal agency, and Malden Mills Industries, Inc., for their generous moral and financial support of this project and for helping to underwrite the exhibition and this catalogue. For additional support we are indebted to Borden Manufacturing Co., Carolina Mills, Inc., Doran Textiles, Inc., E. I. du Pont de Nemours & Co., Lewistown Specialty Yarns, Inc., Monarch Knitting Machine Co., and Unifi, Inc.

ALAN SHESTACK
Director

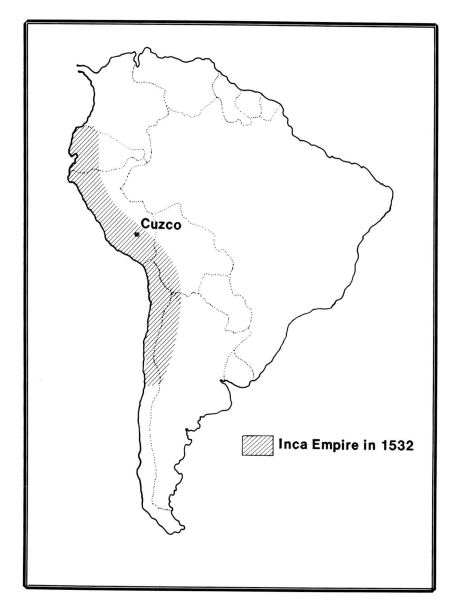

Fig. I.1. South America: The extent of the Inca Empire in 1532
(Drawing by Susan Niles)

Fig. I.2. Major Periods and Cultures of the Ancient Andes

Lithic Period (10,000 B.C.–3000 B.C.)
    Plant-fiber basketry
    (Central Highland site of Guitarrero Cave)

Pre-Ceramic (3000 B.C.–1800 B.C.)
    Twined cotton nonloom textiles, plain weave
    (especially North Coast site of Huaca Prieta)

Early Horizon (1800 B.C.–0)
    Development of all techniques, including triple cloth, tapestry, and embroi-
    dery (especially South Coast: Ica area, Paracas)

Early Intermediate Period (0 –A.D. 500)
    All techniques, especially embroidery and discontinuous warp and weft
    (South Coast: Paracas and Nasca)

Middle Horizon (A.D. 500–800)
    All techniques, especially interlocked tapestry
    (South-Central Highlands to all coasts: Wari and related)

Late Intermediate Period (A.D. 1000–1476)
    All techniques, including slit tapestry, openwork, warp patterning,
    and painting
    (North Coast: Lambayeque, Chimu and related; Central Coast: Chancay, Ri-
    mac; South Coast: Ica)

Late Horizon (A.D. 1476–1534)
    All techniques, especially interlocked tapestry
    (South Highlands to all areas: Inca and related)

Colonial (A.D. 1534–1824)
    Interlocked tapestry (Spanish preference), warp patterning (local continua-
    tion)
    (All areas: Early: neo-Inca, archaizing, 16th –17th century;
    Middle: 17th–18th century, European style dominant;
    Late: 18th–early 19th century, European style dominant)

I. To Weave for the Sun: An Introduction to the Fiber Arts of the Ancient Andes

Rebecca Stone-Miller

It is well known that the Spanish invaders of the Americas, known as conquistadores ("conquerors"), valued gold above all else. Indeed, it was the quest for gold that primarily fueled the search for and ultimately the destruction of what the Europeans saw as a "new" world. However, few realize that the indigenous peoples of the Americas valued other materials more highly. To the Incas, who ruled the Andes of South America, territorially the largest empire in the Renaissance world (fig. I.1), it was the fiber arts that took precedence over other media. As proof, the Incas' first gifts to the European strangers were made of camelid fiber and cotton, not of gold and silver.

The Incas who offered textiles as their most prized possessions were but the capstone to thousands of years of high culture in the rugged and inhospitable Andes; the New World is anything but new. Over the millennia the ancient Andeans had relied heavily on textiles for both survival and artistic expression. In fact, fiber objects have been preserved archaeologically for nearly ten thousand years (Adovasio and Lynch 1973:84–89), that is, since the first evidence of human occupation in western South America (see fig. I.2).

A surprisingly large number of extremely elaborate fabrics still exist, spanning from about 3000 B.C. to the present. They form the longest continuous textile record in world history. Burials in the coastal sand dunes have sheltered these treasures over the centuries (fig. I.3). With this exceptional record come hints of the unsung textile artists who created so many thousands of works of art in fiber.

This publication and exhibition of the remarkable collection of sacred Andean textiles in the Museum of Fine Arts, Boston, mark the quincentenary of Columbus's landfall in the West Indies in 1492 by celebrating indigenous artistic achievement. The title *To Weave for the Sun* encapsulates the Inca belief that the highest form of weaving was made expressly for the sun (*inti*), which they considered the greatest of the celestial powers. They thus endowed woven creations with cosmological power and importance. Although no single phrase could hope to encompass all the nuances of meaning attached to textiles over the thousands of years before and hundreds of years after the Incas, these people serve admirably to summarize Andean traditions as a whole. When the Incas became subjects of the Spanish empire, fine textiles continued to be created and valued despite the many profound changes wrought by the forced melding of cultural opposites. The Incas therefore act as a fitting pivot in the commemorations of 1492, since they stood at the nexus between the ancient and the colonial Americas.

To Weave for the Sun focuses on Andean weavers as creative artists, however unnamed and unknown they may remain. By carefully studying the valued fabrics they so painstakingly wove, we can hope to reconstruct something of their individual contribution to aesthetics, their attitudes, creative process, and the importance they held within their cultures. No artistic system exists apart from its designers, who generate, perpetuate, and innovate within certain cultural boundaries. Through their choices of technology, design, and subject matter all artists reveal themselves and the sociocultural context in which they work, no matter what particular ideas prevail about the role, importance, or individuality of the artists themselves. It is certainly not necessary to adopt a specifically Western definition of the artist in order to call attention to the consciousness behind the finished composition. For example, in the Andes art was largely a collaborative effort, and all pre-Columbian artists, with the exception of a few Inca architects, remain anonymous. Yet this need not interfere in principle with our study of personal contributions to works of art, since strictly biographical knowledge of artistic personalities can be limiting and not necessarily culturally relevant in nonindividualistic societies (Kubler 1962:5–11). Rather, the aesthetic product serves as primary information on an obliterated culture and its artists. It is a fundamental premise of art history that the work of art tells us about the past in a privileged way, if we can learn to read its tale.

How one goes about studying artists through their art alone involves several methods. In particular, clues to the creative process are to be found in unfinished compositions (cat. no. 255, fig. I.4; cat. no. 67, color pl. 9; and cat. no. 71, color pl. 8a,b) and less well preserved pieces (cat. no. 97, fig. I.5). Studies of *series* of similar objects, such as Paracas mantles, are necessary to see how and to what extent people contributed to design in a given period (cat. no. 67, color pl. 9; cat. no. 68, color pl. 12; cat. no. 69, color pl. 5; cat. no. 70, color pl. 13; cat. no. 71, color pl. 8a,b; cat. no. 84, color pl. 10; cat. no. 85, color pl. 6; cat. no. 91, color pl. 7; cat. no. 191, color pl. 11). It is indeed fortunate that the dry sands preserved so many series with which to work! In every case, close observation and analysis are required of all aspects of a piece, from fibers to iconography; yet the scholarly enterprise entails only a fraction of the monumental patience that it took to make the textile in the first place.

In the present catalogue the theme of the artistic presence is explored through various examples: the hands of Paracas embroiderers that can be distinguished through close visual observation (see pp. 25–33); the idiosyncratic Wari design choices that point up widespread interpretation of aesthetic rules by individual tapestry weavers (see pp. 34–42); the multiple substyles within the Late Intermediate Period that suggest a premium was placed on distinctive creative expression (see pp. 43–49); and the varying levels of control over the artist in Inca and early Colonial times (see pp. 50–65). Underlying all these explorations is the identifiable ability of *artists* to determine and interpret design, as opposed to craftspeople approaching fiber via

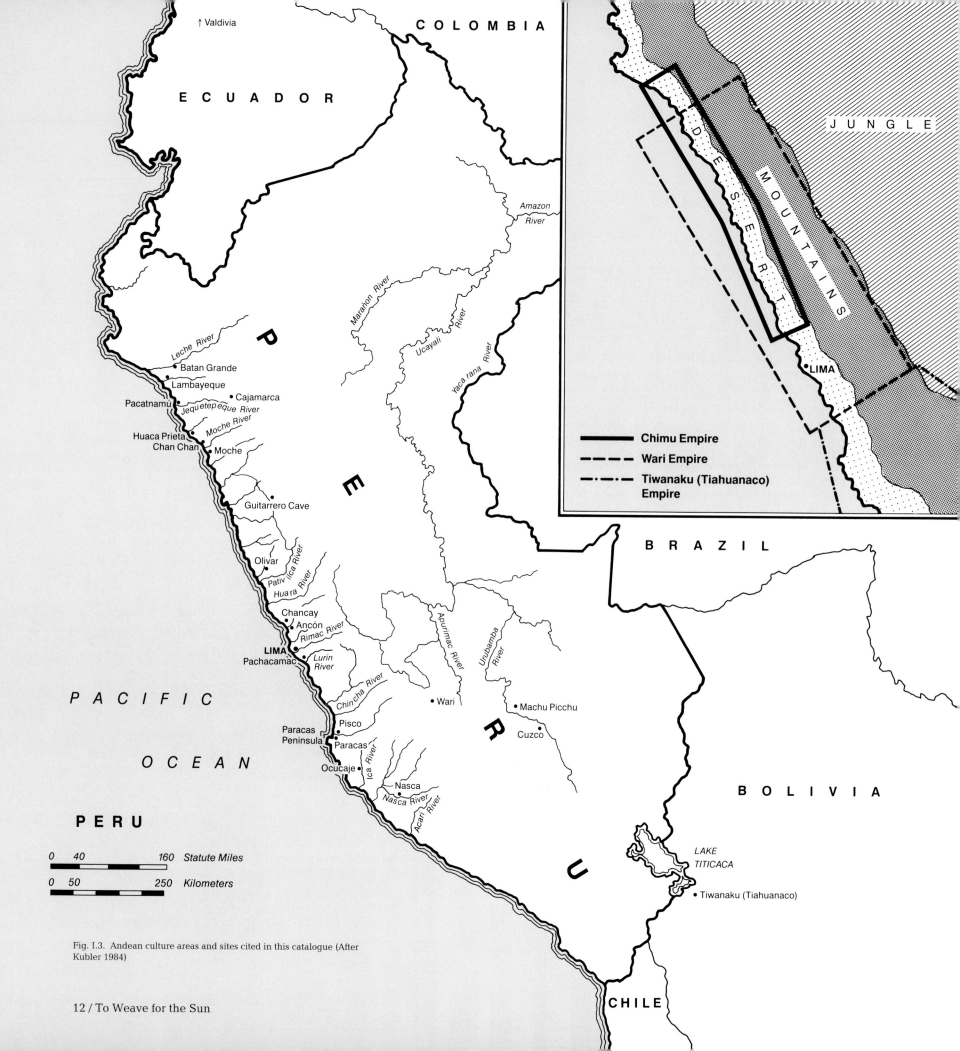

Fig. I.3. Andean culture areas and sites cited in this catalogue (After Kubler 1984)

rote reproduction under the overwhelming weight of "tradition." (Innovation in art is a relative thing; one must use the same criteria for the familiar as for the unfamiliar. For example, in European art there has been an undeniable repetition of a particular mother-and-child scene for over a thousand years, yet we choose to emphasize changes in presentation and details over the obvious continuities of the subject. By contrast, in the study of analogous non-European series of images, continuity is often selectively perceived and change downplayed.)

The great variety of fiber arts created over the ages in western South America certainly should demonstrate that this traditional art form was anything but static. Even individual Andean designs that are predominantly repetitive appear dynamic through creative color patterning and shape asymmetries (cat. no. 312, color pl. 22a,b). And although the textile arts potentially lend themselves to repetitive reproduction of a pattern, because the number of threads in either direction can be counted to make one motif exactly like the last, this practice is not found in the majority of Andean fiber works (see cat. no. 31, fig. I.6; cat. no. 234, color pl. 64; see also pp. 54, 62 with reference to cat. no. 250, color pl. 63). For the sake of visual interest and perhaps to hold the attention of the weavers as they were working, repeated elements are idiosyncratic (see cat. no. 317, color pl. 60b). At a fundamental level such a stress on artistic interpretation in these complex works directs us to look for the person, and the personality, of the textile artist in the dynamic interaction of technique, design, and iconography.

As background, the present essay introduces some of the overarching concepts that characterize the traditions of art weaving in the Andes as a whole. These concepts may be grouped under the topics of textile primacy, technological style, attitudes toward design and subject matter, and relationships of artist to society.

Textile Primacy

Although many artistic media were integral to Andean life and expression, textiles acted as a foundation for the entire aesthetic system to a degree unparalleled in other cultures of the world. Textiles were invented and developed long before other media, played a seminal role in the development of "civilization" itself, and continued their preeminence for thousands of years. They had a profound influence on other media. The intensive efforts involved in gathering and processing materials, the extensive exploration of techniques, and the overall energy devoted to innovation in design show that the entire society was dedicated to fiber. Finally, textiles

were used repeatedly to establish important political and social distinctions.

We can ascertain this pattern of "textile primacy," even in very ancient times, because of the favorable climatic conditions that ensured the archaeological preservation of fibers. Although we speak of the Andes as a region, the narrow backbone of the mountains themselves constitutes only the most physically dominant of three very distinct ecological areas (figs. I.1, I.3). The Andes, the longest and second highest mountain chain in the world, are bounded on the west by the world's driest coastal desert and on the east by the extremely wet Amazonian jungle. It was the practice of burial in the coastal dunes, bereft of all vegetation and lacking in moisture, that allowed the preservation of the fiber history of both the coast and the mountains and even to some extent of the jungle, whose highly valued tropical feathers made their way over the highlands to the coast (see cat. no. 282, color pl. 32; cat. no. 292, color pl. 61; cat. no. 302). In the mountains (except in a few dry caves and frozen burials at high altitude) and certainly in the jungle, moisture destroys perishable materials such as fiber.

Archaeological evidence shows that in the Andes fibers were worked much earlier than other materials, such as fired clay. Textile materials and techniques underwent development over thousands of years before clay was deliberately fire-hardened. This chronological priority is very different from the artistic practices of the Old World, in which pottery was the earliest and most basic art form. Plant-fiber basketry has been found high in the Andes in Guitarrero Cave and Carbon-14 dated to between 8600 and 8000 B.C. (Adovasio and Lynch 1973; see fig. I.3). A later impression of a plain-woven fabric in a lump of accidentally heated clay from the Ecuadorian site of Valdivia reveals a date of 3000 B.C. (Marcos 1979:21, fig. 3). The entire archaeological period from 3000 B.C. to 1800 B.C., termed the "Pre-Ceramic" (the name itself showing an inherent bias toward ceramics), was dominated by exploration of chiefly nonloom cotton weaving. The preeminent known Pre-Ceramic site is Huaca Prieta on the North Coast of modern Peru, from which over nine thousand fabric fragments were recovered (Bird 1963). The patterns on these elaborate twined cotton textiles, dated at about 2300 B.C., include double readings of animal imagery more sophisticated than those on other media. Thus, a generalized progression from plant-fiber basketry to cotton plain weave to patterned textiles can be hypothesized over the first six thousand years of the Andean textile tradition.

Human adaptation to the coast, the mountains, and the jungle was uniquely tied to fiber objects and their creation. It can be argued persuasively that the development of "civilization" itself in all three geographical areas was intertwined with the pursuit of particular fibers. Along the coast the first human settlers survived by fishing in the rich Humboldt Current of the Pacific Ocean. Gradual movement inland to settled irrigation agriculture along the rivers that flow down from the Andes was most probably motivated by the desire to grow rather than gather wild the cotton needed for fishing nets, carrying cloths, protective garments, and the like (Moseley 1975). Later coastal textile traditions continued to be marked by the use of cotton as well as an interest in openwork that seems to have originated with netmaking. In the mountains, the fiber-producing camelids (llama, alpaca, guanaco, and vicuña; see Glossary) made a seminomadic life possible in one of the planet's most formidable environments (Murra 1962; Browman 1974; Stone-Miller 1992).

The hardy New World camel is the key to human survival and to the development of an unparalleled tradition of colorful fiberwork in the Andes. Its ability to exist on the dry, high-altitude grass and little water, while producing silky hair that is easily and brilliantly dyed, as well as its uses as a source of food protein and a means of transportation as a pack animal, make the camelid perfect for meeting the needs of the highlands. Because of the temperature extremes, protective garments are as vitally important here as on the coast. Cloth carrying bags for human and pack animal alike, rather than heavy or breakable containers (see fig. I.7; see also cat. no. 110; cat. no. 174, color pl. 20; cat. no. 265, color pl. 66; cat. no. 274, color pl. 18), allow for the movement from one environmental zone to another that is basic to the human adaptive strategy in the Andes. Here textiles developed beyond practical coverings or means of transporting goods into colorful, densely woven creations with a design tradition distinct from that of the coast. In the jungle, it is assumed that because of the virtual absence of other materials, plant fibers were employed, as today, to fulfill clothing, housing, and furnishing needs (Carlisle 1990, vol. 1:58–59). In all three regions available fibers — with their natural abilities to warm, cool, protect, contain, and support— allowed people to invent products suited to the environment. Aesthetic explorations grew out of practical solutions to become the varied, magnificent fiber arts of the greater Andean region.

Textiles have continued to be preeminent in various ways, from the earliest rudimentary civilization through the growth of mighty indigenous states, from the wholesale restructuring of society in Colonial times to the changes brought by independence in the nineteenth century and the Westernization of today. This can be partly explained by the relative constancy of the environmental conditions that make fiber the solution to human adaptation and the foundation for cultural development. For example, because it is still difficult to travel through the mountains, a fiber bridge over the Apurimac River built by the sixteenth-century Incas (probably on even earlier foundations) is rewoven each year by the modern inhabitants (McIntyre 1973:782–785). Although this example should not create the impression that there have been no changes over time, it demonstrates that fiber still fulfills current needs most elegantly.

An additional aspect of textiles' status is their role as subject matter both in textiles themselves and in other media, as well as their influence on the design of nonfiber arts. Textile subject matter in textiles includes fibers (Cordy-Collins 1979); fiber-producing animals (Stone-Miller 1992); the act of weaving (a scene of a weaver in a figural fiber sculpture in the American Museum of Natural History is illustrated in both Dockstader 1967: no. 145, and Morrison 1979:65; see p. 49, note 8); technical structures (Frame 1986); and garments and their wearers (see cat. no. 12, color pl. 38; cat. no. 69, color pl. 5; cat. no. 217, color pl. 35; cat. no. 282, color pl. 32). The self-referential nature of the medium is marked. Its additional ability to communicate through textile-specific, noniconographic means, such as the significance of a certain dyed color (see cat. no. 210, color pl. 57), represents another aspect of its broad communicative reach.

Other major media that refer directly to the fiber arts or share in their forms include architecture (Stone-Miller and McEwan 1990); sculptural reliefs (ibid.: fig. 8); and ceramic painting (Donnan 1978:21, fig. 36; Anton 1984:122, fig. 90; 222). There are also depictions in ceramics of weaving itself (Donnan 1978:65, fig. 103). Such an aesthetic preoccupation shows the great value, status, power, and significance of textiles for the communication of messages. In addition, what can be seen as textile-related design constraints, based on the natural tendencies of one weaving technique to produce rectilinear designs or another diagonals, are adopted "unnecessarily" in freer media (Stone 1987, vol. 1:45). For example, Wari sculpture and ceramics employ a grid-based design template, not easy to apply to rounded surfaces, which probably originated with the perpendicular relationships of threads in tapestry weaving (on the related Sun Gate at Tiwanaku, see Bennett 1954:76). This shows a deep, structural application of one design system to another, which underscores how the dominant medium of fiber claims precedence.

Another measure of the importance of a particular pursuit to a people is the amount of physical and creative energy they have devoted to it over the millennia. The textile record attests to the fact that Andeans placed a premium on extensive technical exploration and innovation, assigning a great deal of society-wide labor to fiber production. Plain-weave textiles (made by the simple over and under alteration of threads; see Glossary) suffice to produce lengths of cloth necessary for basic household uses (cat. no. 152, fig. I.8). Plain weave continues to be utilized for the ground cloths of embroideries (cat. no. 255, fig. I.4) and other multitechnique pieces (cat. no. 4, fig. I.9).

Fig. I.4, cat. no. 255. A Paracas embroidered mantle border in block-color style. Since the mantle is unfinished, it shows the creative process (outlining the figures, filling in the background, then filling in the figures; see pp. 25–27). The left tunic top of the upper figure is partially filled in.

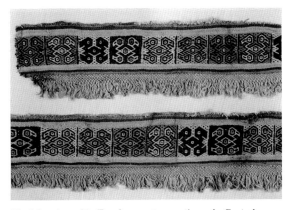

Fig. I.6, cat. no. 31. Two fragmentary portions of a Central Coast border of the Late Intermediate Period, showing characteristic variations in the repetition of the four-headed bird motif in color assignment, measurements, and proportions.

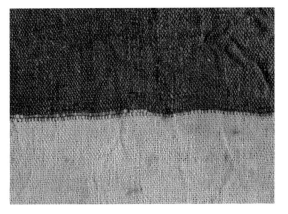

Fig. I.8, cat. no. 152. Detail of a simple carrying cloth, probably from the Central Coast, which conveys the under-over movement of threads in the plain-weave technique.

Fig. I.7, cat. no. 110. Bag, probably from the Chilca area, woven in the Middle Horizon using multiple techniques. It illustrates the importance of textiles as carriers in the Andean highlands.

Fig. I.5, cat. no. 97. A Chancay-style double-cloth panel. Because it is partially deteriorated, it distinctly shows the characteristic dark and light layers of weaving.

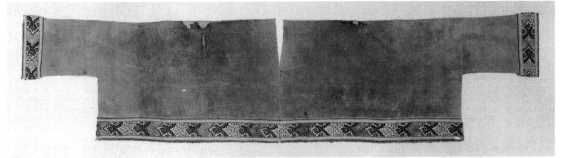

Fig. I.9, cat. no. 4. A sleeved tunic, probably from the Rimac Culture of the Central Coast, which shows the common practice of combining a plain-weave ground with other techniques, here borders in slit tapestry.

Fig. I.10, cat. no. 276. A cap with added camelid fiber "hair" representing one variety within the "wig" tradition. See cat. no. 187, color pl. 33.

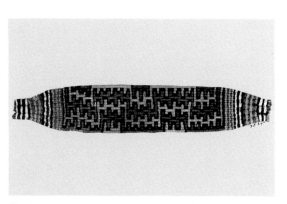

Fig. I.11, cat. no. 168. A fragmentary sling (the long ends have been cut off either side; see Cahlander 1980 for complete versions). It is an example of the wide range of uses to which the Andeans put textiles, including as weapons.

Fig. I.12. A woman spinning yarn with a drop spindle and distaff, while a man plies the spun yarn (Guaman Poma, fol. 57; 1980a, t.1:43).

Fig. I.13. An Andean backstrap loom (Guaman Poma, fol. 215; 1980a, t. 1:150)

Fig. I.14. Upright looms were used for tapestry cloth both before and, as shown here, after the Spanish Conquest (Guaman Poma, fol. 647; 1980a, t. 2:81).

Fig. I.15, cat. no. 149. A miniature mantle (12 x 13 cm) in plain weave with borders featuring weft floats. The mantle exemplifies the tradition of placing tiny garments as offerings in the burials of lower-status individuals. See cat. no. 33, color pl. 56.

However, the archaeological and historical record is filled with pieces made in almost limitless number and combinations of far more complicated, time-consuming, difficult, spectacular, and ingenious techniques, many of which are unique to the region (see Glossary; cat. no. 1, color pl. 46; cat. no. 161, color pl. 52; cat. no. 218, color pl. 34; cat. no. 295, color pl. 14a,b; cat. no. 265, color pl. 66; cat. no. 319, color pl. 21a,b). A widely used classification system of fabric structure has been based almost entirely on this corpus of techniques (Emery 1966). These techniques are applied to innovative forms, as well, such as figural sculptures (cat. no. 40, fig. IV.2; cat. nos. 39, 42, 41, color pls. 55a–c), hats with "hair" (cat. no. 276, fig. I.10; cat. no. 187, color pl. 33; cat. no. 35), and weapons, such as slings (cat. no. 168, fig. I.11; see also Cahlander 1980).

Virtuoso execution, such as in textiles with over 78 wefts per centimeter (over 195 per inch; see cat. no. 322, color pl. 67a,b), goes hand in hand with complexity. We can safely assume that in order to develop creative techniques and maintain this high level of skill, weavers must have been specialists. In other words, they held a privileged social position and probably were supported by others in most, if not all, Andean cultures (see p. 23; p. 45; pp. 51–52).

A great number of people worked to provide the weaving specialists with the necessary materials; the entire society seems to have been involved in the task (Gayton 1973). To grow cotton and produce a textile from it entailed extensive and intensive labor. Work included the irrigation and preparation of the fields; planting, tending, and harvesting the plants; removal of the seeds, cleaning and combing fibers to a uniform direction ("carding") in preparation for spinning and plying mile upon mile of thread (fig. I.12); loom construction, warping, and finally weaving of the threads (figs. I.13, I.14). Dyeing of cotton, not as prevalent as that of camelid fiber but nonetheless existent, involved locating, picking, and extracting dye from plants; in addition, the subsequent wetting, steeping, and drying steps. Camelid fiber requires even more constant and long-term labor: years of herding, with attention to animal fertility and health (Browman 1974; Stone-Miller 1992); sheering, washing, carding, spinning, and dyeing of threads (with the additional task of pretreating the thread with mordants, minerals that prepare fibers to take dye better and effect final color). The final step, tightly packed weaving in intricate patterns, characteristic of camelid fiber pieces, is itself particularly arduous.

To assemble all these materials, interaction between coastal and highland areas and cultures was usually necessary, since many textiles combine the ecologically distinct cotton and camelid fiber threads. There was probably extensive transportation of unspun fiber or finished thread, or both, between geographical zones. Dyes also may have been traded from one region to another, particularly in the case of cochineal, the permanent red dye prepared from parasites on the nopal cactus, which grows only in coastal areas (see cat. no. 62, color pl. 37). Most dye plants grow in lower elevations so that *both* highland and coastal peoples would have had to travel to gather them. Thus, the overall transportation of items related to the Andean textile "industry" must have been widespread. The combinations of various fibers and dyes also imply a trade or organizational system, or both, to unite the coast and the highlands (as well as the jungle and the highlands, in the case of feathers; see entry for cat. no. 282, color pl. 32). This not only means the expenditure of more communal time and effort but also suggests administrative specialization existed to coordinate these interchanges. Indeed, the term "industry" applied to Andean textile manufacture may not be too far off the mark.

There were evidently other political roles in which textiles figured prominently as measures of power within society or over other societies. Cloth primarily symbolized power in the Andes because it directly represented the garnering and organization of so many levels and variations of labor. It follows that the more labor-intensive textiles indicated more power controlled, within non-state-level and state-level cultures alike. As one example, the splendid Paracas mantles (such as cat. no. 303, color pl. 4a,b), heavily embroidered, were mummy-bundle wrappings for the most important people in that village-based culture, individuals whose status merited the hours upon hours of painstaking needlework dedicated to their protection and glorification in death (see pp. 25–33; see also Paul 1990a:37–41, figs. 4.1–4.12). In other cases power over foreign peoples was repeatedly disseminated by spreading fiber works from a central area to conquered or influenced areas. A prime example of this is the Wari state exportation of large numbers of tapestries, recognizably highland in technique and imagery, to the coastal areas during their expansionist period (see p. 35; see also Stone 1987, vol. 1:20–26). The Inca empire especially used textiles in political transactions, as coercive payments, gifts, and rewards, to indicate the loyalty of the conquered, and to maintain social hierarchy, to name a few of the many roles (see p. 53; Murra 1962). In all pre- and post-Conquest Andean cultures social status and role were visually designated through the type of textiles worn and carried.

It is important to note that fiber has a repeated association with high status in particular. People of higher status rated greater numbers of textiles in life and in death, each of which may be of larger size, made with a more time-consuming and perfectly executed technique, prized materials (such as the silky vicuña hair or the color blue, which was hardest to dye; see cat. no. 210, color pl. 57), restricted iconography, and/or masterful design. This elaboration of textiles for the elite can be seen in images of personages (fig. III.8) and especially in the burial goods of the most elaborate interments (see, for example, cat. no. 306, color pl. 42). Textiles were not only dressed or wrapped around the deceased but figured as offerings as well. Some fancy garments show evidence of having been folded for long periods of time; that is, they were placed in that way near the body rather than being dressed over it (see cat. no. 234, color pl. 64; cat. no. 290, color pl. 44). Interestingly, miniaturized versions of garments were fashioned for the more modest in social stature (cat. no. 149, fig. I.15; cat. no. 33, color pl. 56). The inclusion of looms and samplers (related to cat. no. 275, color pl. 47) may have indicated one role played by the deceased during life.[1] These are but a few of the ways in which fiber created and maintained social distinctions both in life and after death.

Finally, as the ultimate measure of importance in the pre-Columbian world view, high-quality textiles themselves were "killed" as sacrifices. The Incas took tapestries woven by the best weavers, as well as the animals whose hair was used to make textiles, and ritually burned them in Cuzco as daily sacrifices to the sun (Murra 1962:714). This practice cements the integral relationship of fiber to cosmic forces and accentuates the great status of the medium, since a people sacrifice what is most important to them in order to propitiate the supernatural realm most effectively. In sum, the antiquity, continuity, influential nature, labor intensity, virtuosity, status, and political significance of Andean fiber arts make them primary sources of information about their makers.

Technological Style

Technology, as it is commonly understood, constitutes the materials, such as camelid fiber and cotton; the tools, such as spindles (cat. no. 257, fig. I.16; see cat. no. 49, color pl. 1) and looms (figs. I.13, I.14); and the techniques, such as tapestry weave, routinely utilized to make fiber objects. However, equally important, it also includes *attitudes* toward materials, tools, and techniques that govern the choices that are made at every step of the creative process. Thus, we can speak of "technological style" just as we do of artistic style, because individuals, societies, and cultures consistently show recognizable patterns of choices in this dimension as well (Lechtman 1984). For example, pre-Columbian peoples chose stone tools even though they had the materials, equipment, and processes in place to produce metal ones. Hardly owing to a deficit of inventiveness, this represents an active choice to approach metals for alternative decorative or symbolic purposes and to employ a simple, very effective

stone-on-stone technology that lacked neither utility nor beautiful results (Helms 1981; Lechtman 1984; Protzen 1985). Andeans used the softer, more colorful metals to signify the status and character of the wearer rather than the harder metals to work other materials. Stone tools had the further advantage that they were readily available to an extensive network of workers, not just to a small number of specialists. Similar choices can be found in the realm of textiles, in fact, technological patterns based on textile primacy also seem to have influenced those in the other media (Lechtman 1984:31–36). Such diagnostic choices in technological style not only reveal to us basic ideas prevalent in the aesthetic arena but also have broad implications for a wide range of conceptual patterns, social organizational schema, and religious belief systems that would be completely lost to us if we did not have the objects that make such ways of thinking manifest (Prown 1980, 1982).

In general, acknowledging that individual cultures actively determine their own technologies, usually fully aware of certain alternatives, leads to greater understanding and appreciation of cultures that did *not* follow familiar Old World patterns. Two of the most limiting "common sense" technological assumptions that hinder our consideration of the uniqueness of Andean technological style are evolutionary schemes and technical determinism.

Evolutionary schemes assume cultures will go through natural progressions from one technological "level" to the next, almost always based on the better-known Mesopotamian or Mediterranean sequences. Although "advancement" from Stone to Bronze to Iron Ages may be expected, fulfillment of this pattern does not corrolate with cultural sophistication: the Incas built some of the world's most stunning and technically transcendent architecture and cannot be judged as deficient by their choice of tools (see Gasparini and Margolis 1980). The same applies to pre-Columbian weaving technology which never "progressed" to the European-style floor loom but nonetheless generated some of the most outstanding textiles the world has ever known.

Nor can the limiting concept of technical determinism, often accepted prejudicially for art of non-Western societies, be applied if active choice is acknowledged to take place at all levels of artistic activity. "Technical determinism" means that the inherent constraints of the chosen technique (this can be extended to materials and tools as well) determine the visual appearance of what is made. Constraints are assumed to be especially powerful and binding in weaving, with its unyielding loom framework. It is obvious that a weaving technique based on a perpendicular relationship of warp and weft threads, such as plain weave or tapestry weave, will easily produce rectilinear patterns, especially plaids (cat. no. 151, fig. I.17), stripes,

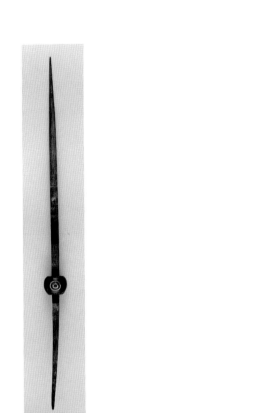

Fig. I.16, cat. no. 257. A spindle with ceramic spindle whorl decorated with concentric circle design, one of the simple tools used to make the thread for the many elaborate Andean textiles. See cat. no. 49, color pl. 1.

Fig. I.18, cat. no. 26. A Chimu-style, slit tapestry-weave border fragment, showing the natural tendency for tapestry to create rectilinear, especially stepped designs.

Fig. I.21, cat. no. 74. Tiny fragment of a border made in crossed-knit loop stitch (see Harcourt 1962: pls. 86–104), representing the interest of Andean textile artists in exploring innovative three-dimensional fiber techniques.

Fig. I.19, cat. no. 21. Detail of a fragmentary Rimac-style border in slit tapestry weave, representing an example of curvilinear designs possible in tapestry, here made possible by the use of eccentric wefts (see Glossary).

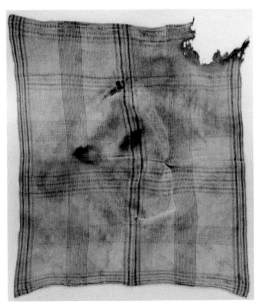

Fig. I.17, cat. no. 151. A plain-weave carrying cloth, illustrating that the technique naturally generates plaid patterns.

Fig. I.20, cat. no. 162. Late Horizon bundle cloth made in the double-cloth technique, with characteristically extreme abstraction (note frontal human figures and two versions of llamas).

Fig. I.22, cat. no. 73. Paracas embroidered border fragment in block-color style, showing the great density and coverage of stitches over (nearly invisible) ground cloth.

and steps (cat. no. 26, fig. I.18). Yet to expect that no indigenous artist can overcome these natural tendencies and produce curvilinear designs instead is misleading (see cat. no. 21, fig. I.19; cat. no. 316, color pl. 24). Andeans maintained a very different relationship of technology to visual effect, one that does not reflect a tyranny of means over ends.

Some of the principal features of Andean technological style in weaving, several of which may be counter-intuitive to us, can be termed as follows: simplicity of means and sophistication of ends, goal-orientation over effort expenditure, technical transcendence, primacy of completeness, and emphasis on combinations. The dimension of design inevitably enters this discussion, since technology, design, and meaning are, after all, inseparable.

Andean weaving technology was also basically "Stone Age" in character, simple in means yet sophisticated in ends. The textile industry was and remains chiefly based on few materials: cotton and camelid fiber, with the post-Conquest addition of sheep's wool, linen, and imported silk (see cat. no. 283, color pl. 72). Tools were deceptively rudimentary: sticks tied together make up the backstrap loom (fig. I.13), the frame loom, and the upright loom (fig. I.14); simple combs, needles, spindles, and bobbins helped move the threads in weaving (see Glossary). The weaver's workbasket in the Museum's collection (cat. no. 49, color pl. 1) shows a typical array from about A.D. 1000 and indicates the degree of elaboration lavished upon such "simple tools."

Given this spare technology, the sophistication of the woven results becomes even more striking. No matter what the specific technique(s) employed, whether structural or superstructural, Andean execution has a certain intensity and elaboration. Structural techniques are those in which the fabric and its pattern are built up simultaneously, as in a tapestry, where threads interlock to create the design (see cat. no. 317, color pl. 60b). Many examples of structural sophistication can be found in the Museum's collection, including techniques that create fabric whose front and back faces display different colors or even different patterns; for example, double cloth (cat. no. 162, fig. I.20, among others) and triple cloth (cat. no. 237, color pl. 2) or complementary warp patterning (cat. no. 218, color pl. 34). Ancient Andeans also thought of cloth as potentially three-dimensional (cat. no. 74, fig. I.21), even sculptural (cat. nos. 39, 42, 41, color pls. 55a–c). Many complex techniques and their combinations took several distinct steps to complete and defy brief characterization, such as discontinuous warp and weft (see entry for cat. no. 289, color pl. 17), "patchwork" tie-dye (cat. no. 319, color pl. 21a,b), or sprang-based double cloth (cat. no. 169, color pl. 16). Superstructural techniques involved the production of an undecorated cloth to which patterning was added, as in embroidery (cat. no. 255, fig. I.4; cat. no. 73, fig.

I.22), painting (cat. no. 146, fig. I.23), resist (cat. no. 148, fig. I.24), or even metal appliqué (cat. no. 306, color pl. 42). In the superstructural techniques as well, the regularity of stitching in an embroidery or the painstaking filling of a cloth with painted motifs share in this quality of technical intensity.

This brings up a characteristic Andean approach that is goal-oriented rather than concerned with efficiency of effort. Paracas embroidered garments may have as much as 75 percent or more of their ground cloth covered with tiny, overlapping embroidery stitches; in a typical mantle this represents many hundreds of square inches of handwork. The borders alone of textiles from different periods constitute an amazing investment of time (e.g., see cat. no. 73, fig. I.22; cat. no. 190, color pl. 15). The creation of a typically complex Wari tapestry tunic entails six to nine miles of different colored thread interlocked as many as 1,500,000 separate times while being woven (Stone 1987, vol. 1:76–77). Labor economy could not have been a primary concern! Instead, the desired visual effects took precedence, especially the aesthetic emphasis on solid areas of color: more embroidery stitches, more closely packed tapestry rows, and the extremely labor-intensive techniques mentioned above all produce more intense or numerous colors, or both. An equally persuasive reason for labor intensity seems to be that it served to praise both the makers of the textile, by showing their ability to create, and its recipients, by showing their merit to receive, something that has taken so much time and effort to produce. Certainly the sacred uses of many textiles as well as textile imagery made it necessary to expend "unnecessary" energy on the act of creation.

A concept allied to labor intensity and goal orientation is what may be termed technical transcendence. In opposition to technical determinism in design, mentioned above, this denotes an innovative attitude that neither bends to the constraints imposed by the loom nor follows previous manipulations of that particular method. Technique can be "transcended" by the very intensity of execution discussed above: a tapestry with a great many threads packed together can display a very smooth curve or accurate circle, since the many steps that make up these shapes are each so tiny (see cat. no. 52, fig. I.25). Other technical limits were routinely circumvented, as well. For example, during many distinct periods weavers wove their compositions sideways (cat. no. 313, color pl. 22a,b), from the back (cat. no. 288, color pl. 62), or even upside down (Conklin 1971) so as to adapt the method to the effect needed. They used highly developed powers of visualization, making use of what is known as eidetic thinking (as opposed to verbal or written information), to maintain a visual image of the final product while weaving under confusing perceptual situations (as dyers also did while dyeing "blind" with indigo; see entry on

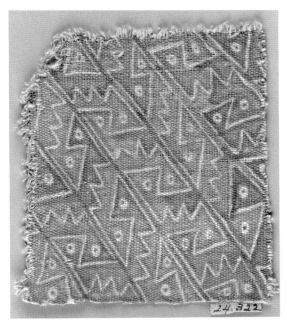

Fig. I.23, cat. no. 146. Small fragment of painted plain weave from the Late Intermediate Period, demonstrating how the pigment is applied to the surface of the cloth.

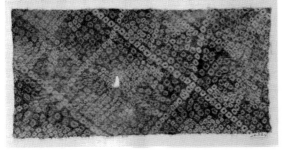

Fig. I.24, cat. no. 148. Tie-dyed plain-weave fragment, illustrating a resist process utilized in Andean textiles. See cat. no. 319, color pl. 21a,b; cat. no. 300, color pl. 51.

Fig. I.25, cat. no. 52. Colonial tapestry panel fragment with design of roses, probably 16th–17th century. Note the circularity achieved and the relative lack of color shading.

Fig. I.26, cat. no. 178. Garment fragment, probably from the Late Intermediate Period Rimac culture, illustrating the widespread Andean practice of weaving shaped textiles rather than cutting cloth to shape.

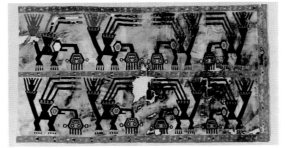

Fig. I.27, cat. no. 304. Chimu-style slit tapestry panels sewn together, a prevalent assemblage method in the Late Intermediate Period. The large birds with human trophy heads in their beaks are an instance of human-animal identification common in the Andean aesthetic system.

Fig. I.28, cat. no. 205. Double-cloth bag, probably converted from another type of piece (all figures are upside down), with a wrapped human hair braid as a "strap" (see cat. no. 187, color pl. 33). This enigmatic assemblage, whose period is unclear, is characteristically Andean in its combination of reused items. (See Harcourt 1962: pl. 31, for a similar double-cloth bag with llama design, with an attached cord rather than a braid and a strap.)

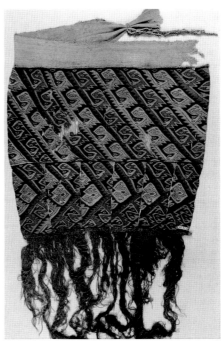

Fig. I.29, cat. no. 180. Loincloth fragment, probably from the Central Coast, showing the dominance of patterning, interlocking meanders, over subject matter, birds, common in pre-Columbian Andean textile design.

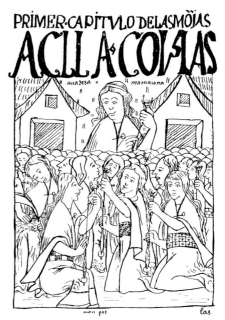

Fig. I.30. Cloistered Inca women spin yarn, directed by an "abbess," within the walls of the *acllawasi* (Guaman Poma, fol. 298; 1980a, t. 1:212).

cat. no. 210, color pl. 57). Another apparently unavoidable loom limitation, size, was also overcome: Paracas weavers somehow produced
a cloth measuring more than 3 by 25 meters (11 by 85 feet; *New York
Times* 1949). Single-web Colonial carpets reach astonishing dimensions as well (see cat. no. 301, color pl. 76).

A further diagnostic feature of the Andean technological style
in weaving may be described as an emphasis on wholeness or com-
pletion. Cloth was almost never woven to be cut and sewn together,
as in Western traditions. (Some pieces that have been cut were muti-
lated by modern dealers; e.g., cat. no. 200A–D, color pl. 26). In fact,
the Incas considered this an extremely sacrilegious act when it was
instituted by the Spanish in the early Colonial years. Primarily, textiles were woven to their final shape, even if this was an irregular one
and extremely difficult to accomplish (cat. no. 178, fig. I.26; cat. no.
206, color pl. 58). Secondarily, separate but completely finished webs
sometimes were sewn together (cat. no. 304, fig. I.27). Great care was
taken to leave no loose ends at the edges of any loom product and only very rarely on the back face (for an exception see cat. no. 268, color
pl. 59). In a typical tapestry the amount of time spent to weave the
visible design may have been almost equaled by that spent to inter-
weave the ends of threads from each color area on the back. In many
cases it even becomes difficult to ascertain which *is* the front and
which the back face of a fragmentary piece because the finishing is
so complete (cat. no. 213, color pl. 25).

Not to be understood as some sort of "compulsiveness," this
stress on entirety should rather be seen as revealing fundamental cultural values that stress verity over visual deception. In other words,
objects (or people or ideas) must be more than a shallow appearance,
they must be unified through and through. Heather Lechtman has
identified this interaction of technique and belief through in-depth
scientific research on metalmaking approaches, which she sees as intimately related to textile technological style (1984). She has coined
the phrase "technology of essence" to describe the fact that objects
reflect on their exterior what may be hidden inside or on the other
side; they do not have a veneer or illusionary surface appearance.
Surface reveals the essence of the core. This total unity can be extended to the relationship between textiles and their wearers (see cat.
no. 288, color pl. 62); a person's "surface" (their mantle with its millions of stitches) describes their own being or essence (in terms of
power, strength, or sacredness). In general terms, clothing always
represents the person, although in the ancient Andean world this
concept has particular intensity because of this essential view of technology.

A final observation on technology that brings together complexity, sophistication, intensity, and concern with finish is the emphasis on combinations of techniques within individual pieces. Samplers overtly display the many methods and patterns controlled by a
given maker (see cat. no. 275, color pl. 47). Individual pieces routinely contain a number of techniques, whether worked on the same
threads (cat. no. 308, color pl. 50), composed by sewing together various parts (cat. no. 67, color pl. 9), or both (cat. no. 265, color pl. 66).
Further combinations are generated through reuse or conversion of
pieces, such as the enigmatic Late Horizon bag (cat. no. 205, fig.
I.28). This technical fluency represents an aspect of the characteristic
virtuosity that one comes to recognize throughout the Andean textile
traditions.

Attitudes toward Design and Subject Matter

In general, the treatment of design and subject matter follows
in many ways that of technological style, since all three work together
to communicate meaning. As in technique, artistic choices in Andean
textiles differ from our own aesthetic traditions to emphasize the
essence of a subject rather than its surface appearance, spatial relationships, or place in a narrative script. Symbolic reality always takes
precedence over perceptual descriptiveness. For example, in a tapestry strip with figures and birds (cat. no. 62, color pl. 37), the white
birds' feathers are shown enlarged, separated, and from above in order to express their "truest" characteristics. In general, actual scale
and consistency in position or angle of view are of secondary importance. A fish placed next to the birds' claws refers to the latter's fishing habits without literally describing the act by overlapping the
forms. However, a fish placed below a bird also symbolizes a relationship of capture by victors or warriors. Birds are also presented as
equivalent to humans by their similar size, by being fitted into the
same rectangular spaces, and especially by wearing identical elite
headdresses. These characteristics obviously do not describe the specific bird (unless perhaps the headdress indirectly refers to head
plumage) but rather portray both figures as high-status victors in
their respective realms. Animals in pre-Columbian art often represent
the powerful, desirable, superhuman qualities of strength, size, feroc-
ity, keen vision, flight, or fertility. Composite human-animals are
common (cat. no. 78, color pl. 36). Animal characteristics, like adjectives, represent both the essential qualities of humans —perhaps fe-
rocity or keen-sightedness— and their aspirations to have these qualities. (This extensive identification with the animal kingdom seems to
continue even in Colonial art, along with overlapping, foreign-influ-
enced animal symbolism [see cat. no. 53, color pl. 70; cat. no. 54, col-
or pl. 78; cat. no. 305, color pl. 80.]) Thus, the textile in question does

not depict a man and his bird out fishing but chooses to symbolize "victor" in both human and animal terms through design and iconographic equivalences.

Another example, a loincloth end panel (cat. no. 308, color pl. 50), demonstrates additional broadly characteristic Andean choices as to shape and color. Although an aspect such as plumage may be assigned the color of the bird in question, it is an equally viable design choice to alternate bird colors in a rhythmic pattern that bears no relation to a group of differently colored birds. In this sense it is the essence of a *pattern* that takes precedence over a visual portrait (see also cat. no. 52, fig. I.25; cat. no. 180, fig. I.29). Even in many Colonial works, color areas themselves are relatively unshaded in relation to European painterly textile traditions; that is, there are few gradations of colors toward the edges to indicate three-dimensionality or shadows.[2] Typically uniform or "flat" color throughout a shape and the bold juxtaposition of contrasting colors in geometric patterns can be seen in the coloration of birds' bodies in the tapestry end of this fragmentary loincloth. This use of color, rather than constituting a limitation, makes Andean textiles from all periods particularly striking, visually rich, and dynamic (see also cat. no. 50, color pl. 71; cat. no. 79, color pl. 19; cat. no. 250, color pl. 63; cat. no. 319, color pl. 21a,b). The stress on symbolism, as opposed to strictly representational art, leaves the Andean artist much freer to explore the fundamental properties of color, design, and meaning (just as the early twentieth-century Euro-American art world discovered, with non-Western art as a catalyst; see Goldwater 1986).

In the realm of shape —which is, after all, an aspect of color, since a continuous area of color is what creates a shape— Andean fiber art freely abstracts, especially with graphic, rectilinear shapes (cat. no. 174, color pl. 20; cat. no. 290, color pl. 44). Abstraction by definition seeks the essence of a shape, reducing it to its most fundamental character, which often in Andean art assumes a geometric appearance (see essay III). Like uniform color, hard-edged shapes are set apart from one another, either through outlining (cat. no. 316, color pl. 24) or strong color contrast (cat. no. 246, color pl. 41), or both (cat. no. 79, color pl. 19). The degree of abstract, graphic, or geometric interpretation certainly varies a great deal, from the rich, curvilinear detail of Paracas embroidery (cat. no. 91, color pl. 7) to the subtle linear stripes and steps of a Late Intermediate Period tunic (cat. no. 285, color pl. 43a,b). Within a particular style the amount of abstraction also varies (see fig. III.1a–c). Extreme stylization often makes these designs difficult to read; so many hard-edged shapes or outlines may be juxtaposed that patterns become nearly impenetrable (cat. no. 303, color pl. 4a,b). Shape and color abstraction can also be used purposely to undermine clarity, as in the Wari graphic vocabu-

lary (cat. nos. 312 and 313, color pls. 23a,b and 22a,b; see pp. 35–36, 38–41). In fact, intentional perceptual ambiguity is a major theme in Andean textile design (e.g., see cat. no. 240, color pl. 53). In any case, a sophisticated, strong, developed control of patterning can be seen as part of this symbolic, aperceptual aesthetic system.

Artists and Social Context

Individual weavers, though important, can never be separated from the sociocultural context in which they create. The collaborative nature of Andean creativity has been mentioned; this forms the first level of context for a particular weaver. In the Andes the group was —and continues to be— of greater importance than any one person. This is in large part owing to the nature of survival in the marginal environments of the Andes: the reciprocal duties and obligations of each group member to the rest make it possible for all to survive. Weaving was one of the major components of this reciprocity; for instance, in Inca times textile production equaled agricultural production, cloth being traded for sustenance itself (Murra 1962:715). Fabric and food were not just treated as everyday, practical, adaptive items but were elevated to high status through art: the Incas fashioned gold and silver corncobs (Jones 1964: figs. 58, 59) and the technically finest handmade textiles in the world (in terms of thread count), while earlier peoples combined food and textile imagery in all their arts (see especially Paul 1990a:79, 83, 101, 119, 131, 142, 147, 156 on bean imagery in Paracas textiles; Sawyer 1979 on agricultural symbolism in Nasca painted textiles).

Social context includes relative social position; high status not only of the weavings but also of the weavers themselves has always been a component of textile creation in the Andes. If the fiber arts were as important as has been argued here and elsewhere, then the people responsible for their creation must have shared in that importance. This can be seen in artists' ability to direct the design of a significant medium; to contribute to and change what is valued highly reflects on their own high value. As mentioned earlier, in many of the Andean cultures other members of the extended group probably supported textile specialists. We know this is true of the Incas (see pp. 51–52) and can infer from archaeological evidence, such as weaving workshops, that it was also true in earlier times to greater and lesser degrees (see pp. 43, 45, 48). Being supported so that they could weave full-time did not take the weavers outside the system of reciprocity. On the contrary, it allowed them to produce surplus, more prestigious, and more perfect types of textiles to satisfy their obligations to personages of higher status, such as local leaders or rulers, and to higher powers, such as the sun. Thus, the everyday and the sacred realms were equally served by the different makers of fabric.

A final corollary of collaboration, reciprocity, and high-status specialization was control over the weaver. It is natural to expect what is most valued in a society to be most strictly controlled, especially when sacred duties are involved. Evidence of this is also found archaeologically: the Inca walled, single-access textile workshops and living quarters for the *aclla* (chosen women who wove for the ruler and the sun) is the most notable example (see p. 52; see also Morris and Thompson 1985:70–71, fig. 8). The Peruvian chronicler Guaman Poma illustrates the crowd of women spinning with an overseer, also female, presiding above (fig. I.30). From pre-Inca times, a Moche ceramic painted weaving scene depicts a group of female weavers supervised by a larger male figure (Donnan 1978:65, fig. 103). However, this control may have been primarily focused on the very top female weavers, since in the Inca case a second echelon of specialist weavers were males, and below them commoners, mostly female, wove everyday cloth unsupervised (see pp. 51–52).

It is hoped that this extremely general discussion of textile primacy, technological style, artistic attitudes, and social context will place into perspective the following essays on the major Andean textile styles represented in the Museum of Fine Arts.

Notes

1. However, see Margaret Young-Sánchez's cautionary note, p. 48.

2. See p. 60 for Susan Niles's modifications of this view. The point is a relative one; compared with pre-Hispanic textiles, Colonial compositions display color shading, but compared with European, they do so only in a rudimentary fashion.

II: Procedures, Patterns, and Deviations in Paracas Embroidered Textiles: Traces of the Creative Process

Anne Paul

For over seventeen hundred years the Paracas fabrics described and illustrated in this catalogue lay hidden from human eyes, buried in dry graves in Peru's South Coastal desert. Then, in 1911, these secret burial sites were discovered by *huaqueros* (grave robbers), who began looting on the Paracas Peninsula: there, conical funerary bundles that held rulers of Paracas society were pulled from the sandy earth.[1] These bundles were constructed of multiple layers of handsomely designed woven garments, each rich in iconographic content. In part because of their antiquity and in part because there was no written language to record details about the people who made them, these fabrics possess an aura of mystery that makes them seem remote from the realm of human activity. Examination of these ancient artifacts, however, reveals traces of the procedural and conceptual steps that underlay their production; these steps reveal the presence of human hands and something about the working of the minds of the Paracas people.

Paracas weavers excelled at making a range of fiber structures, including the impressively challenging discontinuous warp and weft, as seen in cat. no. 295 (color pl. 14a,b), an extraordinary example of Paracas fiber art.[2] The technical hallmark of the Paracas Necrópolis textile style, however, is plain weave decorated with brightly colored embroidered images (see color pls. 3–14). Detailed study of the embroidered textiles in the Museum of Fine Arts, in conjunction with data from earlier studies, has made it possible to determine some of the ways in which Paracas designers and embroiderers carried out their work.

Stitching Images

The images on a Paracas weaving could be constructed in one of several substyles of embroidery, two of which are illustrated in this catalogue: the linear style and the block-color style. In the linear style of decoration (cat. no. 100, fig. II.1; cat. no. 186, color pl. 3; cat. no. 303, color pl. 4a,b), thin straight lines of stitches define figures whose outlines and interior details follow in large part the horizontal and vertical structure of the woven ground cloth. The torsos of primary figures contain smaller figures, and the spaces surrounding principal images are usually filled with numerous smaller images (e.g., felines flank the serpentinelike designs in cat. no. 303, color pl. 4a,b). In linear-style designs the distinction between a figure and its background is minimized because much of the figure is stitched with the same color of thread as the ground, causing the two to become interlocked on the same color plane. This "transparency" of the figure, in

conjunction with the fact that its many narrow lines prevent the eye from focusing on any detail, results in an image that is initially difficult to see. The linear style may have communicated abstract information (Paul 1990a:72).

In contrast to a linear-style design, an image in the block-color style (cat. no. 71, color pl. 8a,b) consists of parts that were each embroidered with one color of thread to create areas of solid color. The delineation of opaque parts and the clear distinction between figure and ground produce an image that is visually clear and legible. The block-color style usually records elements of the visible world, such as costumed human beings, as it was known on the Paracas Peninsula and nearby valleys. It was suited to the presentation of specific information about the roles of an individual in Paracas society and was appropriate for the depiction of cult images (see Paul 1990a:68–69).

The linear and block-color styles are formally, iconographically, and conceptually different, and procedural differences in the stitching of the designs reflect this fact. When we look at a finished linear-style Paracas garment, it is virtually impossible to tell what procedure was followed in the stitching of images. The embroidery on poncho cat. no. 186 (color pl. 3), for example, is so carefully executed that there is very little evidence of how work proceeded on the piece. This poncho has one telling unfinished detail, however: the larger eye rings on one double-headed bird (see arrow in fig. II.2) should have been filled in with red thread, but instead we see the unembroidered, dark blue of the woven ground cloth. This detail is consistent with what is known about the methods of working in the linear style of embroidery, methods that are visible in unfinished textiles, such as the skirt illustrated in fig. II.3.[3]

The unfinished designs of felines stitched on this skirt catch the embroidery work in midprocess. Here, we can readily see that the red background was embroidered first, stitched in sequential parallel rows that were at least as long as one design unit. As the background was worked, the images of interlocking felines slowly emerged as negative forms. Only after the background was complete did the embroiderer begin to fill in the lines of these felines with different colors of thread. Mantle cat. no. 303 (color pl. 4b) is also unfinished; several of the outlines of the two-headed serpentine designs in the borders are still "blank," with the unembroidered, dark blue woven ground cloth visible. Work on all known unfinished linear-style embroideries was carried out in the same way, and the procedure suggests that the design plan of linear-style images was conceived as if the images were to have been woven: to facilitate stitching each row of the background, the embroiderer counted the particular sequence of warps or wefts in the ground cloth to be covered by the embroidery thread, a

Fig. II.1, cat. no. 100. Overall view of an unfinished linear-style skirt with feline motifs

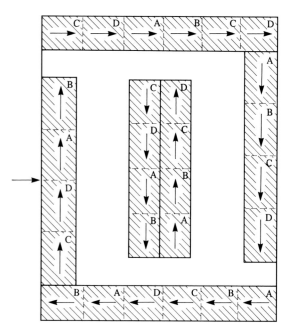

Fig. II.2. Figure orientation and color blocks in poncho cat. no. 186 (color pl. 3). One important feature of an embroidered figure is its orientation, which can be indicated by reducing the figure to an arrow. A symmetrical figure is charted with a straight arrow that shows vertical direction (each bilaterally symmetrical image has the possibility of facing up or down). Color blocks are designated by letters. Linear-style birds decorate this poncho; the arrow at the right side of the diagram points to the only bird on the garment that has an unfinished detail, the larger eye rings.

Fig. II.4. Overall view of skirt cat. no. 67 (color pl. 9)

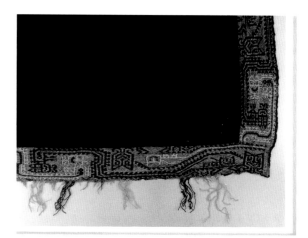

Fig. II.3, cat. no. 100. Detail of skirt in fig. II.1

Fig. II.5. Detail of mantle cat. no. 84 (color pl. 10)

method of working that is analogous to counting the number of warps to be passed over or under by the weft thread in weaving.

Work on an image in the block-color style proceeded differently: instead of forming the background or negative space first, the embroiderer concentrated on identifying the object. For instance, each bird impersonator on mantle cat. no. 71 (color pl. 8a,b) and its matching skirt (cat. no. 67, fig. II.4, color pl. 9) was outlined with one color of thread; once the legs, tunic, arms, head, headdress, staves, and bird cape had been "drawn" in silhouette, the discrete parts could be "colored in" with thread.[4] In another weaving (cat. no. 285, fig. II.5), the outlines of a forehead ornament, circular hair ornaments, and a fist (with the thumb indicated) appear in a partially embroidered anthropomorph. In all these examples the embroiderers are clearly recording the carefully observed shapes of items and beings in the tangible world.

Once the outlines of all images had been finished and, in the case of border areas,[5] the background had been filled in entirely with neat parallel rows of stitches (as in cat. no. 67, color pl. 9), the constituent parts of each image were filled in with different colors of thread, creating the blocks of solid colors that give this style its name.

Aligning Figures

Many Paracas garments carry images in their fields, and these are most frequently aligned in rows and columns to form a gridded pattern. As images were outlined, a problem arose as to how to keep them aligned. The solution is visible in a few unfinished Paracas textiles that have traces of basting stitches whose purpose was to establish a grid that kept figures in their proper places on the ground cloth (e.g., see Paul 1985a:92, fig. 3). An old photograph of mantle cat. no. 71 (color pl. 8a,b) shows basting stitches in three separate areas (see fig. II.6).[6] For example, stitches now no longer present demarcated two sides of a figure identified by arrow 1 in fig. II.6; the vertical basting line marks the right-hand edge and establishes the figure's height, and the bottom line marks the bottom edge and may have originally set the width. (It is possible that at one time it ran the entire width of the figure or even around all four sides, forming a rectangle that marked the limits of the image.) In the upper left-hand corner, along the inside vertical edge of the border bracket, basting stitches (at arrow 2 in fig. II.6, still visible today) mark the figure's height and the border width.

There were also three lines of basting stitches in column 1 of this mantle (at arrow 3 in fig. II.6), but the relation between these lines and the figure they surround is unclear. They appear to form three sides of a rectangle that was to delimit the space for a figure inside. (The height established by the two horizontal lines is the same as the height of the bird impersonator immediately to the upper right.) However, the toes of the unfinished outline do not touch the edge of the basting line, as they should if the image were to fit into the allotted space (compare with the figure at arrow 1), and, even if they did, there is not enough fabric to accommodate the figure's width. The design plan of mantles with images in the field requires that alternate horizontal rows of images extend to the two edges of the mantle between the border brackets, but here there was not enough room to include full-scale and properly aligned figures (in principle there should be two additional figures on the right-hand edge). The upper outlined figure in column 1, whose toes would have been positioned on the top horizontal line of basting stitches had the mantle been longer and the space between the border brackets wider, has been shrunk, but its proportions are the same as the others in the field. The figure immediately below this should also have been made smaller than others on the mantle in order to fit into the space available. Could it be that the embroiderer was in the process of taking out the outlining stitches to start over? Today these stitches are no longer present on the front face of the mantle, but remnants were found on the back during conservation and remounting (Deborah Bede, personal communication, 1991).

An example of what could happen when basting guidelines were not used is visible in the diagram fig. II.7 (cat. no. 191, color pl. 11). The mantle has 150 closely spaced depictions of shaman figures in its field, and although guidelines may have been used in some areas (see the top image in column 17, which has a line of green stitches extending from and marking the edge of the hair), they were not employed in columns 14, 16, and 18. The figures in these columns vary considerably from other shamans on the mantle in height and in spacing, and, as a result, each column has one less figure than the design plan required. The jumble of shaman figures on the skirt (fig. II.8) that forms a set with this mantle suggests that some of its images, too, may have been outlined without the benefit of guidelines.

Filling in with Color

The overall impression projected by Paracas Necrópolis textiles is one of tremendous variety: there are several styles of formal construction, a wide range of iconographic types, and many different color schemes. But underlying this variety are principles of organization that are shared by most Paracas fabrics. One of these systems underlies color schemes and patterns.[7]

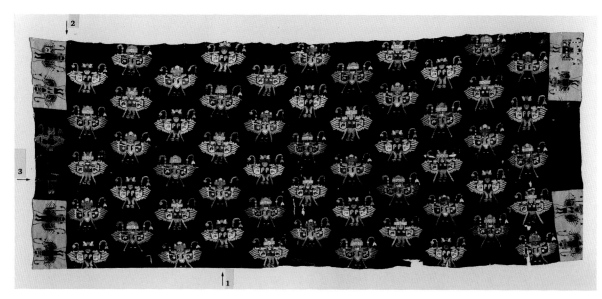

Fig. II.6. Detail of mantle cat. no. 71 (color pl. 8a,b) from a photograph taken in 1917 showing basting stitches (indicated by arrows) as they existed at that time. Stitches at arrow 3 are now gone from the front face, but remnants are visible on the back.

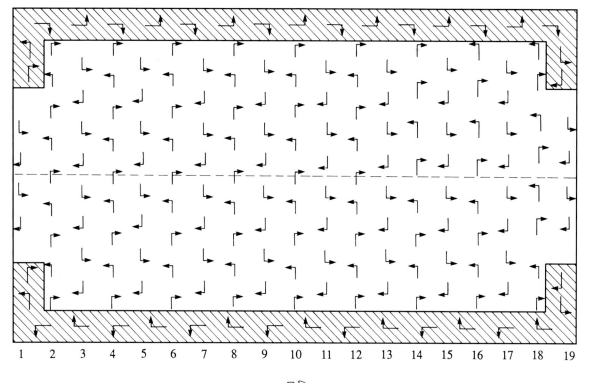

Fig. II.7. Figure orientation in mantle cat. no. 191 (color pl. 11). The asymmetrical figures here are charted with crooked arrows that show vertical and lateral directions; each asymmetrical image has the possibility of facing up or down and left or right. Columns 14, 16, 18 each have one less shaman figure than the design plan required.

Fig. II.8. Overall view of skirt cat. no. 192. This forms a garment set with mantle cat. no. 191 (color pl. 11).

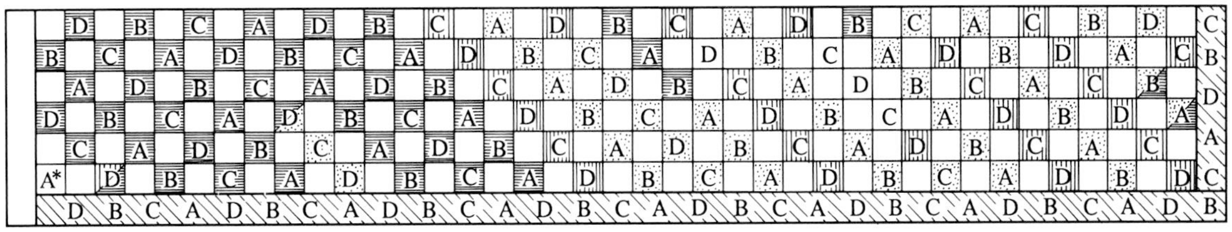

Fig. II.9. Color blocks and hands at work in skirt cat. no. 91 (color pl. 7). At least two and probably three persons embroidered the designs on this fabric. Worker 1 was responsible for images primarily on the left half of the skirt, while the other two workers contributed to the right side.

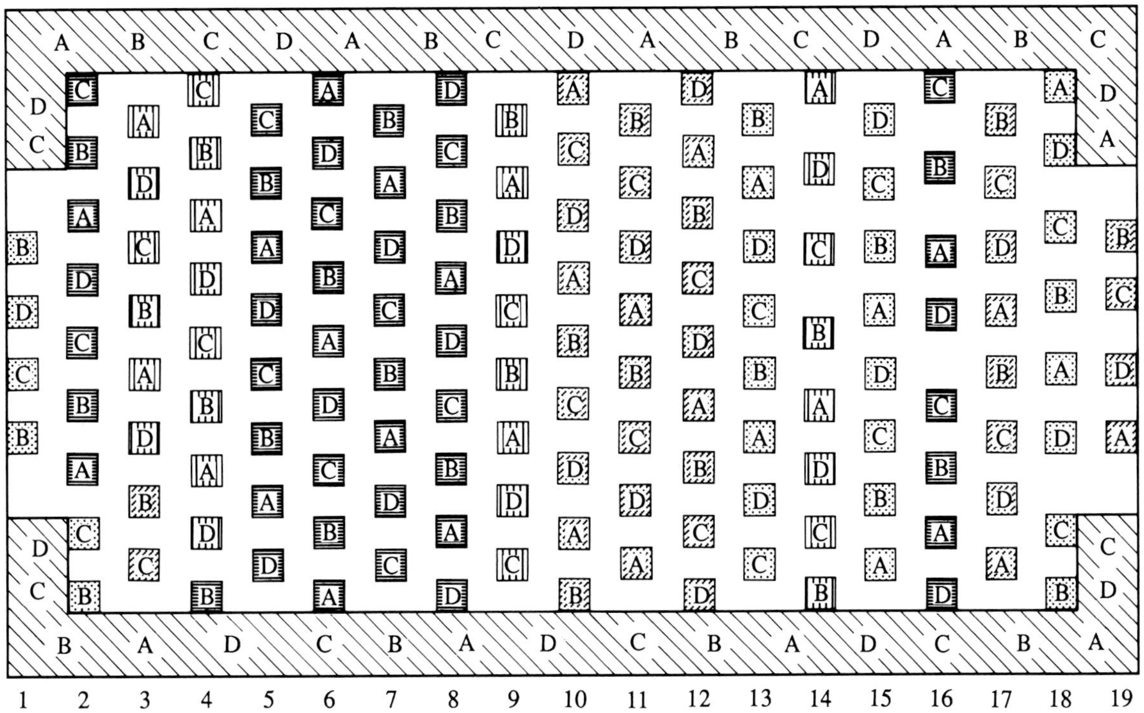

	Worker 1			Worker 3
	Worker 2		*	Unfinished

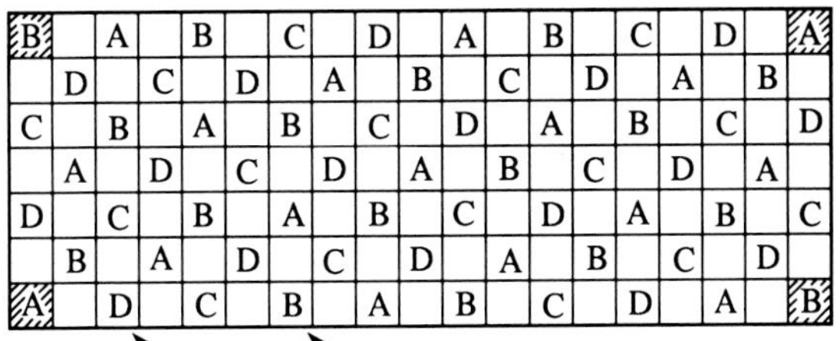

Fig. II.10. Color blocks in mantle cat. no. 69 (color pl. 5). The arrows at the bottom edge of the diagram mark diagonals where the starting color block is out of sequence. The color-block sequence of the one remaining longitudinal border is not indicated on the diagram because most of this border has been reconstructed.

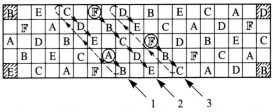

Fig. II.11. a. Ideal, or intended, color-block pattern for mantle cat. no. 68 (color pl. 12). To follow the A–B–C–D–E sequence on the diagonal marked by arrow 1, the viewer must imagine that each color block is a link on a closed moving chain (the starting color block of each sequence is circled). With A as the starting point, the eye moves one notch forward to B and then moves up the "back side" of the diagonal to C at the top; D and E in the next two notches complete the cycle. In the diagonal at arrow 2, wild card F substitutes for A, followed by B–C–D–E. F also substitutes for A in the next diagonal to the right (at arrow 3); this starting position has moved two notches forward from that of the previous diagonal.

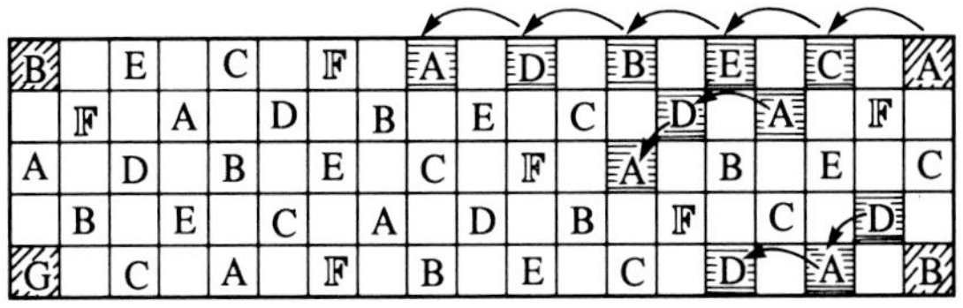

Fig. II.11. b. Color blocks in mantle cat. no. 68 (color pl. 12). Horizontally hatched letters indicate color blocks that are positioned out of sequence, assuming that the ideal pattern presented in figure II.11a was the intended arrangement. Most of these deviations can be "corrected" by a simple shifting of color blocks to the left (see arrows in diagram). For an explanation of color block G in the lower left corner, see my note 8.

Fig. II.12. Color blocks and hands at work in mantle cat. no. 191 (color pl. 11)

	Worker 1			Worker 3
	Worker 2			Worker 4

Color Blocks

The embroidered images on any single Paracas weaving are usually the same iconographically (for an exception, see cat. no. 91, color pl. 7), but this iconographic uniformity is animated by color diversity that prevents rows and columns of repetitious figures from becoming static and monotonous. At the same time, the complex color schemes characteristic of Paracas Necrópolis fabrics are carefully controlled to prevent visual chaos. This can be illustrated by examining the figures in the field of mantle cat. no. 68 (color pl. 12), where there is a finite number of ways to color forty-four images of a fish impersonator. In the third image from the right in the middle row, the upper body of the fish is light blue, the forehead ornament is brown, the limbs are gold, the tunic is dark brown, the loincloth is red, the anklets are blue, and so on. Any other image on the mantle that has a light blue upper fish body will have its other components stitched in the same colors as this figure. I call this specific color configuration of the consitutent parts of an iconographic unit a "color block." In all there are six color blocks in the field of the garment.[8]

The organization of the colors of images by color blocks is basic to the style of Paracas Necrópolis textiles (and is present in all the substyles of decoration), even though the number of color blocks per garment can vary. The linear-style poncho in fig. II.2 (cat. no. 186, color pl. 3), for example, has just four color blocks, and each bird has fewer constituent parts than the fish impersonator just described. But the concept of coloring the images according to a system of color blocks is still basic to its design.

Filling in the Color Blocks

Faced with a large garment covered with the outlines of many images, each having many constituent parts to be colored according to color blocks worked out for that particular fabric, how did the embroiderers keep all of the colors straight? Sometimes they did not succeed: one mantle in the Museum's collection (cat. no. 303, color pl. 4a,b) was designed with four color blocks in mind, but there is an unusually high number of color irregularities. In most cases, however, the embroiderers maintained pattern regularity, and there are tiny clues in an unfinished mantle that show how this was done. Mantle cat. no. 71 (color pl. 8a,b) has depictions of bird impersonators; a few of the details of this iconographic unit and their corresponding colors (as they appear on the borders) are listed here, grouped by color block (letters A_1–D_1):

Color block	A_1	B_1	C_1	D_1
Limbs	green	dk blue	dk green	red
Tunic	dk blue	green	red	dark green
Loincloth	blue	*cream*	cream	olive
Headdress	turquoise	*purple*	brown	dk blue
Striped staff:				
"tape"	green	*red*	dk blue	dk green
tongue	*red*	purple	dk blue	purple
Bell staff				
triangles	green	*red*	dk green	white
Bell:				
top	beige	*gray*	dk blue	red
bottom	dk blue	*green*	brown	green
Trophy head face	*white/ dk purple*	red/ green	blue	cream/ red

Since most of the figures on the longitudinal borders that belong to this mantle are complete, the correct configuration of colors for each of the four color blocks can be established.[9] This permits us to reconstruct the purpose of the snippets of loose thread visible in several of the unfinished figures in the border brackets of the mantle. Scrutiny of the two images illustrated in color pl. 8b reveals bits of thread still caught in the dark blue fabric. These threads are codes for the color that was to have been used in that particular detail of the image. For example, one of the bird impersonators (color pl. 8b, left) has a red thread in the tongue at the end of the striped staff and a trophy-head face that is marked with two threads, white and dark purple (see colors in italics in list above). These color codes, along with details that have already been embroidered, indicate that its color block was A_1. Next to this figure (color pl. 8b, right) is one with a cream thread in the loincloth, a purple thread in the headdress, a red thread in the "tape" of the striped staff, a red thread in a triangle on the bell staff, and one gray and one green thread on the top and bottom sections of the bell, respectively. Each of these colors is consistent with the configuration for color block B_1. This method of color-coding images in order to facilitate correct resolution of the color blocks has been observed on only one other mantle (see Paul and Niles 1985:13), but it is such a sensible and quintessentially fiber solution to an embroiderer's problem that it surely must have been a common practice.

Irregularities in Color Block Details

When data were collected on the garments in the Museum's collection, the "rules" were ascertained for each color block on a piece, and then every image was examined to check for compliance with or deviation from those rules. Consistency and variation between the color blocks on any given garment create intelligible patterns that can help reconstruct some of the procedures followed in the making of that fabric.

Sometimes two different shades of one color of yarn appear on a single garment, the result of dyeing the yarn in different dyebaths; these color variations are visible in the finished garment (for further discussion, see Paul 1990b). This is true in a skirt (cat. no. 91, color pl. 7) that has four different anthropomorphic figures repeated over its surface. (All figures within one iconographic type are of the same color block.) Among the colors of yarn used to embroider the images, red is particularly interesting. Two distinct dyelots of red yarn can be identified, one of which is still in good condition and the other of which has deteriorated either partially or entirely.[10] Both reds are used in all four iconographic types, but they are distributed in discernible patterns over the surface of the skirt.

When the use of degraded versus nondegraded red yarns is plotted separately for each of the four figural types, the following patterns of yarn usage emerge. There are two possible patterns for the figural type A (wearing a turban that hangs to one side): one where a quarter of the figure's face and the trophy-head hair have been stitched in red thread that has been lost (Worker A-1) and another where none of the red threads have deteriorated completely (Worker A-2). Figure B (with a feather headdress) also has two possible patterns: one with the face of the figure and the hair on the trophy head deteriorated (Worker B-1) and another where red yarns in these areas remain in good condition (Worker B-2). Figure C (with a net on the head) has three possible patterns: one in which the yarns of the net and anklets have deteriorated but with the other reds in good condition (Worker C-1); another in which all red yarns are intact (Worker C-2); and a third in which only the anklets have degraded (Worker C-3). Figure D (with a snake headdress) also has three patterns: one in which the snakes and the extended arm have deteriorated but the other reds remain (Worker D-1); one that has no deteriorated red threads (Worker D-2); and a third in which the leg(s) and / or feet, but not the snakes or arm, are deteriorated (Worker D-3).

When the four sets of information are plotted on a single diagram (fig. II.9), the following picture emerges: the figures that have some deteriorated red threads cluster together, as do the figures in which the red threads remain intact. We may infer, therefore, that

Worker 1 for each of the four types was the same individual and also that one person was responsible for the four types filled in by Worker 2 above. Worker 1 consistently used red yarns that came from two distinct dyelots, one with a mordant and one without, while Worker 2 used exclusively unmordanted reds. Worker 3, who embroidered only two of the four iconographic types, used two types of red yarn.[11] In addition to showing that at least two and probably three people embroidered the images on this skirt, this analysis of the distribution of shades of red threads indicates that Worker 1 embroidered chiefly on the left half of the skirt and Workers 2 and 3 worked primarily on the right half, and that the work areas of the three embroiderers were contiguous on S diagonals (see below). In a few areas several figures by one worker, arranged on a diagonal, intrude into the space of another worker, and in four figures the pattern of red yarns suggests that two different workers embroidered on the same figure.

Patterns Produced by Color-Block Repetition

Color blocks bring order to the diverse colors that appear in the designs on a garment, but they function in yet another way: the particular configuration created by the alternation of color blocks in the field of a garment carries a system of order of its own. These color-block alternations do not depict anything in a representational way. Instead, the content of color repeats is more likely about the possibility of arranging color blocks in complicated configurations while adhering to strict rules; the system that governs the arrangement of color blocks on a fabric carries a meaning that extends beyond that of the figures themselves, conveying something about ideas of ordering within Paracas society.

As we have seen, many Paracas garments have field images that are aligned in rows and columns on the surface of the fabric. Although there is variation in the numbers of rows, columns, and figures per textile, there is a limited number of ways to order the images by their color blocks. The system that underlies the organization of the color blocks becomes apparent when diagonal lines are imposed on the rectangular matrix of the field. Using the figures as the matrix elements, a diagonal line is defined as a line that starts with any figure in the field and proceeds in a single oblique direction to connect with any other figure that is simultaneously in the next adjacent row and column. The diagonal line may be drawn either to the right or to the left (i.e., in the S or Z direction). When the figures that are connected along a diagonal are plotted by their color blocks, each of which is designated by a different letter, patterns of color-block repeats are created. These patterns fall into different types, only two of which are described here (Paul 1988 has isolated and discussed these types in collaboration with Mary Frame; see also Frame 1991:139–144).

One common sequence of color repetitions alternates two bi-color diagonals, using a total of four color blocks: in the mantle in fig. II.10 (cat. no. 69, color pl. 5), the S diagonals comprising color blocks A and C start at the top (or bottom) of the mantle alternately with color block A and color block C; the "starting" color block of a B–D diagonal alternates as well. Occasionally the "starting" color block of a diagonal violates the alternation pattern (as in two B–D diagonals on the left side of this mantle, marked with arrows in fig. II.10), causing the pattern of color repeats to be thrown off in the horizontal and vertical directions. These errors support the contention that the patterns are meant to be read along the diagonal defined above: it alone retains the regular alternation of color blocks.

A particularly complex sequence of color repeats was established in mantles cat. nos. 68 and 70 (color pls. 12 and 13). In each of these garments the pattern calls for six color blocks, five of which are arranged in repeating pentacolor diagonals. The design plan requires that all like-facing diagonals have the same sequence of color blocks, but with the color blocks shifting positions from one diagonal to the next, as though they were links on a closed moving chain. In the mantle in fig. II.11a (cat. no. 68, color pl. 12), for example, the sequence of color blocks on the S diagonals, reading down, can be given as A–B–C–D–E. We can select any S diagonal, and the color blocks should repeat this sequence cyclically, with the starting A position shifting two notches forward in the sequence in each contiguous diagonal to the right. A further level of complication in the plan is introduced by the function of the sixth color block as a "wild card": it can be substituted for any one of the other five color blocks in order to achieve the sequencing pattern. Hence, in cat. no. 68 (color pl. 12), F (the wild card) can be placed anywhere on a diagonal to stand for the color block that keeps the A–B–C–D–E sequence from being interrupted. The same pattern unfolds on the Z diagonal, with an A–D–B–E–C sequence reading down.

Mantles cat. nos. 68 and 70 (color pls. 12 and 13) contain several deviations in their color-block alternation patterns. These areas in mantle cat. no. 68 are indicated with horizontal hatching in the diagram fig. II.11b, and arrows indicate how the pattern could be "corrected." The type of color-block pattern created on these two mantles is so unusual and so complex that, in my opinion, they must have been designed and made by the same persons. This would tend to confirm the reports accompanying their acquisition in 1916 (nine years before the scientific discovery of the Paracas Peninsula sites) that the two pieces had been found together in the same Paracas funerary bundle (Paul 1991:33).

Irregularities in Color-Block Patterns

The formulation of the color-block pattern is not resolved correctly on all garments, and when there are enough irregularities on a single garment, it is sometimes possible to detect the distinct work areas of different embroiderers. Mantle cat. no. 191 (color pl. 11), for instance, has dozens of figures embroidered in the field; when I first tried to decode the color-repeat pattern, it seemed that there was none. This was because irregularities in its execution had obscured the intended pattern. The correct pattern of A–C and B–D diagonals is achieved in only a few places (e.g., columns 5–8; see fig. II.12). Several factors contribute to this unresolved arrangement of color blocks. First, three columns (14, 16, and 18) are each short one shaman, and as a result the figures in the top part of the columns are positioned incorrectly on the diagonals. Second, the A–B–C–D sequence of color blocks in vertical columns should read from the bottom edge of the diagram to its top, but in four areas the sequencing is reversed and reads from the top edge down. Third, entire columns of color blocks are shifted one or two positions up or down, throwing the diagonal alternations out of alignment.

As in other mantles for which the hands of different embroiderers have been identified (see Paul and Niles 1985; Paul 1986), the work areas on this mantle were columns or, when one person worked several contiguous columns, vertical blocks. There were probably at least four people filling in all the shaman outlines with colored yarns. The four-column-wide section that contains the observable color-block pattern, along with two other areas, is attributed to Worker 1 (fig. II.12).[12] These are the portions of the mantle that have all color blocks correctly alternating in all directions (vertical, horizontal, S and Z diagonals). Worker 1 probably set the model for the color-block pattern, which was then followed without complete success by other embroiderers.

Worker 2 is assigned to the areas where the bottom-to-top reading of the A–B–C–D vertical sequence is maintained but where the entire sequence shifts one notch down, throwing the color blocks out of alignment on the horizontals and diagonals. Worker 3, like Worker 2, has the A–B–C–D vertical sequence going in the right direction but shifts the entire column out of sequence, either one or two notches up. The columns and parts of columns in which the reading of the vertical A–B–C–D sequence is reversed, so that it reads from the top down, are all attributed to Worker 4.

The profound visual impression that Paracas textiles make on us, as modern viewers, can be enhanced by our realization that these fabrics, in addition to being strikingly beautiful, retain traces of the hands that stitched them and provide glimpses of the amazingly intricate and elaborate programs of the Paracas mind. Some of the pieces discussed in this catalogue reveal less of their past than others (finely executed finished weavings tend to conceal evidence, while unfinished garments offer more that is retrievable; see p. 11), but examination of different aspects of a number of different textiles has made it possible to present a broad picture of the creative process. Integral to this process were the procedures of outlining, aligning, and filling in with color, as well as the more abstract construction of the underlying and pervasive systems that governed the overall design of Paracas fabrics. These fabrics embrace many levels of meaning, and to understand but a fraction of their complexities is to appreciate how supremely important weaving, both technically and conceptually, was to the ancient Andeans who created them.

Notes

Study of the Paracas textiles in the Museum of Fine Arts was made possible by the organization, understanding, and kindness of Deborah Kraak, former assistant curator in the Department of Textiles and Costumes, whose help I warmly acknowledge here. Among the persons who ably assisted me in the department, two deserve special mention: Ellen Averick and Moira Sutherland, volunteers, graciously helped with the sometimes tedious task of recording data. I also thank Susan Niles for her comments during the research phase of the project and Rebecca Stone-Miller for her critical readings of my essay.

1. The scientific discovery and exploration of sites on the Paracas Peninsula has been discussed by Tello and Mejía 1979 and by Daggett 1991. Since the Paracas textiles in the Museum of Fine Arts were not excavated by archaeologists, there is no information concerning their precise provenance. However, their technical, design, stylistic, and iconographic features are so similar to those of fabrics recovered scientifically from graves on the Paracas Peninsula, that there is little doubt in my mind that they, too, came from that area. The textiles recovered from cemeteries on the Paracas Peninsula have been dated roughly to the period 200 B.C.–A.D. 200. For a recent discussion of the relative and absolute chronologies of the Paracas cultural tradition, see Paul 1991.

2. For a review of Paracas weavers' technical accomplishments, see Paul 1990a:13–15. The structure of this weaving (Rowe 1972), though rare, is found among the material excavated from the Necrópolis cemetery on the Paracas Peninsula (see Paul 1990a:78, color pl. 3), and its iconography is standard within the Paracas Necrópolis corpus of images.

3. It is not uncommon to find unfinished textiles among the contents of the Paracas Necrópolis bundles. One plausible explanation for this practice is that many garments apparently were made specifically for one individual, and if that person died before a weaving was completed, it was nevertheless included among the burial wrappings.

4. Usually a figure was outlined in its entirety before the embroiderer began to fill in the parts, but a detail on one skirt (cat. no. 91, color pl. 7) shows that this was not always the case: the person stitching the far left-hand figure on the bottom row outlined the legs and then began to stitch them in before completing the outline of the entire figure.

5. The borders on mantles often take the form of "brackets": each longitudinal border turns both corners and continues along part of the width edge. The "bracket" parts of the borders are embroidered directly on the ground cloth of the garment's field; even though they are not made separately and attached, as is sometimes true for the longitudinal borders, I consider them to relate conceptually to the longitudinal borders. This area of a mantle will be referred to as the "border bracket." An unfinished border background is visible in cat. no. 191, color pl. 11 (top right corner).

6. A letter dated November 21, 1917 (on file in the Department of Textiles and Costumes, Museum of Fine Arts) from Sarah G. Flint, assistant in charge of textiles, refers to the washing and mounting of some of the Paracas textiles acquired in 1916. It is possible that some basting-thread losses occurred during or after this process.

7. Another system determines the orientation of images on a garment (see Mary Frame 1986, 1989, 1991). Both are the subject of an ongoing research project that Mary Frame and I are undertaking.

8. A seventh color block, G, appears only once, in the lower left border bracket. This color block may have "belonged to" a set of color blocks in the borders that differed from the set in the field (see my note 9 on mantle cat. no. 71, for example), although this cannot be proved since no longitudinal borders were acquired by the Museum of Fine Arts along with the mantle.

9. The longitudinal borders, cat. nos. 71b, c, were acquired by the Museum of Fine Arts after mantle cat. no. 71a, but from the same source (Julio C. Tello); they must have been buried with the mantle in a burial bundle, but it is not clear that they were ever attached.
   The faces of border figures have a slightly different set of face markings from those of field figures. The ground cloth of the borders is dark green rather than dark blue. Furthermore, the set of four color blocks in the longitudinal borders and in the border brackets of the mantle (indicated with subscript numbers) differs from the set of four used in the field, an arrangement that is not typical of the Paracas garments I have studied. That the border brackets belong conceptually to the longitudinal borders, even though they are physically embroidered on the field, is indicated by the fact that their color blocks correspond to those of the borders, not of the field.

10. The selective degradation of one of two similarly colored yarns has often been attributed to the use of iron as a mordant for one dyelot. There is, however, no scientific evidence supporting this opinion; indeed, the use of two different mordants would produce two distinctly different colors. Iron is known to cause accelerated deterioration when used in combination with a tannin to produce browns and blacks, but the exact reason for the differential preservation of the two reds is at present unknown (Deborah Bede, personal communication, 1991).

11. It is not entirely clear whether Worker 3 was in fact a third person or whether these figures were stitched in part by Worker 1 and in part by Worker 2.

12. The images in the top half of column 16, by Worker 1, do not align correctly with other diagonals, but this is a problem with their spacing; the color blocks, in fact, are in the "correct" order.

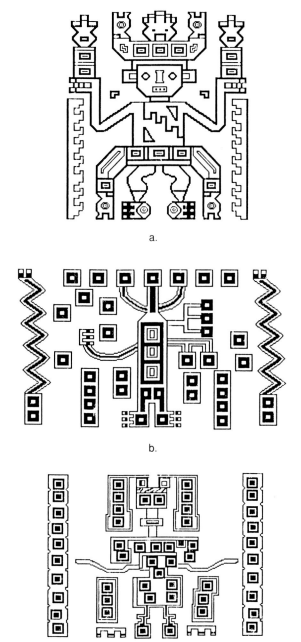

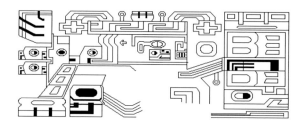

Fig. III.2, cat. no. 262. Overall view of fragmentary band cat. no. 262, probaby converted into a headband, containing abstracted staff-bearing figures. See fig. III.1b.

Fig. III.3a,b. Wari tapestry tunic fragment cat. no. 201
      a. Overall view
      b. Reconstruction of staff-bearer motif (Drawing by Rebecca Stone-Miller)

a.

b.

c.

Fig. III.1a–c. Staff-bearer motifs, at various levels of abstraction, from Wari-related tapestries (Drawing by Rebecca Stone-Miller).
      a. Cat. no. 125, color pl. 30
      b. Cat. no. 262 (fig. III.2)
      c. Cat. no. 278, color pl. 31

III: Creative Abstractions: Middle Horizon Textiles in the Museum of Fine Arts, Boston

Rebecca Stone-Miller

Textiles from the period known as the Middle Horizon (about A.D. 500–800) form an extraordinary corpus of woven works of art (color pls. 21–33). At first these bold compositions seem to celebrate geometry itself; their designs read as grid-based, rectilinear, strikingly coloristic, dynamic, and, above all, *illegible* pattern. This is a valid first impression, one that may well have been calculated by the makers of these stunning tunics, mantles, and headwear (Stone 1987, vol. 1:192, 193). However, by delving deeply into the artistic system it is possible to recognize many of the actual images as well as geometric forms that made up the expressive system of the Wari (Huari), a state that controlled most of what is now Peru during this time (fig. I.3). The iconographic categories represented in the Museum's collection can best be summarized as follows:

Staff-bearing figures
>   cat. no. 125, color pl. 30 (fig. III.1a)
>   cat. no. 201 (fig. III.3a,b)
>   cat. no. 262 (figs. III.1b, 3.2)
>   cat. no. 278, color pl. 31 (fig. III.1c)

Tunic-wearers
>   cat. no. 282, color pl. 32

Frontal faces
>   cat. nos. 200A, C, color pl. 26
>   cat. no. 213, color pl. 25

Profile faces
>   cat. no. 312, color pl. 22a,b

Skulls
>   cat. no. 316, color pl. 24

Animals
>   cat. no. 94 (fig. III.4)
>   cat. no. 214, color pl. 29
>   cat. no. 249, color pl. 27
>   cat. no. 312, color pl. 22a,b
>   cat. no. 313, color pl. 22a,b

Stepped diamonds
>   cat. nos. 200B and D, color pl. 26
>   cat. no. 241, color pl. 28
>   cat. no. 242 (fig. III.5)
>   cat. no. 313, color pl. 22a,b

Stepped triangles and frets
>   cat. no. 272 (fig. III.6).
>   cat. no. 312, color pl. 22a,b
>   cat. no. 319, color pl. 21a,b

It is the artistic process of abstraction —one of the most intriguing in all creative endeavor— that unites readable imagery and relentless pattern into a complex aesthetic. Abstraction, at base, extracts the essence of an image from its surface appearance and, therefore, presupposes an individual interpretative presence to transform shape toward the essential. Two complete Wari tapestry tunics in the Museum's collection, cat. nos. 312 (color pl. 23a,b) and 313 (color pl. 22a,b) most clearly reveal how the creative weavers of the Wari state expressed themselves through abstraction and deviation from formal repetition (figs. III.10a,b, and III.11a,b). The range of other Wari and Wari-related textiles in the collection demonstrates the various techniques and levels of abstraction explored. When the idiosyncratic choices in each composition are uncovered, the creative contribution of particular textile artists can be felt strongly. This essay endeavors to redress a gap in the textile and art historical literature by briefly reviewing this extraordinary abstracting style.

As background for this discussion, the period in question was dominated by an expansive state known as the Wari, which held sway over much of what is now Peru, along with an allied state known as Tiwanaku (or Tiahuanaco), which controlled what is now western Bolivia, northwestern Argentina, and northern Chile (fig. I.3). These two polities shared and exported an iconography that revolved around a staff-bearing figure, as seen most clearly on the so-called Sun Gate at the site of Tiwanaku (fig. III.7). Both groups primarily utilized textiles, specifically, finely woven tapestry garments, to disseminate their message of religious-political control. The militaristic highland Wari conquered the various North and South Coastal peoples, imposing their visual vocabulary along with their state organization, with the aesthetic result that closely related regional versions of the standardized sacred images, such as the staff-bearing figure (fig. III.1a–c), were produced.

The staff-bearer iconography concerns a winged, standing human, human-bird, or human-feline composite figure, holding one or two staffs and wearing an elaborate headdress (fig. III.3a,b). Such figures are found in rows on the Sun Gate (fig. III.7), apparently representing the attendants to the central frontal deity. We may assume that the people wearing this image in the form of a tunic declared themselves as priests or administrators in relation to what was probably a creator deity fused with state authority.

In textile versions, these staff bearers may be more or less readable depending on how extreme the abstraction (compare figs. III.1a–c, III.2, and III.3a,b). It is interesting to reflect that the creation of increasingly illegible versions was *not* the result of increasing misunderstanding of the image, since the various figure parts and their interrelationships are not garbled.[1] In fact, Wari images of the "classic" style are often less legible than those of the peripheral styles, in which such misunderstanding might be expected (Stone 1986).

Rather, the various changes made to the stock elements of the staff bearer and other motifs demonstrate a deeper, wholly artistic understanding of the image's underlying structure. For example, in the staff-bearer motif in fig. III.1c (cat. no. 278, color pl. 31) square-with-in-square shapes seem to multiply, making visual equivalences between the staff segments, costume elements (such as the belt), and facial features (such as the eyes). Nevertheless, these diverse parts maintain their logic: pairs of eye-squares appear on the upper face, while staff segments are stacked to one side of the body.

At this point, when identical shapes stand for decidedly non-identical features, the image has become highly esoteric; only a select group could have identified the subject at all. As levels of abstraction increase, the subject matter becomes the pattern of colors and shapes itself (Stone 1986; Stone 1987, vol. 1:187). Of central importance in the present context is that *artists* are responsible for such an emphasis in a style because it is they who actively extract the visual essence and disassemble the repeated motif. In keeping with the theme of "To Weave for the Sun," creative individuality is revealed in the direction and the wandering of such abstracting vision.

Technique

Wari and Tiwanaku textile artists explored tapestry as the preeminent technique during the Middle Horizon (as did the Incas during the Late Horizon; see pp. 51, 54–64). It was reserved for the highest status, generally official state objects. The key to this preference for tapestry lies in its technical characteristics, which highlight the power of the patrons to control material and human resources. Tapestry in itself is not a complex method of creating cloth, being a variant of plain weave, in which alternate rows of wefts are passed over and under warps. However, since each fine weft thread is packed down to completely cover the thicker warp threads, a huge amount of thread is needed to produce high-quality tapestries. In a typical Wari tunic, for example, between six and nine *miles* of thread are used (Stone 1987, vol. 1:60). In addition, great skill on the part of spinners and weavers is required to produce and manipulate such gossamer-thin thread (cat. no. 312, color pl. 23b). In a Wari tunic over 50 wefts are packed into a centimeter of cloth (more than 125 per inch), and in one related Tiwanaku-style miniature tunic 80 wefts per centimeter (more than 200 per inch) can be counted (Stone 1987, vol. 3:133, cat. no. 167).

Thus, the creation of fine tapestry —regardless of the imagery woven into it— demonstrates that the patron, that is, the state and its officials, has control over vast resources. Controlled materials include coastal cotton for the warps and highland camelid fiber for the wefts, while other resources include the efforts of a multitude of specialists of different kinds (see pp. 14, 17). Further, tapestry as a technique easily produces dense, detailed, intensely colorful imagery, a characteristic that makes it especially suited to the elaborate depictions of a religio-political nature. In a culture characterized by "textile primacy" (see pp. 13–18) these messages of power would not go unnoticed, either within the state hierarchy or by the conquered. Thus, it appears logical that tapestry, particularly in the form of the tunic, was selected for official garments of the Wari representatives as they conquered and administered along the coast.

Other textile techniques were also explored in the creation of an entire ritual clothing ensemble for these high-status individuals. According to ceramic effigy vessels (fig. III.8), tunic-wearers also wore the square hat, such as cat. no. 249 (color pl. 27), and painted their faces in textile-based geometric patterns. Together these layers of geometries made the wearer into a walking pattern (Stone 1987, vol. 1:97). Wearers of this ensemble are found buried in it as well. The tunic is dressed over the mummy bundle (fig. III.9) in which the body is seated in a fetal position and padded with cotton batting inside a rough cloth covering; a stuffed cloth head is then attached to the top. Hats (cat. no. 249, color pl. 27) as well as headbands (cat. no. 241, color pl. 28; cat. no. 242, fig. III.5) are found depicted on the effigy vessels (fig. III.8) and may have been worn on the mummy bundles (fig. III.9). Most headgear was made in cut pile, a technique in which a continuous thread is knotted to form the ground while parallel, discontinuous, dyed threads are left to the outside in loops that were then cut (see Frame 1990). Tapestry headbands, albeit converted from bands and woven in Wari-related styles, are also known (cat. no. 262 and cat. no. 278, color pl. 31). The person's hair was converted into a wig for his mummy bundle's false head (similar to cat. no. 187, color pl. 33). The wig's multiple braids were wrapped at their ends with bands of colored camelid-fiber threads; thus hair, like the rest of the body, was transformed into a geometricized textile.

In addition, brilliantly colored feathers were worked into garments and hangings by tying their quills to threads and sewing these in overlapping rows onto a backing cloth. Tropical feathers were greatly prized, making these highly prestigious works of art, yet they too may refer back to the tapestry tunics and their wearers, as in cat. no. 282 (color pl. 32). Finally, effigy vessels (fig. III.8) show the tie-dyed mantles (cat. no. 235; cat. no. 272, fig. III.6; cat. no. 319, color pl. 21a,b) being worn in the same context as the tapestry tunics. These are known as "patchworks" but actually were made in a complex series of steps involving scaffold threads, tying and dyeing, and sewing (see entry for cat. no. 319, color pl. 21a,b; see also A. Rowe

Fig. III.4. Overall view of Wari tapestry tunic fragment cat. no. 94. The motif features a fanged animal head, handlike form, bird with serrated body. The fragment has been pieced together from various sections of the original tunic.

Fig. III.5. Overall view of Wari-related, thin pile headband cat. no. 242 with geometric motifs. See also cat. no. 241, color pl. 28, and cat. no. 249, color pl. 27.

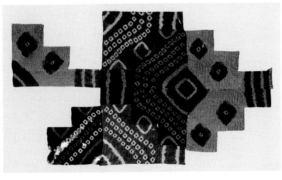

Fig. III.6. Overall view of fragmentary tie-dyed panel cat. no. 272. See cat. no. 319, color pl. 21a,b.

Fig. III.7. The sculpted part of the Sun Gate at Tiwanaku, showing attendant staff bearers, in profile, in rows surrounding central frontal deity (Drawing after Posnansky 1945, vol. 1, pl. 48).

Fig. III.8. Wari ceramic effigy vessel shown wearing a tie-dyed tunic. Museum Rietberg, Zurich, RPB 320 (Photograph by Wettstein and Kauf, Zurich). See cat. nos. 235, 272 (fig. III.6), and 319, color pl. 21a,b.

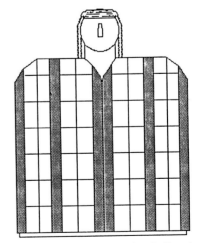

Fig. III.9. Wari false-headed mummy bundle (Drawing by Rebecca Stone-Miller)

1977:31–32). The Museum's stunning example shows yet again the Wari tendency to intermix regular and irregular patterning in whatever technique is chosen (trace, for instance, the diagonals of stepped pieces with gold background).

The Wari Tunic

The tunic, as a central object during this period, deserves in-depth consideration. The collection considered here includes five tunics, two of which are very fine, complete examples (cat. nos. 312, color pl. 23a,b, and 313, color pl. 22a,b), and three of which are well-preserved, representative fragments (cat. no. 94, fig. III.4; cat. no. 201, fig. III.3a,b; cat. no. 213, color pl. 25). Together these demonstrate a range of characteristic motifs and formal combinations. They serve as keys to the textile artist of this period, whose unending creativity within the strictures of set repetition of motifs underlines the importance of individual interpretations even within an official state form. While "creativity within constraints" may seem paradoxical, it is precisely such a rigid iconographic structure that seems to encourage bold formal exploration.

In my consideration of formal irregularities in a Wari tunic, I distinguish between "deviations" and "anomalies." Deviations represent slight irregularities, such as the striping of a different shade of red or the inversion of one shape in a motif; they occur in less than 25 percent of the cases in a given composition. Anomalies consist of more extreme irregularities, such as the introduction of an unprecedented color or a completely different motif; these occur in less than 10 percent of the cases (see Stone 1987, vol. 1:112–113).

On a general note, Wari textile artists worked collaboratively to create these remarkable tunics, according to the evidence of their construction. The two panels sewn together vertically in the tunic as it was worn were in fact woven as webs approximately 240 centimeters wide by 60 centimeters long (8 by 2 feet). This accounts for the unusual sideways direction of the warp in the finished product and contrasts with most ancient Andean textiles woven the long way on backstrap looms (see fig. I.13; p. 20); for Inca and some Colonial exceptions, see figs. V.4, V.5, and V.15). I have previously suggested various reasons for this idiosyncratic choice (Stone 1987, vol. 1:82–85, 88–99). In any case, to weave such a panel would have necessitated more than one weaver to manipulate the very long, heavy loom bars. In addition, the plain areas of most Wari tunics display what are known as "lazy lines," diagonal lines of noninterlocked wefts that signal different work areas. These strongly buttress the idea that different hands were working simultaneously on contiguous portions. Thus, the ground is laid for these different artists to interpret the design in various ways.

Of the two entire tunics, cat. no. 313 (color pl. 22a,b) is the simpler, brighter, and more formally regular. It is typical in its overall layout, with six columns of motifs across the face (including the very narrow side columns). Columns of motifs are outlined in tan then internally subdivided by a white grid of lines and separated from one another by plain colored areas, here in a characteristic rich cochineal red (see cat. no. 62, color pl. 37). A stepped-diamond motif, rather rare in the overall corpus of Wari tunics, alternates with an interlocked double-headed animal (fig. III.10a). The double-headed animal is quite difficult to read: it consists of two interlocked U-shaped forms, each with both ends terminating in an animal head, which has a circular nose, bisected eye, U-shaped mouth, and S-shaped neck element. This motif is quite common among tunics and is found in various degrees of abstraction, of which this one is relatively less extreme. The animal is generally thought of as a puma.

In the presentation of these set motifs, the artists kept to a consistent version; in other words, they did not alter the shapes in any significant way. However, the overall color patterning (the assigning of color combinations in a certain pattern to certain motifs) does have a few irregularities (fig. III.10b). Red and gold stepped-diamond motifs alternate in diagonal pairs with gold and blue motifs, as do pink and light brown double animals with tan and gold ones. Yet there are two intentional deviations from this rule, both found in the narrow column in one corner, in which two golds follow one another out of sequence. In addition, throughout the composition color deviations occur within individual shapes (fig. III.10b): visually prominent striping of different dyelots of blue-green and brown and the substitution of a darker shade of brown for one light brown double animal.[2] There are also two motifs missing in which other deviations may have occurred originally. Although the complexity of the design tends to mask these irregularities, they nevertheless add underlying formal dynamism to the composition.

Cat. no. 312 (color pl. 23a,b) is a great deal more irregular (fig. III.11a,b). Its three alternating motifs include a distinctive version of the double-headed animal, the stepped fret (similar to what is known as the Greek key), and the triangular profile face (characterized by the ubiquitous split eye, a broad headband, nose, and U-shaped mouth; see fig. III.11a). Yet within each of these repeated motifs there are many formal subtypes: there are sixteen versions of the double-headed animal, two of the fret, and four of the profile face. For example, features such as the number of heads, the number of eyes and mouths in each head, and their relative positions create the many double-animal types. There are also thirteen instances of what

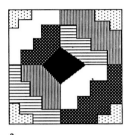

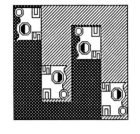

a.

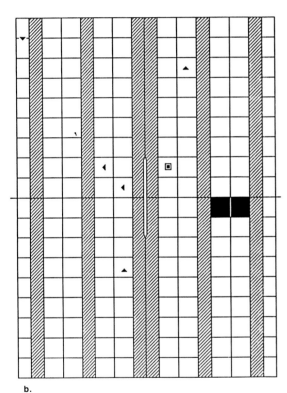

b.

Key:

◙ tan substitution for dark brown

◀ striping in blue-green

▲ striping in brown

▼ two golds in a row instead of alteration 'nation

■ missing portions

Fig. III.10a,b. Wari tapestry tunic cat. no. 313, color pl. 22a,b
(Drawing and diagram by Rebecca Stone-Miller)
a. Stepped-diamond and double-headed animal motifs
b. Formal deviations (see key, color pl. 22b)

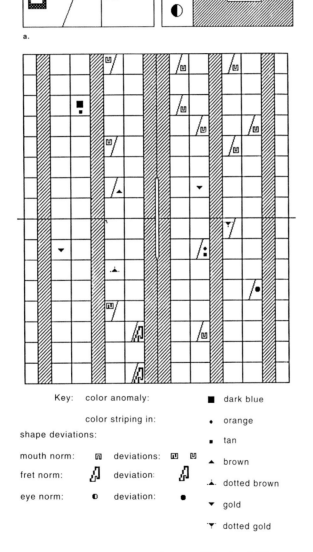

Key: color anomaly: ■ dark blue

     color striping in: ◆ orange

shape deviations: ▪ tan

mouth norm: ⋒   deviations: ⋓ ⋓   ▲ brown

fret norm: ♫   deviation: ♫   ⋏ dotted brown

eye norm: ◐   deviation: ●   ▼ gold

                        ▼̈ dotted gold

Fig. III.11a,b. Wari tapestry tunic cat. no. 312, color pl. 23a,b
(Drawing and diagram by Rebecca Stone-Miller)
a. Stepped-diamond and double-headed animal motifs
b. Formal deviations (see key, color pl. 23b)

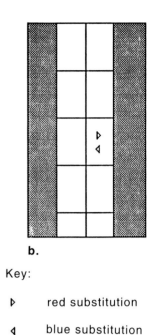

a.

b.

Key:

▷   red substitution

◁   blue substitution

Fig. III.12a,b. Wari tapestry tunic fragment cat. no. 213, color
pl. 25 (Drawing and diagram by Rebecca Stone-Miller)
a. Split-face motifs
b. Formal deviations (see key)

can be seen as shape deviations, that is, individual shapes that differ in some slight but visible way from the rest, such as a filled-in eye or an unusual mouth on a profile face.

This tunic also displays very irregular color patterning (fig. III.11b). There are a number of striping color deviations in gold and brown areas, two of which are striking interrupted lines. Of particular importance is the occurrence of a single dark indigo blue element (see cat. no. 312, color pl. 23b). It is typical of Wari textile design to have such a purposely intrusive element, especially in blue. My research has revealed that almost all Wari tunics contain anomalous shapes or colors (those otherwise unprecedented in the composition and occurring less than 10 percent of the time) and all display deviant ones (those differing in a minor way from the expected configuration and occurring less than 25 percent of the time) (Stone 1987, vol. 1:148–170). Two-thirds of all color anomalies are in the green-to-blue color range. This may be because indigo, which produced these hues, is a notoriously difficult, esoteric, and unpredictable dye (see cat. no. 214, color pl. 29). Therefore, since it is rare and elusive, its inclusion probably connoted prestige, special status, and power for the wearer. It is interesting to note that blue-green continued to play such a role in later Andean textile design (see cat. no. 317, color pl. 60a,b) and was a favored color in other Middle Horizon media (Stone-Miller and McEwan 1990) and in pre-Columbian art as a whole.

This discussion of minute compositional components may appear unnecessarily detailed; certainly, in all art there are deviations from perfect regularity. However, I contend that recognition of these irregularities is essential to understanding the individual creative presence during this period because they are almost entirely *intentional.* In other words, idiosyncracy within and between pieces implies the active participation of their makers in design. Intentionality is visible when, once again, the technique and its application are understood. The creation of a tapestry with a high thread count such as cat. no. 312 would have been slow and considered since hundreds of weft passes were necessary to accomplish every tiny shape. It would have taken a great deal of effort and time therefore to lay down an "incorrect" color; that is, there would have been ample time to notice and remedy an error. Anomalies, by definition, are obvious: How could a weaver accidentally pick up bright red thread after months of working with golds without noticing? The weavers' skill and dedication to consistency were such that literally millions of color changes were completed successfully in every tunic (Stone 1987, vol. 1:75–77). Sloppy, inattentive craftspeople do not produce such dynamic, elaborate, balanced, abstract compositions. Nor is the overall formal regularity attributable to the very natural capacity of tapestry weavers to count threads (for example, crossing exactly fifty warps to build up each staff bearer's hand shape) so as to ensure exact replication. Instead, textile artists repeated extremely complex designs through their extraordinary visual and manual acuity. This lends strength to the argument that when they did vary the shapes or colors significantly, it was intentional. One could argue that weavers ran out of the "correct" color of thread; however, deviations and anomalies occur throughout a given tunic, not disproportionately at the end of the fabric. In short, beyond a very few recognizable errors,[3] the idiosyncratic elements in every Wari design were placed there by design and thus give us a hint of the persons —and perhaps personalities— of the makers.

General comparison of these two striking textiles, cat. nos. 312 and 313, also reinforces the idea of artistic creativity; their similarities and differences show that variation on a theme was central to the Wari textile style. Overall, cat. no. 312 is a more graphic, irregular, and dynamic composition than cat. no. 313. The double-animal motif included in both tunics is presented at two different levels of abstraction: the heads in cat. no. 312 are bold and simple, consisting of rectangles with central circles, while those in cat. no. 313 are curvilinear and complicated, featuring many small elements. The more reductive version reads as pure geometry, while the scale and complexity of the more detailed version also make it hard to interpret. Thus, each has approached illegibility in its own way.

These two pieces also show that certain formal choices, such as color assignment, may remain the same from one tunic to the next, while other formal choices make each composition appear visually very distinct. For example, both have red plain columns and both alternate brown-and-pink double-headed animal combinations with tan-and-gold ones. Yet there are differences between the two in the overall color patterning: cat. no. 313 consistently uses blue-green in its regular color repetition, while cat. no. 312 shows only the one anomalous blue shape within a decidedly irregular design. To counteract this general formal unpredictability, cat. no. 312 continues the color diagonal of one tunic side on the other to unify the two halves (trace, for instance, the brown-and-pink double animals from lower left to upper right). In turn, to add dynamism to its more stable design, cat. no. 313 keeps the two halves more separate visually, neither uniting them into one continuous color scheme nor creating true mirror-image symmetry (note the positioning of the stepped-diamond motifs containing blue-green). Thus, each composition achieves a balance in its own particular way. This is true of the entire corpus of Wari tunics, in which there are no identical pieces among the hundreds known.

The fragments of tunics in the Museum's collection bear out these observations. The remarkable graphic qualities of Wari style are prominent in cat. no. 213 (color pl. 25; fig. III.13a,b), whose motif can be called the split face. A frontal face appears visually "split" by assigning contrasting color combinations to its two halves. Because half-faces on the diagonal from each other share the same color combination, they vie for attention with full faces and thus subvert subtly the coherent meaning of the motif. Faces and parts of faces waver in and out of the viewer's perceptions until there is no stable meaningful unit. The artist thereby emphasizes dynamic pattern over legible motifs even in this simple, incomplete example. In addition, although this fragment comprises less than one-eighth of a tunic, a color deviation appears in the form of a possible mend. Below the upright red and gold face (third from the top on the right) the half-red, half-blue-green triangular point should have been gold (fig. III.12b). Its ancient thread, packed more loosely than the rest, seems to have been added in antiquity sometime soon after the tunic's creation. Even if the blue-green thread was chosen by someone other than the original artists, the status of that particular hue and its anomalous nature remain consistent with the Wari aesthetic system.

Other tapestry tunic fragments, cat. nos. 94 and 201, relate to several of the pieces just discussed. Cat. no. 94 (fig. III.4) consists of a few repeated motifs from the patterned column of a tunic. The facing puma heads in profile, arrayed in the same type of symmetry as the faces in cat. no. 213 (color pl. 25), illuminate the truncated versions of the double animal heads seen in the complete tunics: the familiar split eye, circular nose, and S-shaped element are found here with the more depictive fangs of a feline. In addition, the presence of purple (in four dark background areas) is a rare and significant feature that relates to the aforementioned blue-green; purple probably also indicated prestige, since it would most likely be achieved through overdyeing of indigo and cochineal.

Cat. no. 201 compounds our problems of decipherment by its complexity and its fragmentary preservation (fig. III.3b). From the top down, it consists of the lower front of a figure facing the viewer's left, the back of a figure facing viewer's right, and the upper front of another figure facing viewer's left. The first and third figures together allow the front half to be reconstructed, and, assuming the main difference between those and the second figure is body color,[4] the second provides the back half. The reconstructed image, lacking only a few details of the central body, may still remain visually obscure, but it represents a version of the staff-bearing figure introduced above. The presence of claws (visible on the back foot of the second figure and the front hand of the third) shows it to be a feline, most likely a puma, conflated with the bent-legged, winged staff bearer. Wings, bird heads, and various costume elements, along with probable facial painting further complicate this version of the figure. The bright col-

ors, complex shapes, lack of extensive background, and alternating direction of the figures all add to the visual complexity that serves, in part, to obscure the identity of the figures themselves. Even in such an incomplete composition one can also pick out instances of apparent variation for its own sake (such as whether the left or right half of a split eye is dark). Certainly, tapestry is pushed near its limit here in the creation of visual elaboration and fine detail.

Both readable and abstracted versions of the staff bearer were made in the Wari coastal periphery (cat. no. 125, fig. III.1a, color pl. 30; cat. no. 262; cat. no. 278, color pl. 31). Cat. no. 125 shows the attendant frontally, with bent legs in profile, holding the tops of two staffs, below which are visually analogous filler shapes (fig. III.1a). Dark outlining and a generous amount of background make it easier to separate the figure from its ground than in "central" Wari-style tapestries. In cat. no. 278 the position of the figure and the amount of surrounding background are similar to those in cat. no. 125, but the image is abstracted into a series of nested boxes built up to form staffs, legs, torso, face, and headdress elements (fig. III.1c). In addition, the headband itself would have been worn so that the figures were on their sides, to the further subversion of their inherent meaning. Cat. no. 262 goes even further to completely surround the figure by squares, while the the zigzag versions of staffs have become like decorative borders (fig. III.1b). Yet, since nearly indistinguishable squares representing feet, filler, and face maintain their proper relative positions, the inner logic of abstraction remains upheld even in this extreme example.

The varied textiles of the Middle Horizon period in the collection of the Museum of Fine Arts demonstrate the many faces of abstraction. The virtuosity of the textile artists who created these remarkable compositions is easy to grasp, while the abstracted images themselves are not. This attention to the means of expression, that is, interest in colors and shapes themselves, shows the level of aesthetic sophistication encouraged in a highly developed society. Through this encounter with the illegible we may glimpse the Wari fiber artists' structuring of the formal universe. The fabrication of such a world of bold color and dynamic shape is our clue to the power given to a wholly artistic vision during the ancient Andean Middle Horizon.

Notes

1. There is, however, an interesting exceptional piece found at Pachacamac that combines on the same warps extremely garbled staff bearers with geometric patterns that appear to be later, non-Wari South Coast style (Museum für Völkerkunde-Berlin Va 30961). See Eisleb 1980:123–125, pls. 327a,b; Stone 1987, vol. 3:139, cat. no. 174; vol. 4: color pl. 119.

2. This diagram, which differs from that presented earlier (Stone 1987, vol. 2: fig. 3-112), is based on a reanalysis of the piece applying a narrower definition of striping (as of a visually salient nature) suggested by Anne Paul.

3. Occasional deviations may be seen as errors, such as a tunic in which the inner outline —between two motifs within the same square— is oriented in the "wrong" direction (Museum für Völkerkunde-Munich 18/1363). See Stone 1987, vol. 3:10, cat. no. 4; vol. 2:122, fig. 3-68.

4. Similar staff-bearer tunics, such as Brooklyn 42.87.1, alternate figure direction and body color but maintain other iconographic elements in bascially the same way (with the characteristic shape and color deviations and anomalies). See Stone 1987, cat. no. 62, vol. 3:51–52; vol. 4: color pl. 36.

IV: Textile Traditions of the Late Intermediate Period

Margaret Young-Sánchez

In contrast to the Middle and Late Horizons, the Late Intermediate Period was a time of disunity, when no single political or cultural force dominated the Andean landscape.[1] Textiles and other material remains from this period exhibit pronounced regional diversity. The diversity does not indicate isolation, however, and Late Intermediate Period peoples were in frequent contact with one another (see cat. no. 306, color pl. 42). Exchange between coastal cultures is demonstrated by the presence of North Coast textiles on Peru's Central and South Coasts (Schmidt 1929:482–514; Young 1985:66–74). Grave goods with brightly dyed camelid-fiber yarns (cat. no. 308, color pl. 50) and tropical bird feathers (cat. no. 292, color pl. 61) also indicate that coastal peoples had access to highland and Amazonian products. The camelid-fiber yarns for coastal consumption were apparently spun and dyed in the highlands.[2]

The lack of political or cultural cohesiveness in the Late Intermediate Period dictates a regional approach to the study of its textiles (see figs. I.2, I.3). Archaeological information on the North Coast is relatively abundant, and the traditions of this region are described here first, with emphasis on Lambayeque and the kingdom of Chimor. A discussion of Central Coast textiles focuses on the Chancay style. Despite limited scientific archaeological research, Chancay textiles are plentiful in world collections, and several studies exist (Lothrop et al. 1957:12–25; Fung Piñeda 1978; Young 1985). The cultures and textiles of Peru's South Coast are discussed briefly, owing to the scarcity of accurate information. In addition to describing the stylistic and technical features of each textile tradition, this essay attempts to explain the production and use of textiles within their respective societies. To date no such general summary of the fiber-art substyles of this period has been offered in the literature.

North Coast

Although the general term "Chimu" is often applied to all North Coast culture after the end of Moche dominance (about A.D. 850),[3] much local variation was present. Certainly, the textiles of this region exhibit marked stylistic diversity.

Lambayeque

The Lambayeque textile tradition extends from the La Leche Valley in the north to the Jequetepeque Valley in the south.[4] Batan Grande, which may have been the region's capital, contains monumental religious architecture and shaft tombs with large quantities of metal artifacts. Undoubtedly, textiles were also included among the grave goods, but these are not preserved. Izumi Shimada believes

that organized religion with an important funerary aspect dominated Batan Grande.[5]

Ironically, the largest assortment of Lambayeque-style textiles was discovered in burials at Pachacamac, on the Central Coast.[6] The Lambayeque textile style can be identified by the similarity of motifs in woven and painted textiles to those in other media, such as metalwork, mural painting, and pottery (Bonavia 1985:116–134; Donnan 1984; Carcedo Muro and Shimada 1985). One characteristic feature is a winged or commalike eye shape typical of some figures. The Museum's collection includes several Lambayeque-style textile fragments: cat. no. 12, color pl. 38; cat. no. 62, color pl. 37; cat. no. 78, color pl. 36; cat. no. 217, color pl. 35; cat. no. 254, fig. IV.1.

As in the earlier Moche textile tradition, Lambayeque decorative textiles include tapestries, often with backgrounds woven in white cotton (cat. no. 217, color pl. 35; cat. no. 254, fig. IV.1). Narrative scenes incorporating architecture, animals, and human figures performing a variety of activities occur in painted textiles and tapestries (Schmidt 1929:489, 510), and recall Moche painting on both murals and pottery. Many Lambayeque textiles employ a subdued color palette, in which white, olive-green, gold, and brown predominate (cat. no. 217, color pl. 35). Others are more brightly colored (cat. no. 12, color pl. 38; cat. no. 62, color pl. 37), indicating a temporal or regional variation.

Lambayeque tapestries have long, vertical slits and designs frequently organized into square or rectangular units surrounded by border frames (cat. no. 78, color pl. 36; cat. no. 254, fig. IV.1). Another characteristic technical feature is the assembly of elaborate garments from many narrow, separately woven decorative strips (cat. no. 12, color pl. 38). Contrary to the common Andean practice of weaving each web to the exact length required for a specific garment or textile object, the long, narrow Lambayeque webs were cut to desired lengths. Small, badgelike tapestry appliqués that could be sewn onto plain-weave garments are also typical of Lambayeque textiles (cat. no. 217, color pl. 35); many were excavated by Ubbelohde-Doering at Pacatnamú (Keatinge 1978).

These technical and stylistic features are suitable for piecework production, with individual weavers producing decorative strips, fringes, and badges for assembly into elaborate garments by other workers. Such production at Lambayeque likely took place in specialized workshops (perhaps controlled by political or religious authorities).[7] Both spinning and weaving are depicted in Lambayeque textiles (Schmidt 1929:492, 493; Donnan 1986:110, 111).

Grave lots from Batan Grande indicate that gold and silver objects were restricted to the elite class, while copper was owned by

Fig. IV.1. Overall view of cat. no. 254. The comma-shaped eyes are found in some Lambayeque figures. This trait may indicate "mythical" status (Shimada, in press:6).

Fig. IV.3. Overall view of cat. no. 40. Female Chancay figures have complex facial patterns and wear long garments with horizontal warps and horizontal arm and neck openings. See also cat. nos. 39 and 42, color pls. 55a,b.

Fig. IV.6. Overall view of cat. no. 59. This Chancay tapestry panel once may have formed part of a loincloth. See cat. no. 308, color pl. 50.

Fig. IV.2. Detail of cat. no. 315, color pl. 39. In both the border and the main field the seated animals wear the Toothed Crescent Headdress characteristic of this Chimu style.

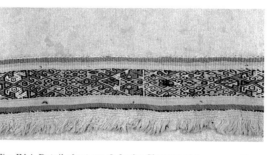

Fig. IV.4. Detail of cat. no. 2. In the Chancay style many cotton garments have colorful tapestry or complementary weft borders, or both.

Fig. IV.5. Overall view of cat. no. 58. See fig. IV.4.

Fig. IV.7. Detail of cat. no. 6. The Chancay taste for weft-patterning techniques is evident in this tapestry and complementary weft panel. (It forms part of a composite textile [see Checklist.])

commoners. Many of the gold objects were probably used ceremonially before their burial with the dead (Carcedo Muro and Shimada 1985:70, 74). Elaborate Lambayeque-style textiles may have been owned and used in a similar fashion.[8]

Chimor

The kingdom of Chimor, centered in the Moche Valley, was a highly stratified society. Much of the valley's population was concentrated in the capital city of Chan Chan and lived in crowded, irregularly planned housing. A small percentage of the population (generally believed to be Chan Chan's rulers and their retainers) occupied large adobe-walled compounds. Within each compound were living quarters, formal courts, extensive storage facilities, and a burial mound. Textile fragments excavated by archaeologists prove that the dead were interred with large quantities of textile goods (Conrad 1982).

Spinning, weaving, and other forms of artistic production were carried out in the cramped quarters of Chan Chan's commoners and in associated workshops (Topic 1982). Weavers were also included among the retainers who occupied elevated living quarters associated with Chan Chan's great compounds (Topic 1990:158–161). Chan Chan's weavers and spinners received their raw materials from the state; finished products were sent to the large walled compounds and then redistributed by the government authorities (Topic 1982:172; 1990:165–166). The large number of textile specialists at Chan Chan suggests that fabrics produced in the commoners' quarters and workshops were destined for both export and local use (Topic 1990:166).[9]

Textile fragments excavated at Chan Chan provide a direct association between several North Coast textile styles and the kingdom of Chimor (A. Rowe 1980). One such style directly associated with Chan Chan is known as the "Toothed Crescent Headdress Style" (A. Rowe 1984:67–93). In the Museum's collection is a delicate mantle, cat. no. 315 (color pl. 39; fig. IV.2), ornamented with seated animals wearing the diagnostic Toothed Crescent Headdresses. Narrow tapestry bands with bifurcated ends and long tassels (cat. no. 284, color pl. 40) are also included in this Chimu style.

Although the kingdom of Chimor was conquered by the Incas in the 1460s, the North Coast textile tradition was neither destroyed nor replaced, and Chimu textiles are found in Late Horizon graves on both the Central and South Coasts. Textiles of this period (A. Rowe 1984:121–143) are characterized by bold, large-scale designs, usually executed in brocade or tapestry (cat. no. 317, color pl. 60a,b). Both human and animal figures frequently wear angular, crescent-shaped headdresses. The ubiquity of certain designs (especially the standing human figures and small profile birds) suggests standardized produc-

tion. The brocade technique employed in late textiles produced large, dramatic designs quickly, and with limited quantities of imported camelid-fiber weft. Possibly the Chimu textiles were manufactured to Inca specifications in state-operated workshops and used as tribute. The garments were then transported to other regions as part of the Incas' complex system of economic redistribution (see p. 51; see also Murra 1962:722).

"Bird Lot Style"

Other North Coast styles defined by Ann Rowe (1984) on the basis of technical and design features cannot be securely dated, nor can their origins be traced to specific North Coast sites. The "Bird Lot Style" includes some of the most visually spectacular of the Andes' ancient fabrics. One example, cat. no. 266 (color pl. 45), is a complex assemblage of tapestry, fringes, openwork, embroidery, and elaborate tassels. Although this textile is merely a fragment of a larger garment, its coloration is extraordinarily well preserved and thus provides a notion of the original magnificence of North Coast fabrics. A subtly patterned shirt, cat. no. 285 (color pl. 43b), is less ostentatious than cat. no. 266 (color pl. 45), but the vivid scarlet supplementary weft yarn contributes exceptional visual beauty. A large panel, cat. no. 290 (color pl. 44), woven entirely with cotton yarns, has soft colors and a large-scale and dramatic design. The crisp outlines and sheer texture are achieved with discontinuous warps and wefts, a technique requiring an elaborate system of scaffold wefts (see entry for cat. no. 289, color pl. 17).[10]

Central Coast

The people of the Central Coast are known primarily through their burial goods. Association data for these objects are usually lacking because few tombs from this period have been scientifically excavated and fully published.

Cultural boundaries on the Central Coast generally correspond to those of pottery and textile styles. Thus the Chancay culture extends roughly from the Huaura Valley in the north to the Chillón Valley in the south. This region may have been politically united as well. A pottery style related to Chancay, found from the Chillón Valley south to the Lurin Valley, is thought to correspond to the thirteenth–fifteenth century Ichimay polity (Shimada, in press:13). Rimac-style textiles have been found in the valley of the same name and at Pachacamac in the Lurin Valley. Since there are no published accounts of their excavation, it is unclear whether Rimac textiles are contemporaneous with Ichimay pottery.

Chancay

Figural sculptures (see cat. nos. 39, 42, 41, color pls. 55a–c; cat. no. 40, fig. IV.3) constructed of reeds, spindles, yarn, and cloth are a unique source of information on the use of Chancay textiles.[11] These dolls were often tucked into the wrappings of Chancay mummy bundles (Kauffmann Doig 1980:512), but groups arranged on cloth cushions were sometimes placed in tombs (Tsunoyama 1977: 197–199). These sculptures, whose exact meaning remains unknown, were created with great care and skill. Their faces are usually woven of tapestry (cat. nos. 39 and 42, color pls. 55a,b), and their garments are made of small cloths woven specifically for this purpose. Female dolls have complex facial patterns (cat. nos. 39 and 42, color pls. 55a,b; cat. no. 40, fig. IV.3), and wear dresslike garments with horizontal arm and neck openings (Young 1985:57–58). They often have openwork cotton headcloths (tiny versions of cat. no. 286, color pl. 49). Males have simpler facial patterns and wear loincloths and shirts with vertical arm and neck openings (like cat. no. 33, color pl. 56; however, this piece was probably made as an offering in itself [Susan Bruce, personal communication to Rebecca Stone-Miller, 1991]).

Utilitarian Chancay garments were made of undecorated cotton plain-weave cloth. Camelid-fiber yarns were a valued commodity on the Central Coast, used only as a colorful patterning element. Techniques that require a great deal of camelid fiber, such as tapestry and complementary weft, occur frequently in borders on cotton plain-weave garments (cat. no. 2, fig. IV.4; cat. no. 58, fig. IV.5; cat. no. 308, color pl. 50). Garments woven entirely of tapestry (cat. no. 59, fig. IV.6; cat. no. 61, color pl. 48; cat. no. 240, color pl. 53; cat. no. 246, color pl. 41) or tapestry and complementary weft (cat. no. 6, fig. IV.7) are less common, although they are disproportionately represented in museum collections because of their sumptuousness. Brocaded textiles (with supplementary camelid-fiber wefts on a cotton ground cloth) employ the imported weft sparingly but to maximum decorative effect. They are among the most beautiful and sophisticated of Chancay textile products (cat. no. 299, fig. IV.8).

The Chancay textile tradition encompasses an unusual variety of decorative techniques that do not rely on the colors of camelid-fiber yarns. Double cloth requires the use of two sets of warp and weft of contrasting value (see Glossary). Chancay weavers generally used cotton yarns for double cloth, either brown and white (cat. no. 159, fig. IV.9; cat. no. 161, color pl. 52; cat. no. 275, color pl. 47) or sometimes blue and white (cat. no. 210, color pl. 57). Chancay double cloth is primarily funerary in character; large shrouds (cat. no. 159, fig. IV.9) and long strips for winding around the bundle are often made of double cloth (Young 1985:64–65).

Women's sheer headcloths are also made with only cotton yarns, relying on contrasts in density for their decorative effect. Often, these headcloths are worked in embroidered square-mesh openwork (cat. no. 286, color pl. 49; cat. no. 287, fig. IV.10; see Emery 1966:216), a technique unique to Chancay among Andean textile traditions. Less frequently, the headcloths are of embroidered gauze or complex gauze. Additional decoration was sometimes applied to the finished Chancay headcloths through dyeing (cat. no. 287, fig. IV.10).

Painting was used to embellish cotton plain-weave cloth. Designs were applied freehand, but carved stamps were also employed (Bird 1973:7). Paint colors are usually limited to shades of brown (cat. no. 170, fig. IV.11) and yellow, but bright orange and yellow mineral pigments are found (cat. no. 296, color pl. 54). One large, lightweight cloth in the collection combines the techniques of painting and resist-dyeing (cat. no. 300, color pl. 51). First, a grid pattern was outlined on the cloth in dark paint, then designs were painted into the fields and borders. Next, fiber was wrapped tightly around small circles of cloth, and the fabric was dipped in a light brown dye. The small wrapped circles did not take the dye; they retain the cloth's original cream coloration.

A final decorative technique that does not require camelid-fiber yarns is featherwork (cat. no. 292, color pl. 61). Some of the feathers applied to Late Intermediate Period textiles come from sea birds, although most are from parrots native to the eastern slopes of the Andes and the Amazon basin (O'Neill 1984:145–184). Feathered tunics reportedly have been found on the North, South, and Central coasts and may have been produced in all these regions. One of the few specimens with secure provenance and association data was found in an early-Chancay woman's tomb (Lothrop et al. 1957:17–18). The tunic's long proportions are similar to those of other feathered tunics (cat. no. 292, color pl. 61) but are unlike typical Central Coast shirts (such as cat. no. 4, fig. I.9). The construction, with vertical neck slit and armholes, is also unlike a Central Coast woman's garment. Many questions thus remain to be answered regarding the production, distribution, and ownership of feather-decorated garments.

The design principles of Chancay textiles are fairly simple and apply to all weaving techniques (e.g., see cat. no. 308, color pl. 50). Motifs are depicted according to standard conventions (for instance, human beings are shown frontally, while birds are typically depicted in profile) and are small in scale. Motifs are repeated in horizontal and vertical alignment throughout the decorative field. No rigid system of color alternation appears to exist, although color is frequently employed to create diagonals in large textiles. Diagonals

Fig. IV.8. Detail of cat. no. 299. The repetition of a single motif is here enlivened by color alternation in a zigzag pattern.

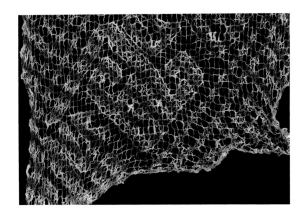

Fig. IV.10. Detail of cat. no. 287. This woman's sheer headcloth is ornamented with both embroidery and painting.

Fig. IV.9. Detail of cat. no. 159. The patterns on adjoining panels of this large double-cloth shroud do not match precisely, probably indicating the hands of several weavers.

Fig. IV.11. Overall view of cat. no. 170. Monkeys, birds, and fish are painted on this technically simple plain-weave cloth.

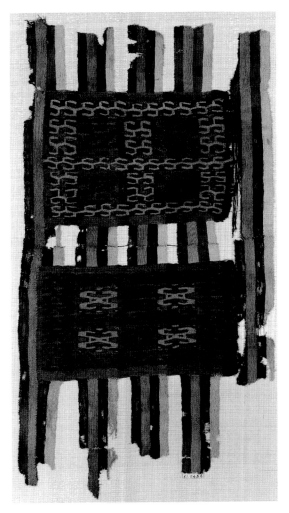

Fig. IV.12. Overall view of cat. no. 267. Interlocked tapestry, found on this Ica garment fragment, is rare among Central and North Coast textiles during the Late Intermediate Period.

are also emphasized in techniques such as painting, double cloth, and square-mesh openwork, where color plays a lesser role.

The simplicity of Chancay design principles and the infinite variety of the finished products suggest that Chancay weavers exercised considerable freedom. Any member of Chancay society could absorb and apply the essential design principles without formal training or supervision. A grouping of Chancay figural sculptures on a cushion portrays a woman seated at a backstrap loom, observed by a small girl, perhaps her daughter (American Museum of Natural History 41.2/5630; see Dockstader 1967: no. 145; Morrison 1979:65; Skinner 1975:75, figs. 7a,b). The Chancay weaving tradition was probably transmitted from one generation to another in just such a fashion.

The learning process for Chancay weavers is also revealed by special textiles that are often termed "samplers." The experimental character of these webs is indicated by the variety of motifs, weaving techniques, and selection of colors, and by their haphazard arrangement. Sampler strips are not incorporated into finished garments, and they are often incomplete. The samplers probably were not created by novice weavers but, rather, were built up over time as individuals practiced new techniques and designs. The completed pattern units then provided the weaver with a visual record for future reference. An unusual double-cloth bag in the collection (cat. no. 275, color pl. 47) shares some traits with samplers. The variety of motifs and the irregularity of their arrangement may suggest a practice piece.

Unlike many contemporary North Coast textiles, Chancay fabrics were made to the dimensions required for specific garments. The assembled character of many North Coast garments, with their multiple decorative strips, is not typical of Chancay textiles. Instead of the piecework production postulated for the North Coast, each Chancay garment was manufactured by a single weaver or household, most often for the use of that same household. Specialized weavers may have also produced garments for their neighbors, and cloth was probably given to local rulers as tribute. It is very unlikely, however, that textile production was rigidly controlled by government authorities.

Rimac

Very little is known about the Rimac textile tradition, but many examples have come from Pachacamac in the Lurin Valley. Rimac-style textiles are usually tapestries woven entirely with cotton yarns. White, together with shades of brown, gold, and blue are the principal colors employed. A few complete garments are known (see Lehmann 1924: pl. 125), but badge or patchlike appliqués are more common. Rectangular patches often depict a frontal human figure surrounded by birds, fish, and plants. The most fascinating of the Rimac tapestries are those shaped like fish (cat. no. 206, color pl. 58). Despite their irregular shapes, the fish appliqués have complete selvages achieved through the use of scaffold warps cut away after weaving. Like Lambayeque tapestry appliqués, the Rimac examples seem to have been stitched to plainer garments or hangings.

South Coast

Textiles were the primary artistic medium of the South Coast, and the influence of textile design is clearly visible in the pottery, murals, and woodcarvings of the region (Kaufmann Doig 1980:517–521). Textile patterns are small in scale, often with intricate, interlocking designs. Frequently, compositions are organized in horizontal strips or diagonals. Stylized geometric birds are the most common motif. Decorative weaving techniques include tapestry, brocade, complementary weft, and complementary warp.

To date, the most detailed study of South Coast textiles of the Late Intermediate Period focuses on rectangular garments from the Ica Valley (A. Rowe 1979). Most are executed in interlocked tapestry (cat. no. 267, fig. IV.12; cat. no. 268, color pl. 59), although some examples include complementary weft or supplementary weft patterning as well. Organized into horizontal registers, the motifs are often geometrically stylized and outlined in black (cat. no. 268, color pl. 59). The pottery styles of the valleys from Chincha in the north to Acarí in the south are related to one another, and their decorations bear a strong resemblance to the Ica rectangular garment patterns. The people of these valleys were in frequent contact, but the region may not have been politically unified until its later incorporation into the Inca empire.

Weaving Implements

Weaving implements are frequently found in Late Intermediate Period tombs; they include workbaskets and spindles (cat. no. 49, color pl. 1; cat. nos. 257, 258, 263, and 264), yarn, loom parts, and complete looms with unfinished webs (Cahlander and Baizerman 1985: color pl. 1). One study of looms from ancient graves indicates that many were never truly functional but were constructed specifically as offerings (Skinner 1975:69). Since looms were probably employed by most Late Intermediate Period households, their presence in tombs does not indicate the graves of professional weavers any more than maize in a tomb necessarily signals that the deceased was a full-time farmer.

In all the traditions discussed here individual cloths are relatively narrow, rarely exceeding 75 centimeters (about 30 inches), and could be produced by a single weaver on a backstrap loom (see fig. I.13). This technology is suitable both for household production and for the specialized piecework production characteristic of the North Coast. At the household level, more than one weaver may have collaborated to produce large garments (such as mantles, wrapping cloths, and hangings). Evidence of such collaboration is found in the frequently imperfect match of patterns on adjoining panels (cat. no. 159, fig. IV.9; cat. no. 161, color pl. 52). Weavers from several households or workshops manufactured the variety of patches, fringes, strips, and tassels found in North Coast fancy textiles. Assembling these materials into elaborate garments was probably a specialized occupation as well.

Stylistically, the fabrics of the Late Intermediate Period exhibit a liveliness and freedom quite foreign to some of the rigidly formal Wari and Inca styles of the Middle and Late Horizons (e.g., compared with cat. no. 312, color pl. 23a,b, or cat. no. 250, color pl. 63). The broad Wari and Inca tunics required two or more weavers to work together on the same loom, closely coordinating their efforts to ensure uniformity. Within these complex, formal styles, scope for individual creativity existed but was limited to certain aspects of design (see pp. 38–41). The Late Intermediate Period weaver had wide scope for individual expression in the choice of color, pattern, and color sequencing. Designs were distorted at will to accommodate them to the available space, and small filler motifs were arranged to suit the weaver's fancy (cat. no. 161, color pl. 52). The colorful patterns of Late Intermediate Period textiles, even those manufactured in North Coast workshops, express the taste of individual weavers. Their exuberance and variety reflect a love of display in the cultures to which both weavers and wearers belonged.

Notes

My research on Late Intermediate Period textiles at the Museum of Fine Arts was facilitated by several members of the staff of the Department of Textiles and Costumes, including Deborah Kraak, former assistant curator, Nicola Shilliam, curatorial assistant, and Jane Hutchins, former conservator. My work has also benefited from collaboration with Susan Niles and Rebecca Stone-Miller.

1. In the accepted chronological scheme for the ancient Andes (J. Rowe 1962b), the Late Intermediate Period (about A.D. 1000–1476) is defined as the time interval be-

tween the Middle and Late Horizons.

2. Although unspun cotton fiber is common on the coast, camelid fiber is almost always discovered already spun and dyed into a narrow range of yarn sizes and colors (Topic 1982:163; A. Rowe 1984:25).

3. The term "Chimu" can also refer specifically to the people and culture of Chimor, a kingdom that included all the North Coast and extended as far south as the Chancay Valley. It is in this latter sense that "Chimu" is employed here. See J. Rowe (1948:26) for a discussion of the origins and usage of "Chimu" and "Chimor."

4. When referring to the Middle Horizon–Late Intermediate Period culture of this region, Shimada now prefers the designation "Sican" to the more commonly used term "Lambayeque" (Shimada, in press:3–4). I will retain the term Lambayeque here because a "Sican" textile tradition is not yet precisely defined, and thus a broader term seems appropriate for textiles without archaeological provenance.

5. Shimada characterizes this organization as "an economically and politically active 'Vatican-like,' state-level religious polity" (Shimada, in press:12). He dates this polity to approximately A.D. 900–1100 (ibid.:5, 13).

6. In the collections of the Museum für Völkerkunde-Berlin are numerous Lambayeque-style textiles from Pachacamac (Schmidt 1929:488–493). They are currently under study by Carlos Zalles Flossbach.

7. Carcedo Muro and Shimada infer that specialized craft workshops at Batan Grande manufactured goods for powerful patrons. Goods produced include adobes for religious constructions and a range of metal artifacts, such as gold masks, cups, and *tumi* knives (Carcedo Muro and Shimada 1985:62, 65–74).

8. Donnan (1986) describes an elaborate tapestry fragment excavated at Pacatnamú. Depicted on the textile are a variety of ceremonial activities as well as several weavers. On the basis of archaeological and ethnohistorical data, Donnan believes that dancing, ceremonial drinking, llama sacrifice, and weaving took place in the Major Quadrangle, where the textile fragment was found. Physical evidence of weaving there includes the presence of balls of yarn, bobbins, and spindles.

9. According to Topic, large-scale production of textiles and metalwork at Chan Chan began about A.D. 1300–1325. He suggests the intriguing possibility that the initiation of this large-scale production corresponded with the Chimu state's conquest of the Lambayeque region and the relocation of Lambayeque artists to Chan Chan (Topic 1990:149–150).

10. Late Intermediate Period textiles in this technique continue a tradition that was present on the Central and North-Central Coast in the latter half of the Middle Horizon. Discontinuous warp and weft textiles from Ancón and Supe have large-scale geometric motifs and incorporate brightly colored camelid-fiber yarns (Reiss and Stübel 1880–1887, vol. 1: pl. 15; see also textiles from Supe in the Robert H. Lowie Museum of Anthropology, University of California, Berkeley.

11. Although Chancay figural sculptures are distinctive and clearly recognizable, they are part of a widespread and long-lived tradition. Miniature garments of both male and female types were found in Middle Horizon tombs at Pachacamac (VanStan 1961, 1967). Miniature garments were also included in a Late Horizon mummy bundle from Ancón (Stothert 1979a, 1979b, 1981). A study of Late Horizon Central Coast pottery figures dressed in miniature garments suggests that they were placed in tombs as substitutes for female human sacrifices (Schuler-Schömig 1984). A large number of miniature garments that seemingly date from the Late Intermediate Period were found at Pacatnamú, on the North Coast. Both the miniature garments and miniature pottery vessels were deposited as offerings in tombs associated with an *audiencia* (U-shaped administrative structure) there (Bruce 1986:95–108).

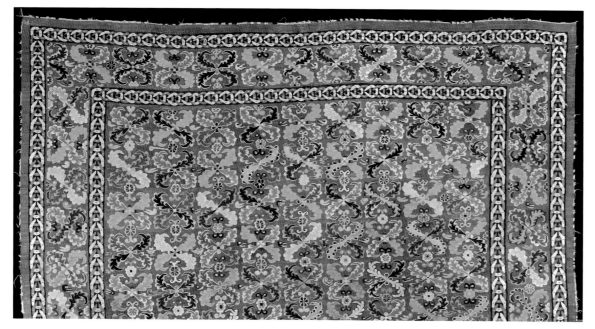

Fig. V.1, cat. no. 314. A large Colonial tapestry carpet. See also cat. no. 301, color pl. 76.

Fig. V.2. Inca and Colonial Inca Styles of Dress

c. Lower-level Colonial Inca functionary, with native-style tunic, mantle, and pouch, and native decorations on the brimmed Spanish hat. Shoes, breeches, and a rosary are likewise from Iberian costume (Guaman Poma, fol. 753; 1980a, t. 2:164).

a. Inca-style male dress, showing a *tocapu*-waistband tunic with embroidered hem, plain mantle, and carrying pouch (Guaman Poma, fol. 86; 1980a, t. 1:61).

b. Inca-style woman's dress, showing a wrapped one-piece dress (*anaco*), *tocapu*-patterned mantle pinned in front, and a cloth headdress (Guaman Poma, fol 134; 1980a, t. 1:97).

d. Colonial dress of an Inca noblewoman, showing the traditional *anaco* and pinned mantle with Spanish headdress, jewelry, and sleeved underdress (Guaman Poma, fol. 757; 1980a, vol. 2:167). Except for this one, all of Guaman Poma's depictions of Colonial Inca women show them in dress little influenced by Spanish costume.

V: Artist and Empire in Inca and Colonial Textiles

Susan A. Niles

About the middle of the fifteenth century A.D., the Inca polity began to dominate the social and economic life of the Central Andes. Based in the southern highlands of Peru, Inca culture was transported from the capital at Cuzco north as far as Colombia and as far south as central Chile (figs. I.1, I.3) by the soldiers, artisans, administrators, and colonists who explored and helped to expand the limits of their world. The Incas perfected a system of tribute designed to move raw and finished products among the diverse environmental zones of the Andes; these goods sustained the corps of administrators and soldiers and likewise supported Inca cults and maintained the royal families. The arrival of Spanish soldiers in 1532 initiated a process of European domination of established patterns of production and exchange in the Andes. By 1565, when the Spanish conquered the Philippines, Andean artisans had entered into a system of trade that spanned two oceans and four continents (see cat. no. 66, color pl. 79).

The story of the economic and political transformation of the Andean people as they confronted two expansionist empires is one that can be read in their cloth. The Spanish recognized the high quality of Andean textiles and soon pressed native artisans to produce cloth for them. With the consolidation of overseas trade routes, Andean weavers gained inspiration from new materials —silk, linen, sheep's wool, and metal-wrapped threads— and from new ideas — engravings from Flanders and textiles from China— and quickly incorporated them into items produced for native and Iberian use (e.g., see cat. no. 283, color pl. 72). So important were textiles to the flow of goods within the Spanish empire that the parish priest in Livitaca, in the hinterlands of Peru, writing in 1689, could list among the assets of his church: vestments from Milan and from Castille, an amice of Breton linen, a chasuble and curtains of Chinese silk, linen altar cloths from Rouen, and curtains and a pallium of gold-fringed Milanese cloth (Villanueva 1982:333–334).

Patterns of Production

For the Incas the production of cloth was intimately tied to notions of control, both of people and of resources (e.g., see Murra 1962, 1989); demands for raw material and finished garments were integral to their system of tribute. A Jesuit priest, Bernabé Cobo, who lived in the Andes early in the seventeenth century, describes the labor-intensive preparation of cloth that characterized the pre-Conquest Andes (book II, chap. 11; 1990:223–226). In highland Inca garments the wool of native camelids was used, including the coarse fiber of llamas, the softer wool of alpacas, and the silken wool of the vicuña; coastal people made clothing, for themselves and for Inca

overlords, from domesticated cotton. The fibers were first dyed then spun with a drop spindle, most commonly by women (see fig. I.12). Some spinners used a distaff, while others wound the fiber around the wrist. After the fiber was spun, it was plied. In Inca, as well as in Colonial times, old men, children, and others not capable of hard work, helped with the plying (Diez de San Miguel 1964:61). Cobo describes two kinds of native looms: staked looms set up out of doors were most common; tapestry-weave textiles were warped on a four-sided frame set vertically against a wall (see fig. I.14). Traditional backstrap looms were also known (see fig. I.13).

Five categories of camelid-fiber cloth are described by Cobo (book II, chap. 11; 1990:225–226). The coarsest, *chusi,* was used for blankets and rugs. Everyday garments were made of a cloth called *abasca,* probably rendered in warp-face plain weave, perhaps with supplementary warp patterns (J. Rowe 1946:242). A finer category of cloth, known as *cumbi,* was probably rendered in tapestry weave (J. Rowe 1946:242). Use of *cumbi*-cloth garments was restricted to "the kings, the great lords, and all the nobility of the kingdom, and the common people could not use it" (Cobo, book II, chap. 11; 1990:225). A fourth kind of cloth was made by fastening tiny, colorful feathers onto the surface of *cumbi* until it had the texture of velvet. Three pieces in the Museum's collection, cat. no. 282 (color pl. 32), cat. no. 292 (color pl. 61), and cat. no. 302, though not identical to Inca featherwork, illustrate how feathers can be attached to a ground cloth. One final kind of cloth was entirely covered with small pieces of gold or silver that were attached to the surface of a *cumbi*-cloth garment. Two earlier pieces (cat. no. 306, color pl. 42) show how silver can be attached to cloth.

For the Incas the worth of a garment was measured by the delicacy of its workmanship and the rarity of the material that went into its manufacture. The extremely fine fiber of the vicuña, reserved for royal garments (Cobo, book II, chap. 36; 1979:245), resulted in textiles likened by the Spanish chroniclers to silk. Some of the feathers used in the intricate designs of featherwork were the minuscule chest feathers of hummingbirds (Cobo, book II, chap. 11; 1990:226). Cobo reports that the deceptively plain gray tunic and mantle of the imprisoned Inca king, Atauhualpa, was made of bat wool (Cobo, book II, chap. 36; 1979:245).

The production of cloth was part of the Inca system of requisitioning labor and goods from throughout the empire. Because special skill was required to produce tapestry-weave clothing suitable for an Inca, *cumbi* production was left to experts. In some provinces, groups of male weavers, known as *cumbicamayos* ("*cumbi*-cloth makers") prepared this cloth (Cobo, book II, chap. 11; 1990:225), while others from their province wove *abasca*-cloth garments (Diez de San Miguel

1964:106). The finest *cumbi* cloth was made by the *acllas,* specially chosen cloistered women (see fig. I.30), taken from throughout the empire and trained from childhood to prepare food, maize beer, and garments for the use of the ruling Inca and for the principal shrines (Cobo, book II; chap. 11; 1990:225; book II, chap. 34, 36; 1979:236, 245). Close kinswomen of a king-designate were expected to prepare garments for his installation ceremonies (von Hagen, chap. 7; 1976:35). Additionally, wives of provincial officials were expected to make garments to be sent to the ruling Inca (J. Rowe 1979:239–240).

The arrival of the Spanish did little to change established Andean patterns of requiring the production of cloth by subject peoples. Quickly recognizing the skill of native weavers, the Spanish commissioned *cumbicamayos* to produce hangings with coats of arms for them, such as cat. no. 283 (color pl. 72) (see Cobo, book II, chap. 11; 1990:225). The Spanish tax system likewise incorporated demands for clothing and introduced money to the native system of reciprocity. In the Lake Titicaca region, one thousand sets of clothing were to be produced annually, half of *cumbi* cloth and half of *abasca*. The tax was reckoned through local lords, who oversaw the production of the cloth and acted as intermediaries with agents of the Crown (Diez de San Miguel 1964). Elsewhere, the tax was overseen by *encomenderos,* Spaniards who were licensed to command the work of tributaries and who profited from the exchange with the Crown's agents (J. Rowe 1957:159–161).

In areas of the Andes where camelid fiber was not produced, the tax included other kinds of cloth. In coastal Ecuador, women wove cotton clothing and lengths of cloth as payment in the sixteenth and seventeenth centuries (Hagino and Stothert 1983:20). In 1567, women of the Sama Valley on Peru's South Coast produced fifty cotton outfits a year, helped by young boys (Diez de San Miguel 1964:126–127). On Peru's North Coast, the tax was reckoned in native-style garments and household goods of cotton, most of which were sent to Lima for sale to Indians; some of the cloth also went into the export market, going to Chile, Ecuador, Panama, and Mexico (Zevallos Quiñones 1973:119–120).

The Inca system of textile production by cloistered women seems to have been adapted by the Spanish as well. Felipe Guaman Poma de Ayala, a member of the native elite who wrote and illustrated a chronicle of Andean life early in the seventeenth century, accused the religious orders of rounding up unattached women to produce *abasca* and *cumbi* garments and household furnishings for sale (fol. 546[660], fol. 648[662]; 1980a, t. 2:80, 82; and see fig. I.14). Much cloth in Colonial Peru was made in *obrajes,* factories in which native weavers worked for little or no compensation (J. Rowe 1957:177–179). In 1689, some *obrajes* still turned out Indian-style

garments for both men and women, although whether these were of *cumbi* or other kinds of cloth is not noted (Villanueva 1982:276; Urubamba parish).

From the point of view of most weavers, there was probably little difference between demands for cloth by the Inca rulers and demands for cloth by the Spanish Crown. Theoretically, the raw material was issued to the weavers —the cotton was given to Ecuadorian women by the *encomendero* (Hagino and Stothert 1983:20), while the camelid fiber for the textiles of Chucuito province came from community herds (Diez de San Miguel 1964)— and the tax itself was given in the work of weaving cloth to the specification of another. However, the Spanish tax was reckoned in amounts of garments, while the Inca system was based on the amount of time devoted to the preparation of garments. Tributaries in Chucuito, at least, complained that meeting the Crown's demands for cloth took so much time that they were unable to clothe their own families.

We do not have precise estimates of the time needed to make Inca-style cloth. Pedro de Cieza de León, writing in the middle of the sixteenth century, claimed that the women who made the clothing for a royal installation were required to spin and weave four garments (two mantles and two shirts) in the same day (von Hagen, chap. 7; 1976:35). This comment seems incredible in light of a Colonial investigation that concluded that one and a half to two months were required for a woman to weave an outfit of *abasca* (Diez de San Miguel 1964:216); additional labor was required to prepare the fiber.[1] Undoubtedly, the preparation of a complicated *cumbi*-cloth outfit would have taken even longer.

Perhaps the greatest transformation in Andean textile production effected by the Spanish Conquest was the changed context of the cloth, particularly tapestry cloth, that weavers were required to produce. *Cumbicamayos* were recruited to make household goods rather than clothing for Iberian tastes. The Museum's collection of Colonial tapestries includes carpets (cat. no. 301, color pl. 76; cat. no. 314, fig. V.1), a probable chair seat or cushion cover (cat. no. 53, color pl. 70), and many covers (cat. no. 47, color pl. 77; cat. no. 50, color pl. 71; cat. no. 51, color pl. 74; cat. no. 54, color pl. 78; cat. no. 293, color pl. 73; cat. no. 305, color pl. 80). Contemporary drawings and paintings show the importance of such items in Spanish Colonial households. For example, Guaman Poma generally depicts the interior of Spanish houses with patterned floors, windows, furniture, and domestic textiles such as tablecloths (fol. 770; 1980a, t. 2:178), covered chairs (fol. 603; 1980a, t. 2:46), and small, fringed rugs (fols. 757, 759; 1980a, t. 2:167, 169). Colonial paintings from the Cuzco school also show patterned cloth used as rugs ("San Ginés"; De Mesa and Gisbert, fig. 5), tablecloths ("La Misa de San Gregorio" and "Retrato del Obispo

Manuel Mollinedo y Angulo," De Mesa and Gisbert, figs. 28, 83; "San Pascual Bailón," De Mesa and Gisbert, fig. 120), and bed canopies ("La Muerte Benigna en Casa del Pobre," De Mesa and Gisbert, fig. 130). Patterned or lace-edged cloth is often used to frame the central image in Colonial religious art ("Virgin of the Rosary," Kelemen 1971, no. 23; "Our Lady of Pomata," Kelemen 1971, no. 26; "Christ Bearing the Cross," Kelemen 1971, no. 13; "Virgin of Merced," Kelemen 1951, pl. 135b); it is interesting that lace-related patterns are found around the edges of many Colonial textiles as well (cat. no. 47, color pl. 77; cat. no. 52, fig. I.25; cat. no. 53, color pl. 70; cat. no. 54, color pl. 78). Perhaps the most intriguing examples of domestic cloth are the huge pieces shown hanging from windows and balconies of Cuzco in paintings depicting the Corpus Christi processions of the seventeenth century (De Mesa and Gisbert, fig. 59; Kelemen 1951:pl. 65b). Separated from their everyday context, they become a decorative backdrop for the religious pageant in the streets.

Although the use of textiles for household furnishings was foreign to their tradition, the Incas were accustomed to displaying cloth for special occasions. For the wedding of the Inca king Huascar, "all the houses of the dead Incas were covered with feather cloth, and the walls were hung with fine cloth, of *cumbi* and of cotton, and the towers of the plaza were decorated the same way" (Murúa, cap. 43; 1962–1964, t. 1:123).

It is known that the production of cloth was enforced in both the Inca and Spanish empires, but we have little documentary evidence of how work on textiles was ordered. Under Inca rule, conscript labor was theoretically organized in decimal units, with a gang of ten workers overseen by a foreman, five gangs of ten workers overseen by a boss, and so on up to ten thousand citizens (Cobo, book II, chap. 25; 1979:198–199). Such organization was related to the census, inventory of goods, and the base ten system of counting in the Inca language. In Inca architecture, it is possible to recognize provision for gangs of workers in construction details (Niles 1987). However, Inca textiles rarely show how the labor of weavers was organized or whether they worked in groups or alone. Some textiles, such as women's belts, probably required the labor of only a single weaver. Similarly, the backstrap looms used in some areas do not lend themselves to the simultaneous work of groups of artists. Yet some phases of textile production could involve groups. For example, Guaman Poma depicts an "abbess" directing a fleet of *acllas* as they spin yarn (see fig. I.30). The only depiction we have of a *cumbi*-cloth loom shows a single, elderly male weaver in front of it (fig. I.14), although the wide loom width used for many Inca and Colonial tapestries would accommodate the simultaneous work of several weavers. As will be seen, some textiles show evidence of multiple hands at work.

Inca and Colonial Costume

In the pre-Conquest Andes, a garment was an important statement of the owner's social identity, and local peoples were expected to retain their native costume (Cobo, book II, chap. 24; 1979:196; von Hagen, chap. 19; 1976:71). Rulers also made use of both Inca and provincial dress in matters of state. Upon assuming rule, Huayna Capac (r. about A.D. 1493–1527) sent emissaries from the capital to visit provincial dignitaries and to take them gifts, including Inca-style clothing (Betanzos, I parte, cap. XL; 1987:179). Shortly thereafter, the new king himself made a visit to the provinces. As he entered each town, he was met by its local lord and was given a native outfit, including a wig arranged in the local style; the Inca king donned the costume before entering the town so that he might appear to be a native of it (Betanzos, I parte, cap. XLIII; 1987:186).[2] Such reciprocity involving costume undoubtedly served several functions. The gift of Cuzco-style clothing to the native elite would have the effect of equating Inca-style garments with prestige. The local lord would gain prestige by his association with Cuzco's overlords, and Inca style would gain a certain local acceptance because of its association with the hereditary ruler of the province. Murra characterizes such gifts of Inca cloth as "the initial pump-priming step in a dependent relationship" (1989:293). The donning of native garb by the Inca king may also have been a sort of "Ich bin ein Berliner" diplomacy effected in Andean terms.[3]

Costume was an important marker of the wearer's place in the hierarchical social system of the empire. Garments received in tribute were redistributed according to strict sumptuary laws: a nobleman's military prowess might be rewarded with gifts of fine clothing (Murúa, lib. II, cap. 87; 1962–1964, t. 2:7), while the men and women who worked on construction projects were issued coarse mantles to use as carrying cloths during their work so that their own garments would not be spoiled (Betanzos, I parte, cap. XIII; 1987:61–63). Captives taken in battle were stripped of their native dress and forced to wear long red tunics covered with tassels as a sign of their humiliation, while the victorious Inca warriors paraded in their finest feather garments (Betanzos, I parte, cap. XIX; 1987:94–95; cap. XXIII; 1987:120).

Pre-Conquest Inca costume is described by chroniclers and is depicted by Guaman Poma (see figs. V.2a, V.2b). Both documentary and pictorial accounts show that Inca-style garments continued to be produced after the arrival of the Spanish and probably became even more widely disseminated in the Andes since Inca-style clothing was sold to Indian laborers who did not make their own garments. In addition, some pre-Conquest clothing was carefully preserved, such as the salvaged waistbands from Inca tunics (A. Rowe 1978; and see cat. no. 234, color pl. 64) and the safeguarded heirloom cloth in Inca style (J. Rowe 1979:244; Murra 1989:292).

Iberian costume influenced the dress of the native Colonial elite more than that of commoners and men's dress more than women's (figs. V.2c, V.2d). However, by the middle of the seventeenth century, minor concessions to European values had influenced ordinary women's dress. Father Cobo comments that the traditional style of wearing the wrapped dress left women's legs and thighs exposed when they walked, but "now that the women are Christians and profess more decency, they are in the habit of sewing up the side in order to avoid that immodesty" (Cobo, book II, chap. 2; 1990:188). Such a subtle change in costume would hardly be noticeable in the textiles themselves.

The Andean textile tradition shows the intimate relation between the patterning of work and the design of the finished garment. Because Inca garments were produced in tribute for later redistribution, they also show the relationship of those who commanded the work to both the weaver and the ultimate owner of the piece.

Inca-Style Tunics

The tapestry-weave tunic is the symbol *par excellence* of the relationship of artist to object under the Incas, exemplifying the control that the lords of Cuzco had over textile production and exchange (J. Rowe 1979:240–241). Three items in the Museum's collection are tunics, or parts of tunics: cat. no. 234 (color pl. 64); cat. no. 250 (color pl. 63); and cat. no. 309 (color pl. 68). One of these, cat. no. 250, decorated with a black and white checkerboard pattern and red yoke, exemplifies a standard tunic design described for the Incas (J. Rowe 1979; A. Rowe 1978), which was probably associated with owners of relatively high status (J. Rowe 1979:259). As is typical for this style of tunic, cat. no. 250 has camelid-fiber warps (A. Rowe 1978:7) and conforms to standard Inca measurements: 84.5 centimeters in length and 78 centimeters in width, as worn. The side seams are finished in tight figure-8 stitch, and the hem in a cross-knit loop stitch, both types of embroidery making a pattern of alternating stripes. Remnants of zigzag running-stitch embroidery with two strands, one red and one gold, decorate the bottom edge of the shirt. The regularity of the tunic's pattern seems not to have been achieved by counting warps and wefts, because the number of each per square differs considerably. Rather, it appears that a set unit of measurement was used as a template to order the pattern of the design. A system of ordering tunics of a set number of designs, each of a specified size, would ensure that garments requisitioned from throughout the empire

would be of uniform size, despite variations in the thickness of threads used for warps or wefts or the tightness with which wefts were packed.[4]

A second item, cat. no. 234 (color pl. 64), is a pair of stepped-diamond-motif waistbands that originally were part of a striped cotton tunic (a style discussed by J. Rowe 1979:251–257; A. Rowe 1978). Although some aspects of the design and edge finish of cat. no. 234 are aberrant (A. Rowe 1978:14), the bands were from a common Inca tunic type, one perhaps associated with relatively humble social status (A. Rowe 1978:14).

The third Inca-style tunic in the Museum's collection, cat. no. 309 (color pl. 68), is not described as a standard tunic type; nonetheless, aspects of its design are characteristically Inca, including the red-embroidered zigzag side seams and the striped neck binding. Its width, 76.2 centimeters, is within the parameters for Inca tapestry tunics (J. Rowe 1979). The design of small squares outlining a stepped neck is reminiscent of an Inca tunic depicted by Guaman Poma (fol. 194; 1980a, t. 1:135) and an Inca-style shirt of probable Colonial date illustrated by Reid (1986:57, pl. 39).

The Inca tunic is a garment that appears to be devoid of complex iconography. Yet its very simplicity belies the powerful symbolism that its production and design entail. The Incas divided their social world into halves that were seen as complementary; two parts were required to make a whole. Similarly, the garment has two identical sides (front and back) and two identically finished faces (inner and outer), but each is necessary to the integrity of the whole. Even the zigzag stitching on cat. no. 309 (color pl. 68) becomes a microcosm for this duality: two complementary threads (each made of two strands) work together, zigzagging so that as one is unseen, the other is seen, as that disappears, the other appears. The two strands are never on the same face at the same time, yet both are needed to bind the garment.

The overall design of the checkerboard tunic, cat. no. 250 (color pl. 63), likewise encapsulates the Incas' world view. As is typical for tunics of this design (J. Rowe 1979:247), front and back each have a pattern ten (or nine and two-halves) squares in width, and ten in height, surmounted by a red, stepped-pendant triangle. Recalling the Inca system for reckoning tribute and organizing work in groups of ten overseen by a foreman, we might see in the design of this tunic a constant reminder that the service of ten is to be ordered by one.

Provincial-Style Garments

Inca style, which developed and spread with the Inca empire and endured well into the Colonial Period, cannot be associated with

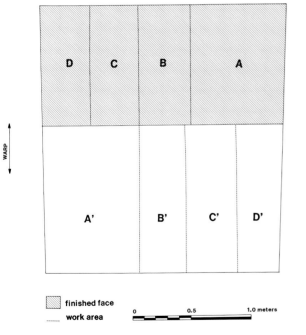

Fig. V.3, cat. no. 288. The probable draping of the mantle (see color pl. 62)

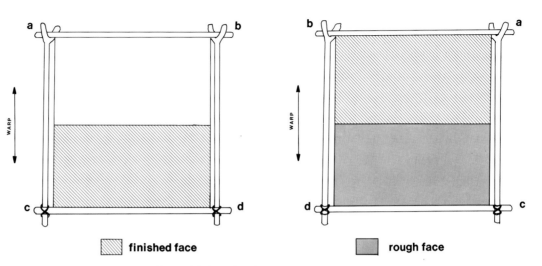

finished face

rough face

Fig. V.4. A possible configuration of an upright loom for cat. no. 288, color pl. 62
Left: Weavers could prepare the first part of the cloth while seated on the ground.
Right: Work would then proceed on the opposite side of the loom to complete the piece, probably while weavers sat on a high bench or scaffold.

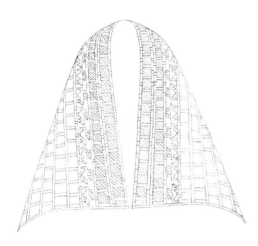

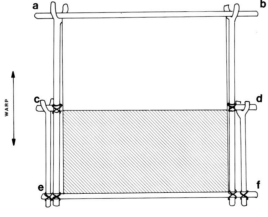

Fig. V.5. A possible configuration of a folding loom for cat. no. 288, color pl. 62
Left: Weavers could prepare the first portion of the cloth.
Right: The loom would then be folded, and work would proceed on its opposite side while the weavers remained seated.

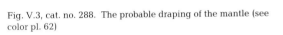

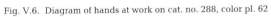

finished face
work area

0   0.5   1.0 meters

Fig. V.6. Diagram of hands at work on cat. no. 288, color pl. 62

a single ethnic group or a single point in time; similarly, many local styles that developed in the Late Intermediate Period (see IV pp. 43, 45) persisted into the Late Horizon and beyond. Some of the textiles in the provincial Late Horizon styles use exotic fibers and innovative technology and show the ability of the person who commissioned the piece to command the work of superior weavers.

One such textile is a mantle, cat. no. 288 (color pl. 62). Probably from the far South Coast of Peru, it is similar to other known pieces, including a tunic fragment in the Museum's collection (cat. no. 173; figs. V.7, V.8) probably fashioned from a mantle.[5] The style they share is characterized as a local tradition that flourished during the Late Horizon (A. Rowe 1978:24). The overall design of the mantle includes three main fields: two red ones with a green one between, separated by a narrow dark blue band with a line of yellow felines. The central field includes rectangular blocks with geometric patterns in complementary weft weave (see Glossary). In the two other main fields, groups of three similar complementary weft blocks are bounded by tapestry-weave eight-pointed stars.

The design of the mantle is intimately related to its production. In contrast to Inca *cumbi,* where both surfaces of textile are equally well finished, this textile has a neatly finished and a less neatly finished face. But unlike Colonial textiles, which have an obvious "right" and "wrong" side, this piece, as woven, combines "right" and "wrong" on each surface, exemplifying the interrelatedness of textile production to garment design that is typical of Andean weaving. A narrow red line in the center field marks the point where the face of the textile changes: on one side of the line, the neatly finished face is visible; on the other, the less neatly finished face is visible. The garment must have been made to be folded over in order for the "right" side of both surfaces to be visible to viewers (fig. V.3). If the garment were worn this way, a line of felines would march around the wearer's shoulders, and the bottom band of designs on the inner layer of the mantle would be visible.

It is intriguing to imagine what the loom used to produce this piece might have looked like. We must posit one that could accommodate the 219-centimeter width of the mantle and that allowed the weavers to change the working surface of the textile as they proceeded (assuming they always faced the "right" side of the piece), while at the same time maintaining an even warp tension. If we assume the coastal weavers were working on an upright loom of the sort used to make highland *cumbi* cloth, we could imagine that, as they reached the midpoint of the piece, weavers turned the loom or, more likely, moved to the opposite side of the loom to continue their work (see fig. V.4). Because it would have been difficult for workers seated on the ground to reach this new area, there must have been a raised

bench or scaffold where they could sit. (Such a scaffold is shown in the twentieth-century loom depicted in fig. V.17). Alternatively, we could posit a hinged loom, oriented horizontally or vertically, that would allow workers access to each face.[6] As weavers reached the midpoint, the loom could be turned and folded so that they could work on the opposite face while still seated on the ground (see fig. V.5).

The width of the piece would accommodate several weavers, and, indeed, the textile shows four work areas on each face of the textile. Such clues as ridges where the work of two weavers interlocks, slight disjunctures in the tightness of warp packing, and evidence that they drew from different dyelots of thread show us where workers were seated. The four work areas, A, B, and C, and D, on face 1, are not of equal size. Work area A is roughly twice the width (79 centimeters) of each of the other areas, and each of the others is approximately equal in width (42, 43, and 40.5 centimeters, respectively). Assuming that four individuals worked simultaneously, we can suggest that weaver A was a faster or more skilled weaver and worked twice as fast as the others to build up the web.[7] On face 2, it is also possible to recognize four work areas, A', B', C', and D'; and, again, A' is about twice the width (78.5 centimeters) of the work area of the other three (38.5, 41.5, 35.6 centimeters, respectively). The arrangement of work areas shown in fig. V.6 suggests that the relative positions of workers remained unchanged as the piece was turned over to accommodate work on the second face. We do not know how many others might have been involved in preparing the fiber or in warping the loom, but at least the weaving of the entire garment seems to have been done by the same team of four workers or by the same relative positioning of four weavers.

As mentioned earlier, the style and some of the distinctive technical features of this mantle are also seen in cat. no. 173, which represents one face of a tunic that was cut from a larger piece, probably a mantle (see figs. V.7 and V.8). Like that of the mantle, its design is composed of complementary warp-patterned blocks of geometrically rendered birds. It also shares with the mantle such technical features as multiple warps on the bottom selvage and thick double warps on the side selvage. Similarly, a thin red line barely visible along the top, cut edge of the tunic corresponds to the red lines on cat. no. 288 that set off the main pattern areas (fig. V.7). A similar placement of multiple workers is also indicated on the tunic, with ridges indicating at least three work areas. As in the mantle, one area is nearly twice the width of the other one that can be measured (71.6 centimeters compared with 40.5 centimeters). The refashioning of the garment makes it impossible to tell whether this piece was originally designed to be worn folded like cat. no. 288.

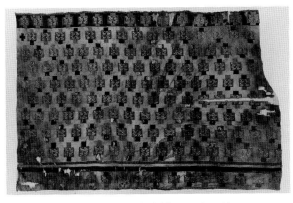

Fig. V.7. Overall view of a provincial Inca tunic cut from a mantle, cat. no. 173

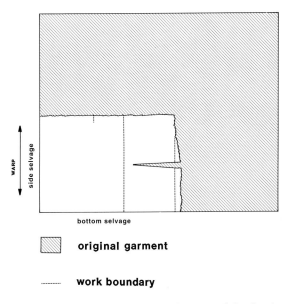

original garment

------- work boundary

Fig. V.8 Reconstruction of cat. no. 173 (see fig. V.7) showing the placement of the tunic on the original garment from which it was cut, assuming proportions similar to those of cat. no. 288, color pl. 62. The location of ridges marking work boundaries is indicated with dashed lines.

Both the mantle and the recut tunic show a high quality of workmanship, lavish use of camelid fiber, and evidence of the handiwork of multiple weavers, yet they are not made in Inca style. They are testimony to the fact that some provincial elites retained a certain amount of autonomy and privilege within the Inca empire.

The Persistence of Inca Style

During the time of Inca hegemony in the Andes, access to Inca-style goods was strictly regulated. Although elements of Inca style found their way into local, high-prestige ceramic and textile traditions, it is unlikely that wholesale counterfeiting of Inca goods would have been tolerated by the Cuzco elite or by their local representatives. After the Spanish Conquest, such regulation of the use of Inca-style objects disappeared. In devising their response to the absence of Inca control, local artists selected elements of pre-Inca design as well as Inca style to incorporate in the objects they made. In the Ica Valley, on Peru's South Coast, a resurgence of local pride was manifested in a distinctive ceramic style that emphasized elements of pre-Inca design while retaining some aspects of Inca style (Menzel 1976).

In other cases, artists produced objects that liberally mix their native tradition of manufacture with aspects of Inca style associated with the rulers' prestige. For example, a cotton tunic in the Museum's collection, cat. no. 248 (color pl. 65), shows a combination of Inca and local styles. The sleeveless tunic was adopted by coastal people from their highland conquerors, as was the Inca design of a pendant triangle decorating the neck slit. However, the coastal tradition of garment manufacture is evident in the piece in its coarse cotton weave, its painted decoration, and its design of diagonal rows of bird heads. Possibly dating from the Late Horizon, this garment could have borrowed from the highland tradition to bring the cachet of foreign overlords to the local person who wore or displayed it. Alternatively, the garment could have been made after the Conquest, when artists worked in a tradition that represented a century of Inca influence on their native style.[8]

A similar appropriation of Inca ideas is seen in a Colonial mantle in the Museum's collection, cat. no. 322 (color pl. 67a,b). The piece demonstrates that even after the Conquest a native tradition of elite textile manufacture persisted, based on fine tapestry weave and careful planning of a garment's overall design. The textile measures 172 centimeters in length by 119 centimeters in width. The well-preserved lower left corner of the piece shows the vivid colors of the original, with two tones of a lively blue-green, along with red, white, dark blue, and yellow, on a dark brown ground (color pl. 67b; cover).

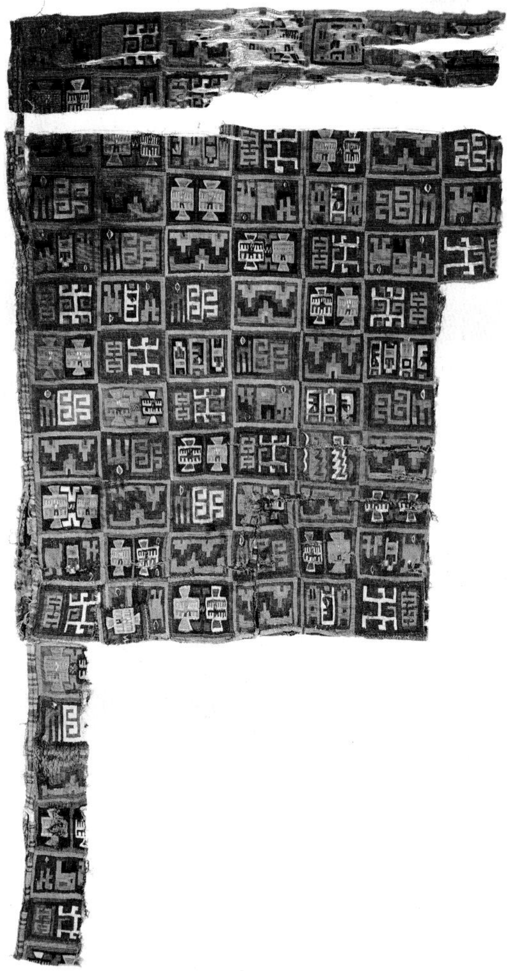

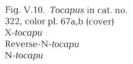

Fig. V.9. Allover *tocapu*-patterned tunic fragment, Textile Museum 91.535 (A. Rowe 1978:21, fig. 30) (Courtesy of The Textile Museum, Washington, D.C.)

X – *tocapu*

Reverse – N – *tocapu*

N – *tocapu*

Fig. V.10. *Tocapus* in cat. no. 322, color pl. 67a,b (cover)
X-*tocapu*
Reverse-N-*tocapu*
N-*tocapu*

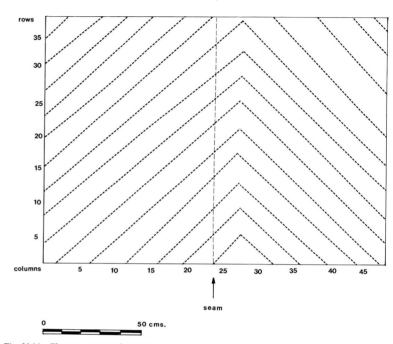

seam

rows

columns

0   50 cms.

seam

Fig. V.11. Chevron-pattern layout in cat. no. 322, color pl. 67a,b (cover)

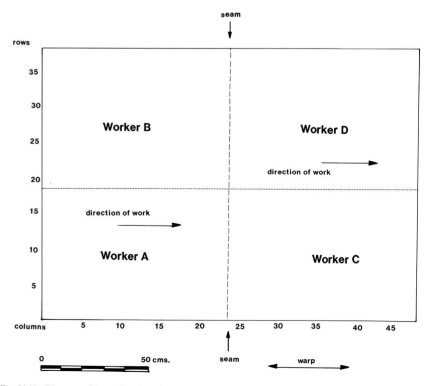

seam

rows

Worker B

Worker D

direction of work

direction of work

Worker A

Worker C

columns

0   50 cms.

seam

warp

Fig. V.12. Diagram of the order of work on cat. no. 322, color pl. 67a,b (cover)

This was probably a man's mantle;[9] like the mantles of pre-Conquest Inca men, it was woven in two parts and joined with a seam in the middle (Cobo, book II, chap. 2; 1990:187). The allover pattern on this textile has not been reported for pre-Conquest Inca-style men's mantles, nor do Guaman Poma's depictions show patterns on any men's mantles. Cieza's descriptions of the outfits required at the installation of a new king suggest that mantles were plain and that, in some cases, the color of the mantle and of the tunic contrasted (von Hagen, chap. 7; 1976:35). Guaman Poma's descriptions of royal male outfits similarly include plain mantles of various colors that contrast with patterned tunics (Guaman Poma, fol. 87–116; 1980a, t. 1:62–85). The elements that make up the pattern have Inca antecedents, however.

The 1,824 small patterns on this textile include rectangular designs alternating with diamond-shaped elements. The rectangles are probably Colonial versions of *tocapus:* geometric patterns that decorate Inca-style tunics in Guaman Poma's depictions of pre-Conquest royal dress. Most commonly, *tocapu* designs in Inca and Colonial-Inca style textiles form allover patterns (see fig. V.9 and a tunic from Dumbarton Oaks, B.518; see Lothrop et al. 1957: pl. CLXI) or are arranged in bands at tunic waists or on women's mantles (see fig. V.2a,b).[10] *Tocapu* designs also occur as isolated design elements on Colonial men's tunics, such as on one found on the Island of Titicaca now in the American Museum of Natural History (B/1503; see Kelemen 1943: pl. 191c).

The design of the Museum's mantle shows how it was put together and how, if it was a garment, it might have been worn. It is easiest for the contemporary viewer to imagine the pattern of designs arranged in 38 rows and 48 columns; for the ancient weavers, too, the design would have been composed on horizontal and vertical planes. The patterning of these designs permits several "readings" of the finished garment. First, the alternation of *tocapus* with diamond motifs permits readings of diagonal lines of diamonds alternating with diagonal lines of *tocapus.* An additional patterning based on color includes white in every other diagonal of *tocapus.* A final reading involves the patterning of the seemingly random *tocapu* designs: alternate diagonals of *tocapu* designs are themselves composed of alternations between an X-*tocapu* (fig. V.10), and a reverse-N-*tocapu* (fig. V.10) or N-*tocapu* (fig. V.10). This final patterning results in a chevron design that has column 27 as its apex (fig. V.11) and that gives us the most insight into the production of the textile, as well as its possible use.

The two pieces that make up the mantle are nearly the same length: one is 85.5 centimeters and has 23 *tocapu* columns; the other is 86.2 centimeters in length and has 25 *tocapu* columns. In planning the textile, special care was taken to assure that the overall diagonal patterns and chevron pattern of the *tocapu* elements were maintained even though the visual center (i.e., the apex of the chevron) is not identical with the physical center of the textile (i.e., the seam that joins the two parts) or its exact middle (which would fall slightly to the left of the seam line). This attention to the planning of the overall pattern is shown in the small compensations made by the weavers, such as compressing *tocapus* near the center seam (column 23) or expanding them near the edge of the piece (columns 37 and 38). Such adjustments suggest that weavers needed to maintain a particular number of *tocapus* in order to complete the overall design, without exceeding the preplanned length of the textile. These adjustments also suggest that work proceeded from the edge toward the center (i.e., from col. 1 to col. 23) on one piece and from the center to the edge (i.e., from col. 24 to col. 48) on the other. The *tocapu* elements in columns 1 and 2 are especially well worked and even in size. According to my analysis, this would have been the first portion of the textile to be woven and could have been prepared by experts to set the overall pattern; the basis for all the diagonal patternings of designs could have been set in just two columns.

The widthwise warping typical of Inca tunics is seen also on this mantle. The loom width of 119 centimeters would have been too great for a single worker to use with ease, and slight irregularities in the spacing of *tocapus* between rows 19 and 20 suggest that two weavers worked side by side (see fig. V.12). The fact that the two worked the same amount of the textile and left no trace of lazy lines suggests that they were about equally skilled and wove at similar rates. The analysis of work patterns shows that the overall conception of a textile —its dimensions, its pattern, and the planning of a complex design arrangement— was integral to its manufacture.[11] The analysis of the hands at work on this mantle likewise reveals the Andean attention to complementarity shown in pre-Conquest garments: one whole is composed of two slightly unequal "halves," each of which is itself made up of two work areas.

The way in which this garment may have been worn similarly shows Inca design principles. Inca and Colonial men's mantles were worn lengthwise across the shoulders, with no fold at the top. On this mantle, the apex of the chevron pattern could be placed at the wearer's nape, so that the flare of the chevron would have exaggerated the width of the bottom edge. Such an illusion has an analogy in Inca architecture, which uses both entasis and slightly inclining profiles on doorways, niches, and walls to enhance the appearance of massiveness in building foundations.

Transformations in Design and Technique in Colonial Textiles

The skill of earlier Andean weavers is shown in techniques such as double cloth (e.g., cat. no. 162, fig. I.20) and in aesthetic devices such as complex rotations of images around an axis (see cat. no. 205, fig. I.28). Despite such unparalleled technical mastery, innovation and artistic inspiration seem not to have been highly valued by the Incas or by the Spanish. Under Inca rule, weavers of *cumbi* cloth produced garments of standard sizes with stereotyped designs (J. Rowe 1979). The Spanish brought catechisms and engravings to the Andes, which inspired some of the images in Cuzco-style painting (Kelemen 1951:200–213); similiar sources may have governed the production of some Colonial textiles (Cavallo 1967, vol. 1:182).[12]

The Spanish were impressed by the range of dyes perfected by Andean weavers (von Hagen, chap. 54; 1976:177). Nonetheless, Colonial textiles often give the impression of being more colorful than Inca weavings. This impression comes partly from the Colonial weavers' use of colors in new ways. For example, many Colonial weavers expanded their palette by alternating colors in adjacent wefts, as on three pieces in the collection: cat. no. 50 (color pl. 71), cat. no. 53 (color pl. 70), and cat. no. 54 (color pl. 78). Other weavers used strands of two colors as a single weft without plying to achieve a similar impression, as on cat. no. 48 (color pl. 69a,b), where red and white, red and yellow, and brown and beige wefts are woven in pairs (see buds surrounding the siren in fig. V.13). Two pieces, cat. no. 66 (color pl. 79) and cat. no. 47 (color pl. 77), use both the double-strand weft and alternate-color weft techniques. These two-color variations are restricted to small pattern areas. For example, the hair of the sirens in cat. no. 47 (color pl. 77, fig. V.19) is composed of strands of red and gold woven as a single weft (middle siren, bottom row) or in alternate wefts (left and right, bottom row).[13]

Color can be used in Colonial textiles to give an illusion of three dimensions, an effect that is not part of the earlier Andean weaving tradition. Color is used in this way to outline blocks of color and to give shading, as, for example, on the belly of a Chinese mythical animal, the *xiezai* (cat. no. 66, color pl. 79; see Camman 1964:26–27), or on the haunches of a quadruped and edges of an armorial design (cat. no. 283, color pl. 72). Use of adjacent blocks of a light gold color and a dark gold color is common and seems intended to mimic the dimensionality of the carved giltwork typical of Colonial churches, as, for example, in a carpet, cat. no. 301 (color pl. 76), and a cover, cat. no. 293 (color pl. 73). The tapestries that draw inspiration from Ming silks, such as cat. no. 66 (color pl. 79), emulate the red background favored by Chinese weavers (ibid.:28).

New materials available through the Spanish are seen in the Museum's Colonial textiles, but not in great number: cat. no. 283 (color pl. 72) has some silk and linen; cat. no. 48 (color pl. 69a,b) has metal-wrapped threads attached to the border. Such exotic fibers as linen and sheep's wool were introduced from Spain. Raw silk, silk threads, and whole textiles were carried to the New World on the Manila galleons (Cammann 1964:24). Design motifs from imported Asian objects are seen in several pieces in the Museum's collection, among them two large tapestries: cat. no. 50 (color pl. 71), with a motif possibly inspired by squirrels and grape vines (ibid.:32), and cat. no. 66 (color pl. 79), with its peonies and dragons (Cammann 1964). The long-legged birds that appear in medallions in the border of a third piece, cat. no. 293 (color pl. 73), likewise might have Asian antecedents. Despite liberal borrowing of design, only one, cat. no. 66 (color pl. 79), makes lavish use of a foreign fiber, with most of the light green areas worked in silk.

Most of the Museum's Colonial textiles are inspired by European artistic conventions, and some show both technical mastery and a sophisticated understanding of source images. For example, cat. no. 324 (color pl. 75), which probably dates from the late seventeenth or early eighteenth century, successfully communicates three-dimensionality in the scrollwork of its four design fields and includes clear depictions of guitar-playing mermen in the corners of its dark blue design band (fig. V.14). Other pieces in the Museum's collection that are roughly contemporaneous demonstrate similar familiarity with the European textile tradition (e.g., cat. no. 305, color pl. 80, and cat. no. 51, color pl. 74).

It is an earlier piece that most clearly reveals the transformations in design and production from pre-Conquest to post-Conquest times. This garment (cat. no. 48, color pl. 69a,b) combines traditional notions about costume and the organization of design with exotic images, colors, and fibers. The mantle is unique in the Museum's holdings as a post-Conquest woman's garment. It is warped in cotton with wool wefts, and the border has traces of both silk and metal-wrapped cotton. Among the Iberian images on the mantle are the siren, a flat rendition of an armorial, and a multiplicity of flowers and birds. The mantle is composed of seven design bands, arranged symmetrically around the midline of the piece. Similar arrangements of designs in three, five, or seven registers are seen on other Colonial women's mantles.[14] The native inspiration for such a design arrangement is suggested by a pre-Conquest mantle that likewise has seven registers, arranged around a midline (A. Rowe 1977:71, fig. 81).

In contrast to a pre-Conquest mantle, which is both reversible and symmetrical around either a horizontal or vertical axis, cat. no. 48 has only one finished face and one "correct" orientation: all the

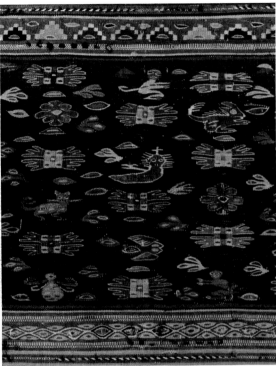

Fig. V.13. Detail of cat. no. 48, color pl. 69a,b. The central image, nearly unrecognizable, is a siren with an outstretched arm.

Fig. V.14. Detail of a guitar-playing merman in cat. no. 324, color pl. 75

Upper register												
A	B	C	(E)	I	H	C	(○)	○	I			
D	G	D	C	(C)	D	(L)	(D)	(I)	○	B		
B	C	I	K	B	A	B	C	D				
E	H	A	D	L	J	D	A	C				
C	F	D	H	E	D	A	F	B				
A	B	J	E	B	I	L	D	D				

horizontal axis

- -

Lower register											
A	B	J	E	B	I	L	D	D			
C	F	D	H	E	D	A	F	B			
E	H	A	D	L	J	D	A	C			
B	C	I	K	B	A	B	C	D			
D	G	D	C	F	D	E	D	B			
A	B	C	H	I	H	C	H	I			

Fig. V.15. Diagram of the patterning of images on the upper and lower registers of cat. no. 48, color pl. 69a,b. Within each register there are diagonal patternings of armorial motifs (indicated by dots) and floral-faunal motifs (indicated by letters). The images in the two registers reflect along the horizontal axis, although orientation in each is constant with respect to the warp selvage. Violations of the rules of patterning are circled. The floral and faunal motifs include: A–cat; B–catfish; C–vizcacha; D–flower; E–monkey; F–red creature; G–walking bird; H–flying bird; I–owl; J–spider; K–siren; L–lizard.

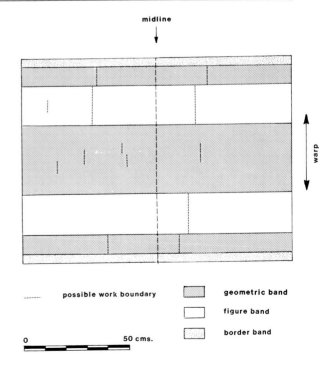

- - - - - -	possible work boundary

geometric band

figure band

border band

0   50 cms.

Fig. V.16, cat. no. 48. Work areas on the Colonial woman's mantle (see color pl. 69a,b)

figures are right-side up as the garment probably would have been worn, with two corners of the wide edge pinned at the neck (see fig. V.2b). The unidirectional orientation of figures is characteristic of post-Conquest mantles. Yet there are some aspects of the design arrangement that place it firmly within the Andean tradition. In this piece, the design elements in the broad figured band do not depict a scene or central image, as is common on similar mantles, but rather include arrangements of animals or flowers alternating with armorial designs and arrayed in columns, with empty space filled with buds, flowers, and small animals. The overall pattern of figures can be "read," as can the Inca-style Colonial man's mantle, cat. no. 322 (color pl. 67a,b), as diagonal lines of armorials alternating with those of floral and faunal motifs (see fig. V.15). The placement of figures on the piece is governed by mirror-image symmetry: viewed in columns, as the weaver would have seen the pattern during the weaving process, the figure nearest the midline is the same on both upper and lower registers, the second nearest figure is the same, and so on, with very few exceptions. This arrangement differs from that seen on most other Colonial mantles, in which the upper and lower figured registers are exact copies rather than mirror images of one another. Each of the geometric design bands, too, is premised on a reflective symmetry of geometric images around an axis, in this case, the midline of the band.

In most of this mantle, the rendering of the figures suggests a lack of understanding of the iconography of the source image. Renditions of alien motifs as forms, rather than as images whose import is understood, is in keeping with the notion that Colonial textiles were produced by corvée labor or by weavers following a two-dimensional design they did not understand. Close examination of the mantle allows us to suggest how that labor might have been organized (fig. V.16). Lazy lines abound on this and on most other Colonial tapestries probably because of the many colors of the wefts used in the figured ground. More useful in determining the placement of workers on this textile is the examination of the iconography, to see how similar figures are rendered and how their arrangement differs in the various parts of the piece. In the narrow border bands, for example, there are systematic differences in the way certain figures are rendered, as, for example, in the orientation of animals, their proportions, and the rendition of their tails. Other registers of the mantle give similar evidence of multiple hands at work, in slight changes in the patterning of colors or in the dyelots (see fig. V.16 for a summary of the places where such disjunctures appear). Much of the work on the mantle appears to have been allotted with respect to the midpoint. This would give a work width of about 64 centimeters to each of two weavers sitting side by side.

Despite the irregularities in the rendition of the design, there is regularity in the size and placement of elements within the textile. Such uniformity seems to have been achieved by counting warps and wefts, since there is great consistency in the number of threads incorporated in equivalent design areas throughout the piece. This method of planning the pattern is different from that observed on the Inca tunic (cat. no. 250, color pl. 63) discussed earlier, as is the provision for multiple workers. Whether these differences are related to the garment type or a changed context of production is not known.

Patterns of Work on Colonial Tapestries

Like the woman's mantle just discussed (cat. no. 48, color pl. 69a,b), the large Colonial domestic tapestries in the Museum's collection show evidence of multiple weavers at work. For example, cat. no. 50 (color pl. 71) has a seam down the center, parallel to the direction of the warp. If the seam was related to the manufacture of the textile, rather than the result of later cutting and repair (see Cavallo 1967, vol. 1:189), the piece would have been planned so that the design would be bisected and the two component parts woven separately.

More common is evidence of multiple work areas across the width of a piece. Adolph Cavallo notes the presence of ridges on a number of the Museum's Colonial textiles (1967, vol. 1:184–185). As he observes, the ridges tend to be evenly spaced across the width of the textile and are the result of either interlocked or dovetailed wefts that suggest the web of the textile was built up in sections. Cavallo concludes that constructing a large textile with many wefts by this means would help to achieve a flat, unpuckered surface in the finished piece (1967, vol. 1:184). It is also possible for such ridges to result when a single weaver builds up the web in sections, a technique that is suggested for the similarly styled piece depicted in the turn-of-the-century loom shown in fig. V.17.[15] However, on some of the examples in the Museum's collection, close observation reveals that multiple weavers indeed contributed work. In most of the Colonial tapestries in the Museum's holdings, these work areas follow the design fields. In cat. no. 54 (color pl. 78), ridges define as work areas the outer band and borders, the center field with pomegranates, and the center-field medallion. The work areas so defined are very close in size, varying from 30.5 to 33.5 centimeters in width.

In cat. no. 56 (fig. V.18), with an overall pattern composed of three major design fields separated by decorative bands, the four major ridges align with (left to right): the outermost design field, the middle design field and its outlining bands, the center field, the mid-

Fig. V.17. Hiram Bingham's crew, photographed near Machu Picchu, Peru, poses in front of an upright loom little changed from its pre-Conquest form (see fig. I.14). A lone male weaver sits on a scaffold and follows a drawing that hangs at eye level. (Courtesy of the Peabody Museum of Natural History, Yale University.)

Fig. V.18, cat. no. 56. Overall view of the Colonial tapestry. See also cat. no. 54, color pl. 78.

dle field and its outlining bands, and the outermost design field. A narrow ridged area (upper left) contains an extra section of the border design and seems to have been added to complete the outermost design band. On this tapestry, we can suggest that the areas outlined by ridges were woven by different workers, rather than by a single worker building up the web in sections. Identification of the hands of different weavers is made possible by examining technical detail (different dyelots of fiber were used in adjacent work areas, suggesting that weavers drew from different workbaskets) as well as iconography (there are subtle variations in the design in different fields). For example, the worker of the left-most area renders the main design elements as isolated units; the pairs of podlike motifs that separate them are always shown striped, and the floral motif on the adjacent border band is rendered as a three-lobed bud. Two different workers probably contributed to the work area on the right side of the tapestry. Toward the bottom of the piece, the pod designs are spotted, and the floral motif on the interior band has four or six lobes; while toward the top, the pod designs vary, and the floral motif is half of an eight-lobed flower.

Another tapestry, cat. no. 47 (color pl. 77), shows a more consistent placement of workers (fig. V.19). Here, ridges outline five work areas, each between 37 and 40 centimeters in width and, again, following design areas. In the middle three areas (shown in fig. V.19), workers rendered the mermaids in different ways. The right-most worker's figures clutch their tresses and have low-hanging breasts and no navels. The middle worker's mermaids are svelte and long-necked and have free-hanging curls. The left-most worker again shows figures holding their hair, but this weaver provides them with navels. That the weavers did not fully understand the iconography of the source image is suggested by the fact that the inverted mermaid at the top of this worker's field has upside-down breasts and one figure (second from the left in the lower register) has three navels.

An examination of the large Colonial carpets in the Museum's collection provides additional insight into the patterning of labor on post-Conquest textiles. In both of the large carpets, cat. no.

Fig. V.19, cat. no. 47. Detail of the central panel of the Colonial tapestry, showing mermaid figures (see color pl. 77).

301 (color pl. 76) and cat. no. 314 (fig. V.1), there is a different kind of evidence for the placement of workers. There are no obvious ridges on the carpets, but on each the border areas have obvious lazy lines at regular intervals. In cat. no. 301 (color pl. 76), the lazy lines appear between 38 and 43 centimeters apart across most of the width of the piece (one edge is too worn to observe). In cat. no. 314 (fig. V.1), most of the lazy lines appear 33 or 34 centimeters apart, and all fall within the range of 31 and 38 centimeters. Whether these lines define the work areas of different weavers or show the attempt of a single weaver to build up the web is uncertain. Only cat. no. 314 (fig. V.1) shows an obvious iconographic disjuncture and change of dyelots that would suggest the presence of different workers. The join point is near the midline of the piece, 193 centimeters from the left and 188 centimeters from the right selvage.

The patterning of hands at work on these post-Conquest tapestries suggests that the textiles themselves were conceived as composed of nested rectangular design fields of fairly standard width (approx. 30–40 centimeters). The fields also coincide with different work areas, and in some cases different workers seem to have been involved in the manufacture of single textiles. We do not know with certainty who produced these textiles, where they were made, or, in most cases, exactly when. The size and design of the textiles would have made it possible for multiple weavers to work on the pieces either simultaneously or sequentially. Although such a pattern could be in keeping with the organization of *obrajes*, most such factories used treadle looms of the European type to make yard goods (J. Rowe 1957:177). The patterning of work shown on the textiles is in keeping with an interpretation that they were made by families or small groups of workers meeting the demands of a tribute-collector (an *encomendero* or owner of an *hacienda*) or preparing the pieces for sale.

The production of textiles was important in both Inca and Colonial society. Fiber artists were pressed into service in similar ways: through the institutions of cloth production by *cumbicamayos* and *acllas,* or in *encomienda* shops and *obrajes*, the products of their looms served to advance the social and economic goals of two empires. Throughout the Andean tradition, the structure and design of textiles are closely related to the technology by which they are produced. In documentary evidence and in the Inca and Colonial textiles themselves we see further the link between iconography and the patterns of labor by which they were produced.

Notes

I am indebted to the staff of the Department of Textiles and Costumes of the Museum of Fine Arts for facilitating my study of the pieces described in this essay. Deborah Kraak, former assistant curator, and Deborah Bede, associate conservator, especially, provided assistance and good advice. In addition, I benefited from the comments of Anne Paul, Margaret Young-Sánchez, and Rebecca Stone-Miller in the preparation of the essay. The essay was written during my tenure at the School of American Research in Santa Fe as a Resident Scholar supported by a grant from the National Endowment for the Humanities. This support and especially the help of Jane Gillentine and Jim Duncan at the School's library are gratefully acknowledged.

1. The Indians who complained to a legal investigator about the abuses of Spanish and local-level leaders gave higher figures for the time spent in cloth production. The leaders from Anansaya moiety of Acora, for example, said it took three to four months to produce one of the two-piece outfits required by the authorities and that they were so busy complying with the tax that they hired other weavers to make clothing for their families (Diez de San Miguel 1964:91).

2. A similar strategy of dressing in local costume was followed when the Inca entered the realm of the vanquished Chimu peoples (Cieza de León, in Murra 1962:721) and when Tupa Inca set off on the Chinchaysuyo campaign (Sarmiento, cap. 44; 1960:249).

3. Old World textiles quickly became part of the Inca system of elite gift-giving: Paullu, set up by the Spanish as a puppet ruler, was asked to entice his kinsman, Sayri Tupa Inca, head of the Inca government-in-exile, to leave the jungle. Paullu's emissary approached Sayri Tupa with gifts of "gems and jewels of gold and silver and silk and other valuable cloth," which were repaid with gifts of "fine pieces of gold and silver, excellent cumbi cloth" and other tokens (Cobo, book II, chap. 21; 1979:178).

4. Another Inca tunic type, the "Inca Key Checkerboard" (J. Rowe 1979:248–251; A. Rowe 1978:6–7), likewise usually has a design ten squares in width.

5. Related pieces include the following: a tunic from the Textile Museum, 91.843, discussed by A. Rowe (1978:24, fig. 34, and see note 25); a mantle in the Cleveland Museum of Art, 40.497; two fragments from the Museo Amano (Tsunoyama 1977: pl. 143; Maeyama 1976:59, pl. 81); a fragment from the "Schmidt Collection, Paris" (Harcourt 1962: pl. 9); a tunic in the Metropolitan Museum of Art, 33.149.100 (Kajitani 1982: pl. 120); and a mantle in a private collection in Lima (Kosok 1965:62; chap. VI, fig. 34). This last piece has been analyzed as an ancient calendar (Kosok 1965:61–62; Zuidema 1977:225–226), although it appears to have been cut and repaired.

6. Margaret Young-Sánchez, who examined this textile with me, first suggested the possibility of a hinged loom.

7. Alternatively, work area A could have involved the work of two weavers who worked with identical speed and skill and passed the shuttle back and forth to build up a unified area on the textile, without the telltale signs of interlocking that are seen at the join of other work areas.

8. Another painted cotton tunic showing elements of both Inca and coastal style is illustrated by Kelemen (1943, vol. 2: pl. 182a).

9. Sawyer has provided a compelling argument that the mantle was intentionally prepared as a shroud for a sacrifice (Sawyer 1988). He also provides an analysis of the diagonal and chevron patterning of *tocapus,* and offers a discussion of the probable date of the piece. He suggests it was made for a child. My observations of the design of the textile and patterns of work on it were made independently.

10. See Textile Museum tunic 1960.137 (A. Rowe 1978:19, fig. 26), American Museum of Natural History tunic 41.2/523 (in A. Rowe 1978:19, fig. 27), and one illustrated by Reid (1986: pl. 39), and in design bands of Colonial women's mantles (cf. my note 14 and see fig. V.2b).

11. Sawyer followed a different line of argument to come to a similar conclusion, including comments on the importance of the apex of the chevron to the ultimate use of the textile (Sawyer 1988).

12. Cavallo comments on the importance of cartoons to the European tapestry tradition (1967, vol. 1:18, 30), noting that specialists, many of them in Brussels, prepared cartoons based on paintings or designs that could be used to direct weaving. No information exists on the use of cartoons in Colonial Peru (Cavallo 1967, vol. 1:182). Brussels was also the center of distribution for most of the prints of religious and secular art sent to the New World (Kelemen 1951:211–213).

13. The siren, a symbolic figure derived from Greek mythology, is represented in the art of the Colonial Period as part woman, part fish. According to legend, sirens lured mariners to destruction by their sweet singing. In the form of mermaids, such figures were frequently used, with various symbolic meanings, in coats of arms. Sirens as mermaids (sometimes in shapes that are difficult to identify) are extremely common in Cuzco-style Colonial art, appearing in a range of arts from such humble domestic ornaments as doorknockers to the gold-leafed wood pallets on which saints are carried. Two sirens appear in cat. no. 48 (color pl. 69), one with a cross above her head (fig. V.13, central image).

14. Reading down from the wide edge, these seven bands include a narrow border band with animal figures, a register with geometric motifs, a broad band with figures, a broad band with geometric motifs and a figured band on the midline, another broad band with figures, another register with geometric motifs, and another narrow border band.

Guaman Poma's illustrations of pre-Conquest queens show them either in plain mantles or in three-band mantles, while his drawings of Colonial women show either plain or five-band mantles, in which there are three broad, plain bands separated by narrow figured bands.

Similar mantles are depicted in paintings of the Cuzco school, including a portrait of an Inca princess, dating from the latter half of the seventeenth century (Kelemen 1951: pl. 149d), and "The Marriage of Beatriz Coya and Martín de Loyola" (De Mesa and Gisbert 1962: fig. 61).

Colonial mantles are illustrated by Posnansky (1933: fig. 2); and see Kubler 1946: pl. 92; Dockstader 1967: pl. 179. Kajitani (1982: pl. 125) illustrates one from the Cooper-Hewitt (1902-1-782; gift of J. P. Morgan). Kelemen (1961: fig. b) shows a detail of a partial mantle in the Textile Museum (91.432).

15. My interpretation assumes that the photograph accurately depicts a pattern of work (one weaver, building the web in sections) and is not simply a staged composition. The photograph shows the work areas following the design field, as is common in the Museum's large Colonial tapestries. The sketched design that apparently directs the weaver's work (upper right on loom) appears to include only a portion of the overall design.

COLOR PLATES

NOTES TO THE READER

Arrangement of the Catalogue: The color plates and accompanying catalogue entries are grouped by time period and culture. Initial numbers refer to those of the color plates. Catalogue numbers refer to those in the Checklist, which is arranged by accession number. In a few cases, accession numbers are out of sequence because separated fragments of the original textile have been reunited here for the first time.

Dimensions: Overall maximum height precedes maximum width (or maximum circumference) in centimeters. Dimensions given are those of the entire textile, including fringe, even when a photograph shows a detail or folded portion of the textile. Height and width are determined by the orientation of the piece in the accompanying photograph.

In most of the essays and catalogue descriptions, dimensions are given in centimeters followed by inches (approximate) in parentheses.

Technical Description: for warp and weft, respectively

> material (camelid fiber, cotton, etc.)
> spin-ply direction:
> > \ = single ply, S-spun
> > / = single ply, Z-spun
> > /\ = two-ply, Z-spun, S-plied
> > \/ = two-ply, S-spun, Z-plied
> > /\/ = two Z-spun, S-plied threads replied Z
> > \/\ = two S-spun, Z-plied threads replied S
> > /3\ = three Z-spun threads plied S
> > \3/ = three S-spun threads plied Z
> > pair of /\ = pairs of two-ply, Z-spun, S-plied
> > threads (traveling together but unconnected)
> > three /\ = three two-ply, Z-spun, S-plied
> > threads (traveling together but unconnected)
> thread count per centimeter (randomly taken, not necessarily the maximum)

For fuller information on technical terms, see Glossary.

Exhibitions: Under this heading are listed exhibitions (earliest to most recent) in which the textile was shown. If the piece was published in a catalogue of an exhibition, the pertinent reference is given in short-title form under "Publications." Following is a complete list of the exhibitions referred to:

"25 Centuries of Peruvian Art, 700 B.C.–1800 A.D." Peabody Harvard and MFA, October 4–November 5, 1961
"Peruvian Textiles from the Museum's Collection," MFA, April 1–May 2, 1965
"Colonial Peruvian Tapestries," Textile Museum, October 12, 1968–April 30, 1969
"The Gold of Ancient America: Masterpieces from the Pre-Columbian World," MFA, December 5, 1968–January 12, 1969
"Tapestries of Colonial Peru," MFA, December 1, 1971–February 6,1972
"Paracas and Nasca Textiles, 500–200 B.C.", MFA, March 20–May 27, 1973
"2500 Years of Peruvian Weaving" MFA, March 21–July 11, 1978
"From Fiber to Fine Art," MFA, July 30–September 28, 1980
"Chimu Textiles," Textile Museum, February 3–May 20, 1984
"Textile Masterpieces," MFA, September 27–December 31, 1989

"Connections: Brice Marden," MFA, March 23–July 21, 1991

Publications: Works containing references to the Museum's textile are listed in alphabetical order by author. For full citations, see Bibliography.

Related textiles: Recorded here are closely related pieces in the Museum's collection (abbreviated as "MFA"; see Checklist), followed by pieces from other collections (parts of the same original, when applicable, precede other related pieces). Museums are listed alphabetically, followed by private collections and dealers; published references that do not indicate a location are listed last. The locations listed under this heading are those given in the published references. It has not been possible to confirm the present locations of all the textiles. Quotation marks indicate the last-known location of textiles published early in this century.

The following institutions are included:

> American Museum of Natural History, New York
> The Art Institute of Chicago
> British Museum (see Museum of Mankind)
> Burrell Collection, Glasgow, Scotland
> The Brooklyn Museum of Art
> The Cleveland Museum of Art
> Cooper-Hewitt Museum, The Smithsonian Institution's National Museum of Design, New York
> The Detroit Institute of Arts
> Dumbarton Oaks Research Library and Collection, Washington D.C.
> Field Museum of Natural History, Chicago
> Herbert Hoover Presidential Library-Museum, West Branch, Iowa
> The Metropolitan Museum of Art, New York
> Michael C. Carlos Museum, Emory University, Atlanta
> Musée de l'Homme, Paris
> Museo Amano, Lima
> Museo Arqueologico Regional, Huaraz, Peru
> Museo Nacional de Antropología y Arqueología, Lima
> Museo Oro del Peru, Lima
> Museo Regional de Ica, Ica, Peru
> Museum für Völkerkunde-Berlin
> Museum of the American Indian-Heye Foundation, New York
> Museum of Art, Rhode Island School of Design, Providence
> Museum of Mankind, The Ethnographic Department of the British Museum, London
> Museum Rietberg, Zurich
> Ohara Museum of Art, Kurashiki, Japan
> Peabody Museum of Archaeology and Ethnology, Harvard University, Cambridge
> Robert H. Lowie Museum of Anthropology, University of California, Berkeley
> Royal Ontario Museum, Toronto
> Seattle Art Museum
> Städtisches Museum für Völkerkunde-Frankfurt
> Staatliches Museum für Völkerkunde-Munich
> The Textile Museum, Washington, D.C.
> The University Museum, University of Pennsylvania, Philadelphia
> Victoria and Albert Museum, London

Plate 1
Weaver's Workbasket and Implements
Cat. no. 49

Late Intermediate Period, Chancay, Central Coast
A.D. 1000–1476
H. 32.5 cm, w. 13.7 cm, d. 9.5 cm
Basket: plaited totora reeds over split canes
Contents: 154 wooden spindles, picks, shed sticks, and bobbins (some wound with camelid fiber and some with cotton, \, /, /\; large skein of cotton plied with unidentified vegetal fiber; 16 loose painted wooden spindle whorls; unspun camelid fiber; ceramic dish; camelid or deer bone pick; spine needle; two pieces of chalk.
Gift of Charles H. White
02.680

Exhibitions: 2500 Years.
Related: MFA spindle whorls: 51.573 (cat. no. 257); MFA 51.574 (cat. no. 258); MFA 51.579 (cat. no. 263); MFA 51.580 (cat. no. 264); Amano (Tsunoyama 1977:196, color pl. 229; Bird et al. 1981:137, top); Victoria and Albert T.312/1-41-1910 (Victoria and Albert 1926: pl. XIV); Larsen 1986:53, fig. 39; Taullard 1949:23, top right.

Discussion: pp. 18–20, 46.

The Museum is indeed fortunate to have in its collection a weaver's workbasket, dating from the Late Intermediate Period, apparently found in a woman's grave. The basket, overflowing with bobbins, spindles, and whorls, gives us a direct understanding of the creative process and further conveys an idea of the Andean textile artists' attitudes toward their tools. The technical and design feats found throughout the long history of Andean weaving become even more impressive when the elegant simplicity of the means is appreciated. No more than simple wooden sticks and a few other implements were needed by spinners and weavers to transform raw fiber into the most elaborate textile masterpieces. It cannot be stressed enough that technological simplicity does not correlate with inferior aesthetic results.

The basket contains elements from the entire process of textile production: unspun fiber, spinning tools and finished thread, bobbins to pass threads across in weaving, and a needle for sewing, finishing work, or embroidery. The scale and type of objects included indicate that the owner was a skilled spinner and weaver who worked primarily with very fine thread. The small ceramic cup would support the delicate spindles used to spin and wind extremely fine thread without breaking (Susan Bruce, personal communication, 1991). Lumps of chalk, the small one rubbed against the larger to produce the powder (note how the two fit together), served to dry and smooth passage of fiber through the spinner's fingers, permitting the creation of a perfect, gossamer-thin thread. Other tools are on a noticeably small scale as well: the teeth of the bone pick could only beat down very closely spaced threads; the long needle has an almost infinitesimal hole; and the shed sticks are of the size to pull up only a few threads in an intricate weaving pattern. These are the implements of a master weaver.

In keeping with this high level of skill, the tools themselves are painstakingly decorated and finely finished. Many spindles are painted

along the shaft, although this portion would not be seen when the spindle was used (see cat. no. 288, color pl. 62, on the idea of essence over appearance). Spindles often retain their matching spindle whorls, whose designs include birds, fish, stepped frets, circles, stepped-diamond shapes, jar-forms, and human effigies (see second bobbin from the left and third loose whorl from the top in the photograph). Some spindles with whorls are decorated in matched pairs, suggesting that the Andean preoccupation with complementarity may have extended to weaving tools as well. (It is particularly tempting to imagine that the colors of threads playing complementary roles in a weaving were worked off matching bobbins.) Thread colors include browns, golds, and tans, as well as the red and blue, which required special dyeing expertise, a further indication of this particular weaver's status (see cat. no. 214, color pl. 29, on indigo, and cat. no. 62, color pl. 37, on cochineal).

Perhaps several hundred Late Intermediate Period workbaskets are known and appear to be fairly standardized in form and contents (Susan Bruce, personal communication, 1991). When documented, they are known to come from women's burials. Thus, female identity was closely enough tied to textiles to require that a woman's workbasket remain with her in the afterlife. Tools, when elaborated and found interred like other precious offerings and belongings, certainly hold more than utilitarian connotations. That even the basket itself was finely worked is in keeping with deeply held pre-Columbian ritualism; all steps of a process were revered. The essence of the finished product contained all the actions necessary to achieve it, thus those actions themselves became worthy of praise. Careful burial of the weaver's implements acknowledges the many people (from herders to weavers) and many skills (from dyeing to spinning) involved in accomplishing a masterpiece in fiber.

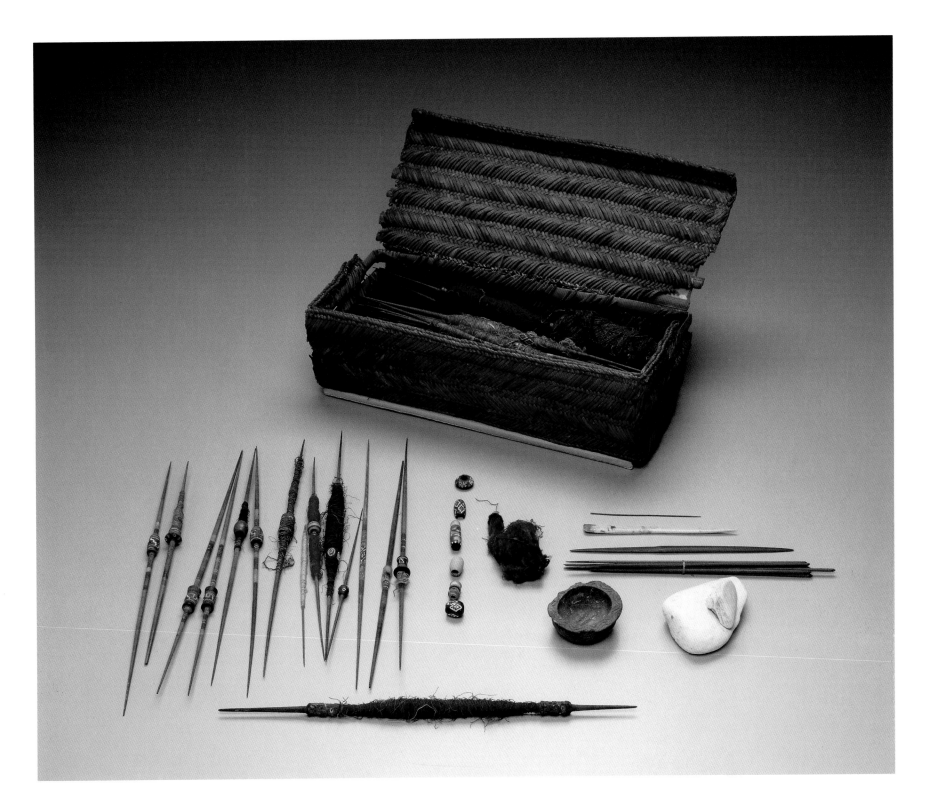

Plate 2

Two-Faced Triple-Cloth Border Fragment with Faces
Cat. no. 237

Early Horizon, Phase 9, early South Coast, probably from Ocucaje, Ica Valley
About 500 B.C.
11.4 x 6 cm
Plain weave; two-faced triple-cloth band
       warp: camelid fiber, ∧, 4.7/cm
       weft: camelid fiber, ∧, 4.7/cm
Mrs. Samuel Cabot's Special Fund
47.1084

Exhibitions: 2500 Years.
Related textiles: Probably part of the same original with University Museum (Wardle 1944:416, pl. IIa,b); University Museum 41-15-13 (A. Rowe in Cahlander and Baizerman 1985:12, fig. 2-12a,b).

Discussion: p. 20.

This tiny fragment of a band holds dual distinctions as the earliest in date and rarest in technique of all the Andean textiles in the Museum's collection. It was woven in a variant of the triple-cloth technique about 500 B.C., making it as much as 2,500 years old. Such antiquity again underscores the perfect conditions for preservation that prevail along Peru's desert coast. Several narrow bands in the same colors and technique bearing closely related designs were found at the site of Ocucaje in the South Coast Ica Valley and dated to phase 9 of the Early Horizon (King 1968; the piece illustrated in Wardle 1944:416, pl. IIa,b, is probably part of the same original).

      We are indeed privileged to glimpse one of the early achievements of the world's longest continuous textile tradition. Yet this piece makes it clear that great antiquitiy itself does not bespeak rudimentary technical or design status; textiles considerably older than this one show great complexity in all aspects (e.g., the twinings from Huaca Prieta dated at 2300 B.C.; see Bird 1963). Here the spectacularly convoluted technique of triple cloth and the abstract geometric motifs, seemingly based on masks, do not signal the hesitant attempts of a nascent artistic endeavor.

      This band of triple cloth was woven as a border to a larger, brown plain-weave textile; the solid brown edges comprise a single layer, while the decorated section is made up of three layers of cloth. Triple cloth, as the name suggests, is one layer more complex than double cloth (see cat. no. 210, color pl. 57); three distinct planes of cloth are woven simultaneously off the same warp threads (see A. Rowe in Cahlander and Baizerman 1985:12–14). Here camelid-fiber threads in yellow, dark brown, and green (the last is now difficult to distinguish; see reconstruction drawings on facing page) all appear on the top face (see photograph). Only yellow and green are interwoven in the invisible center layer and on the visible back face: where green appears on the back, yellow is woven as the center level, and vice versa. The front face design is the most complex, while the back face pattern does not represent all the motif parts and even floats threads across from one motif to the other (see drawing on right).

Because of this dissimilarity of the faces, this specific type of triple cloth is "two-faced" (as opposed to "true" triple cloth, which is double-faced, i.e., identical except in color assignment on front and back [see Emery 1966:165]). Nevertheless, it is astonishing to think of the weaver simultaneously coordinating three distinct planes of cloth, forming three different patterns in two different color schemes. Such multilevel visualization on the part of the weaver can be likened in complexity and character to playing three-dimensional chess.

Key:

■ brown

▣ green

☐ yellow

▤ floats
green
and
yellow

▥ floats
yellow

obverse

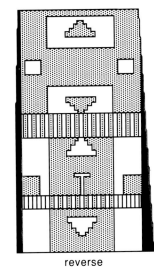

reverse

Early Horizon, Phase 10 (?), Paracas, South Coast
100 B.C.–0
64.8 x 50.8 cm
Plain weave with stem-stitch embroidery; fringe
    plain weave
                warp: camelid fiber, ∧, 14/cm
                weft: camelid fiber, ∧, 14/cm
            embroidery, fringe: camelid fiber, ∧
Mary Woodman Fund
31.496

Exhibitions: 25 Centuries; Paracas and Nasca.
Publications: Dwyer 1973: no. 5; MFA 1961: no. 269.
Related textiles: MFA 1972.353 (cat. no. 303, color pl. 4a,b); American Museum of Natural History (Stafford 1941: pl. XXIIID); Cleveland Museum 46.227 (Paul 1990a:77, color pl. 2); Museo Nacional bundle 310-41 (Paul 1990a:74, color pl. 22); Museo Nacional (Lavalle and Lang 1980:32–34); Museo Nacional (Lavalle and Lang 1980:35);University Museum SA4602 (Stafford 1941: pl. VI).

Discussion: pp. 25, 26, 30; fig. II.2.

This small poncho would have reached to about the midchest when worn; larger versions went to waist level. Its absolutely pristine condition after more than two thousand years is a testament to the perfect preservation conditions in the Paracas peninsula sand dunes, where it was buried as part of the voluminous wrappings of a mummy bundle (see Paul 1990a:35–46). Although such an immaculate appearance might signal that this poncho was created expressly for burial, other Paracas garments show signs of wear, and in all likelihood many were worn on special ceremonial occasions (ibid.:63–64).

The intricate nesting of abstract, transparent images characteristic of linear-style embroidery is nowhere more apparent than in this ingenious composition. A double-headed bird motif has been interpreted in six distinct ways throughout the design. Each motif in a rectangular color area contains four versions, and two others are found in the edging around the neckslit ends and along the inside of the fringe. In a block with a dark blue background, for example, the second one from the top to the right of the neck slit, the main upright bird (with two hexagonal heads facing outward and triangular wings to each side) is outlined in yellow. Inside its rectangular body is the second bird, a slightly simpler, upside-down version in red, while the third bird, in green, is upright inside the second (it has become two heads and four lines below, representing the wings and sides of the body). A tiny sideways red bird, reduced to a single head and three lines for wings and tail, is placed in each wing of the main bird. The two types embedded in the edgings would be unrecognizable, since they are reduced to mere crosses and lines, if the progression to elemental heads and body were not visible in the first four interpretations. Abstraction and the creative interlocking of shapes, such as seen here, allow us to glimpse the formidable aesthetic imagination of the long-dead Paracas textile artist.

Plate 4a,b
Linear-Style Mantle with Oculate Beings
Cat. no. 303

Early Intermediate Period, Phase 1, Paracas, South Coast
0–A.D. 100
133.4 x 288.3 cm
Plain weave with stem-stitch embroidery; fringe
    plain weave
             warp: camelid fiber, ∧, 8/cm
             weft: camelid fiber, ∧, 8/cm
      embroidery: camelid fiber, ∧
      fringe: camelid fiber, ∨
J. H. and E. A. Payne Fund
1972.353

Exhibitions: Paracas and Nasca.
Publications: Dwyer 1973: no. 1.
Related textiles: MFA 31.496 (cat. no. 186, color pl. 3); MFA 67.85 (cat. no. 294); American Museum of Natural History (Stafford 1941: pl. III); Brooklyn Museum (Stafford 1941: pl. IV); Hoover Library, "Hoover Mantle" (Paul 1990a:71, fig. 6.6); Museo Nacional 01434 (Kajitani 1982:28–29, pl. 29); Museo Nacional (Lavalle and Lang 1980:40–44).

Discussion: pp. 17, 23, 25, 30.

Unlike the Paracas block-color style, the linear-style pieces deliberately eschew the freedom inherent in the technique of embroidery. Instead of "sketching" curvilinear designs independently of the cloth ground, the makers of this mantle closely followed the grid of warp and weft to construct a design based completely on vertical, horizontal, and diagonal straight lines. As in other linear examples, almost all of these lines are only one stitch wide (Paul 1990a:69). The creative process is also directly opposed to that of the block-color style. Here the embroiderers counted the threads of the ground cloth to pass over and under as they constructed the background areas of the pattern row by row (Paul 1985a:93–97). The process thus imitated a woven technique rather than reflecting the superstructural nature of embroidery. The outlines of the figures that had been left as bare ground cloth were subsequently filled in, whereas in block-color-style embroidery the figural outlines were the first to be laid out. Linear style is also distinctive in its severely limited palette (there are only four colors here as opposed to nineteen in cat. no. 68, color pl.

Plate 5 (overleaf)
Embroidered Mantle with Staff-bearing Figures
Cat. no. 69

12) and its noninnovative stance (there is little, if any, change in this style of depiction over time). Paul has explored the larger implications of these characteristics and argued that they ensure the communication of abstract, controlled, traditional meanings relating to the supernatural sphere (ibid.:69–73). The two complementary Paracas embroidery styles were basically contemporaneous; they are often found together in the same mummy bundles over a long period of time. Therefore one approach did not supplant the other; rather, their distinctive processes, styles, and subjects were developed for different purposes. The lack of a single creative approach to the embroidery process underscores the importance of artistic choice over technical determinism.

This stunning mantle is embroidered everywhere except for the areas of plain dark blue; the effort that was expended on a mantle of this size is quite incredible. Interlocking S-shaped motifs ending in heads of the Oculate Being (named for its large eyes; see color detail) dominate the complex design. Triangular spaces are filled in with felines, which in turn contain smaller felines within their bodies (like the nested double-headed birds in cat. no. 186, color pl. 3). Through the many nested series of lines, the small number of colors are transformed into a varied, dynamic whirlwind of pattern. Although the motifs are repeated exactly, variation in one major instance of color assignment adds further life to the composition: in the columns that demarcate the mantle center, the motif third from the left forms staggered chevrons rather than diagonals of the same color (the gold is most easily distinguished). A recurring characteristic of woven Andean textile designs, such an obvious formal deviation is interesting to note in the embroidery style that is created most like a weaving.

Early Intermediate Period, Phase 1, Paracas, South Coast
0–A.D. 100
134.6 x 255.3 cm
Plain weave with stem-stitch embroidery
      plain weave
               warp: camelid fiber, $\wedge$, 19/cm
               weft: camelid fiber, $\wedge$, 19/cm
          embroidery: camelid fiber, $\wedge$
Denman Waldo Ross Collection
16.32

Exhibitions: Paracas and Nasca.
Publications: Dwyer 1973: no. 10; Flint 1916:41; Means 1932:56, specimen 29, figs. 48, 49; Stafford 1941: pl. XIII.
Related textiles: MFA 16.33 (cat. no. 70, color pl. 13).

Discussion: pp. 11, 14, 25, 29, 32; fig. II.10.

The style of figures in this checkerboard-patterned mantle is distinctive in relation to that of the other Paracas mantles in the Museum's collection. It is less detailed and precise in design, and the stitches are executed less regularly than in most embroideries; however, the staff-bearing figure is nonetheless very expressive and the composition lively. With its special characteristics, this mantle helps demonstrate the range of artistic visions and abilities of the Paracas embroiderers (see Paul and Niles 1985). Lower technical quality may signal that the textile owner was of a moderate social status; nevertheless, the person merited a large and time-consuming burial wrapping.

Several interesting features of the figure's costume and accoutrements are worthy of mention. In one hand the person holds a long staff with a tiny monkey at the top, which has been called a spear thrower, although Paul doubts this attribution (Means 1932:56; Anne Paul, personal communication, 1991). The figure's headdress consists of what appear to be the head and skin of an animal, possibly a beaked bird, so that two sets of eyes are superimposed. Although the figure is otherwise human, the mouth emanation seen on many Paracas images (e.g., cat. no. 67, color pl. 9) gives a fantastical effect. This one is studded with tiny human trophy heads and ends in a somewhat larger version of one with its characteristic long, flowing hair. Along with the knife in the other hand, these references to warfare and head-taking are typical of Paracas iconography in general. The owner may have proclaimed his status as a warrior through the adoption of this design on his mantle.

Plate 6
Mantle Border Fragment with Pampas Cats
Cat. no. 85

Early Intermediate Period, Phase 1, Paracas, South Coast
0–A.D. 100
20 x 80 cm
Plain weave with stem-stitch embroidery; fringe
  plain weave
        warp: camelid fiber, ∧, 15/cm
        weft: camelid fiber, ∧, 15/cm
    embroidery: camelid fiber, ∧
    fringe: camelid fiber, ∨
Denman Waldo Ross Collection
21.2557

Exhibitions: 25 Centuries; Paracas and Nasca.
Publications: Dwyer 1973: no. 4; Means 1932:58, specimen 33, fig. 55; MFA 1961: no. 264.
Related textiles: Museo Nacional 310-26 (Paul 1990a:75, color pl. 24; 107, fig. 7.49).

Discussion: p. 11.

The image repeated in this fragmentary border of a large mantle is that of a fantastical, abstracted, double-headed pampas cat. This native Peruvian cat (*felis colocolo*) was familiar to the Paracas embroiderer and is seen in other compositions (see Paul 1990a:84, color pl. 12; 79, fig. 7.1; 131). The pampas cat is distinguished by banded legs and a spotted torso, pointed ears, facial markings resembling elongated whiskers, and a diagnostic crest of longer hairs along the backbone. In this embroidered rendition notice the long, gently curving whiskers, the stepped pattern around the eyes, and the triangular ears. In particular, the abstract treat-

ment of the layers of fur as a nest of multicolored jagged outlines lends a strongly three-dimensional sense to the figure and accentuates the cat's identifying backbone crest.

However, the image was not primarily meant to be an accurate description, since it sports a head on each end and incorporates anthropomorphic allusions. Each head holds near its mouth a small human trophy head, thereby making a visual analogy between predatory human practices —the taking of enemy heads in war— and those of the carnivorous wild cats. Thus, the image probably served to reinforce metaphorically the prowess of the cloth's owner. The use of animals' traits as "adjectives" to describe humans, by the making of composites in unnatural configurations, can be seen as a form of highly abstract thinking. The overall congruence between the animal and human kingdoms, which makes it possible to combine freely categories we see as separate, falls within the fundamental pre-Columbian belief in the interconnectedness of all nature.

Another abstraction of the two-headed cat motif is included along the edge of the fringe, where the same motif has been reduced meticulously to a minute, 52-stitch-long version. The entire image consists of one curved whisker to each side, a white line for teeth and two for eyes, and a "railroad track" line for the backbone crest. This restating of the theme in parts of the design almost too tiny to be visible is seen, for example, in cat. no. 186 (color pl. 3) and seems to be characteristic of Paracas creativity.

Plate 7
Embroidered Skirt with Four Figure Types
Cat. no. 91

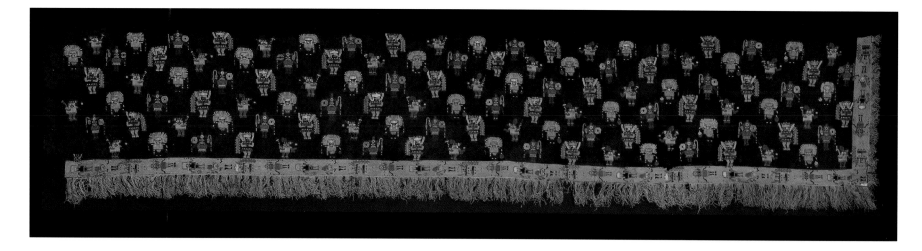

Early Intermediate Period, Phase 1, Paracas, South Coast
0–A.D. 100
60.8 x 286.7 cm
Plain weave with stem-stitch embroidery; fringe
     plain weave
             warp: cotton, /\, 13–15/cm
             weft: cotton /\, 13–15/cm
       embroidery, fringe: camelid fiber, /\
Denman Waldo Ross Collection
21.2563

Exhibitions: 25 Centuries; Paracas and Nasca
Publications: Dwyer 1973: no. 11; MFA 1961: no. 270; Townsend 1932:61, 63, figs. 2, 3.
Related textiles: American Museum of Natural History 41D/1500 (Stafford 1941: pl. IX); Lumbreras 1974:91, fig. 102.

Discussion: pp. 11, 23, 25, 29–31, 33; fig. II.9.

This skirt is exceptional both in size and in iconography: it is 8 centimeters (3 ⅛ inches) longer and 35 centimeters (13 ¾ inches) wider than the average, and it is decorated in the main field with four distinct types of figures. Originally, the ground cloth would have appeared as purple — also an unusual feature — with accents in gold and green; however, the purple has faded to brown, making the greens particularly difficult to distinguish. Probably this fading occurred because the fabric is woven in cotton, which does not absorb and maintain colors as well as does camelid fiber. Characteristic of the skirt format, embroidered borders along the lower edge and one short side would have been visible when worn; the original ties have been lost (see cat. no. 75; cat. no. 67, color pl. 9). The long, multicolor fringe is especially beautiful and would have seemed even thicker when the skirt had been wound around the wearer several times.

Four different ritual or cult impersonators are shown, whereas in almost all Paracas embroideries variations on a single type are found (see cat. no. 84, color pl. 10). Dwyer explains what distinguishes impersonators from supernaturals: "they do not have the peculiar features of mythical representations such as flying pose and flowing appendages, but are shown instead wearing and carrying the paraphernalia associated with the mythical forms" (1973: entry no. 11). Paul has differentiated the four according to headgear: A has a long turban hanging to one side, B a feather headdress, C a net over his head, and D a group of snakes projecting from one side of the head (see p. 31). This iconographic variety is balanced by strong, formal regularity. A single upright and frontal orientation of the figures, as opposed to the four possible directions seen in many pieces (e.g., cat. no. 191, color pl. 11), in addition to the consistent assignment of colors keep the design stable. The artists have even balanced the arrangement of figures with symmetrically placed arms and those with an asymmetrical pose.

Like quite a few Paracas embroideries, this piece remains somewhat unfinished. In the lower left-most corner of the central field one of the embroiderers had only begun to outline in gold and fill in the legs of a type A impersonator. Since all the other figures are entirely filled in, this provides a clue that the work generally progressed from right to left in this piece. The arrested final touches to this magnificent skirt bring us closer to the talented people who stitched it painstakingly for its owner so many centuries ago.

Plate 8a,b
Embroidered Mantle with Bird Impersonators
Cat. no. 71

Early Intermediate Period, Phase 1B (?), Paracas, South Coast
A.D. 50–100
a: 101 x 244.3 cm
b (border below): 13.3 x 241.9 cm
c (border fragment above): 14 x 25.2 cm
Plain weave with stem-stitch embroidery
      plain weave
           warp: camelid fiber, ∧, 13/cm
           weft: camelid fiber, ∧, 13/cm
      embroidery: camelid fiber, ∧
Denman Waldo Ross Collection
16.34a–c

Exhibitions: 25 Centuries; Gold of Ancient America; Paracas and Nasca; 2500 Years;
From Fiber to Fine Art; Textile Masterpieces.

Publications: Dwyer 1973: no. 9; Flint 1916:40–41; Harcourt 1962:183; pl. 105b; Lecht-
man 1984:13, fig. 8; Means 1932:57, specimen 31, figs. 52, 53; MFA 1961: no. 263;
MFA 1964:342–343; MFA 1976:394–395; MFA 1984:394–395; MFA 1989:[8]; Salmon
et al. 1980:60–61, no. 60; Stafford 1941:23; 37–38; 45; pl. VIII; Townsend 1932:61;
Washburn 1988:265, fig. 7.17.
Related textiles: Part of same garment set with MFA 16.30 (cat. no. 67, color pl. 9).

Discussion: pp. 11, 25, 27, 28, 30, 33; fig. II.6.

The most celebrated of all the Museum's Andean textiles, this stunning
embroidered mantle was reportedly "found [in a cemetery] three or four
miles south of Pisco" (Sarah G. Flint, letter of November 21, 1917;
Department of Textiles and Costumes), a town just north of the
Paracas peninsula (see fig. I.3). Julio C. Tello, one of the most important
early archaeologists of Peru, sold it along with other pieces to the Museum thirteen years before the landmark find in 1929 of the Paracas

Cavernas and Necrópolis cemeteries, filled with over five hundred wrapped mummy bundles (Paul 1991:33). Two fragmentary portions of its borders match it exactly in iconography and generally in color patterning, but, interestingly enough, not in the color of the ground cloth (green instead of dark blue). This was apparently a common practice, possible precisely because the embroidery completely obscures the ground cloth (Anne Paul, personal communication, 1991; see essay II, note 9). Since the Museum's skirt cat. no. 67 (color pl. 9; fig. II.4) matches this piece so exactly, these two are presumed to form a garment set (see also cat. no. 191, color pl. 11, and cat. no. 192).

The magnificent rendering of detailed bird-impersonating figures, averaging only 12.7 centimeters (5 inches) in height, demonstrates embroidery at its best. Evenly wrought rows of tiny stem stitches create very dense color areas through the overlap of brightly dyed threads. The stem stitch consists of taking a forward stitch from the fabric back across the front face, then half a backward stitch from the front across the back face, and beginning again. In this way overlapping, slightly diagonal lines are laid down, thousands of which define the many parts of the fifty-five finished bird figures. Besides its perfectly completed figures, this tunic reveals several important stages of the creative process in its unfinished portions (see p. 27). Its matching skirt is also unfinished, to a greater degree than the mantle (see fig. II.4).

Bird impersonators sport an elaborate headdress with gold forehead ornament (for actual ornaments see Lavalle and Lang 1980:45), mask, loincloth, tunic and feathered cape, the last two with trophy head images. They carry in one hand an actual trophy head and in the other a snake-headed baton. Even the tiniest of details are visually sophisticated: for instance, the long feathers of the cape begin as miniature trophy heads, a device that represents an example of what has been called a kenning (J. Rowe 1962a:15). Thus, the feather takes on a second simultaneous reading as the hair of the trophy head victim. Double messages such as this are found throughout Andean art from earliest times (ibid.). The many layers of meaning played out in visual form give ancient Andean art its formidable subtlety and depth.

Plate 9
Embroidered Skirt with Bird Impersonators
Cat. no. 67

Early Intermediate Period, Phase 1B (?), Paracas, South Coast
A.D. 50–100
Skirt: 50.8 x 289.8 cm
Ties: 8.8 x 101.5 cm; 8.8 x 99 cm
Plain weave with stem-stitch embroidery; oblique interlacing; cross-knit
loop stitch (ties)
       plain weave
            warp: camelid fiber, ∧, 10/cm
            weft: camelid fiber, ∧ 10/cm
       embroidery and ties: camelid fiber, ∧
Denman Waldo Ross Collection
16.30

Related textiles: Part of a garment set with MFA 16.34a–c (cat. no. 71, color pl. 8a,b);
MFA 16.38 (cat. no. 75).

Discussion: pp. 11, 22, 25–27; fig. II.4.

This skirt belongs with the previous mantle, cat. no. 71 (color pl. 8a,b), as
part of a matched garment set. Although we tend to associate skirts as an
item of female dress, they were worn by males in Paracas society. The extremely wide garment (fig. II.4) was wrapped many times around the
body and tied, probaby at the front, so that the elaborate tassels hung
down and the embroidered border on the short side was visible (see Paul
1990a:55–57, figs. 5.14–5.17; cat. no. 75). (Here, for conservation reasons, the ties have been placed in their approximate original positions
but not sewn down.) When worn, it would have resembled a kilt, which
these skirts often have been called. There were many different ritual garment types found in the Paracas mummy bundles, including mantles
(e.g., cat. no. 303, color pl. 4a,b), ponchos (cat. no. 186, color pl. 3),
loincloths (cat. nos. 87, 88, 89), turbans (cat. no. 189), and tunics (Paul
1990a:47–64).

     Like that of its mate, the embroidering of the skirt was unfin-
ished when it was interred with its wearer. The bird-impersonator figures
have been outlined in gold and the gold background of the border filled
in around them, as is usual in the Paracas block-color style embroidery
process. The next step would have been to fill in the many colored details
of the figures, their costumes, and accoutrements, as seen in the mantle.
It is as if the skirt had been whisked out from under the embroiderer's
needle, presumably because of the untimely death of the person who
commissioned it. Over two thousand years later we are privileged to see
how the magnificent textiles of the Paracas culture were created, precisely because the process was interrupted.

Plate 10
Embroidered Mantle Fragment with Masked Figures
Cat. no. 84

Early Intermediate Period, Phase 2, Paracas, South Coast
A.D. 100–200
83.8 x 253.4 cm
Plain weave with stem-stitch embroidery
 plain weave
   warp: camelid fiber, ∧, 13/cm
   weft: camelid fiber, ∧, 13/cm
  embroidery: camelid fiber, ∧
Denman Waldo Ross Collection
21.2556

Exhibitions: Paracas and Nasca.
Publications: Dwyer 1973: no. 12; Harcourt 1962:183; pl. 105a); Means 1932:54, specimen 26, figs. 42, 43.
Related textiles: MFA 21.2563 (cat. no. 91, color pl. 7); parts of the same original: National Museum of Natural History 289614 and Royal Ontario Museum 916.7.3.

Discussion: pp. 11, 25, 26; fig. II.5.

This colorful embroidery constitutes most of the top part of a mantle: as seen, its height is about half of the average mantle measurement of 130 centimeters (51 inches), and the left side lacks around 30 centimeters (12 inches) where the green border should turn the corner to form a bracket, as occurs on the right top edge (Paul 1990a:51). Anne Paul has located additional parts of the original mantle in the National Museum of Natural History and Royal Ontario Museum collections and generously shared the following reconstruction (personal communication, 1992). Originally there were five rows of embroidery, each with figures facing the same direction and displaying distinctive facial coloration(from the top down): gold, gold and maroon striped, maroon, scarlet and light blue on diagonal, and pink. Thus, the two figures with scarlet and light blue faces seen to the lower left in the photograph represent fragments from the lower portion of the mantle (placed in their original row if not their exact position). The large fragment of the mantle now in the National Museum of Natural History includes most of the rest of the row of figures with scarlet and light blue faces plus a fifth row of figures with pink faces and blue birdlike eye markings. Each of the five remaining larger figures Along the upper green-background border has a distinctive facial coloration as well. Although such a profusion of facial decorations and an odd number of rows is not particularly common in Paracas mantle compositions, several other similar examples are known.

 Other notable idiosyncratic features include unfinished shapes, a deviation in figure orientation, and an emphasis on three-dimensional effects. The most apparent unfinished shapes are also found in this top row (notice that the five right-most examples have blank forehead ornaments and/or earring circles instead of light blue ones). A figural orientation deviation —a maroon-faced figure faces left instead of right— is seen in the lowest right corner. An exceptional interest in three-dimensional effects (rare in pre-Columbian art as a whole) can be noted in the predominance of clearly overlapping objects held and worn by each figure. Notice, for

example, in the figures' left hand (viewer's right) how naturalistically the fingers wrap around the baton; how the sling drapes around the wrist, its end trailing in front of the snake appendage coming off the belt, which itself goes behind the leg. Such sensitive passages betray the hand of a master designer, whose vision and execution contrast with those of other artists of the time, much as the lyrical three-dimensional treatment of garment folds in the famous Yaxchilan Lintel 24 sets it apart from the work of other Maya sculptors (Schele and Miller 1986:187, pl. 62a).

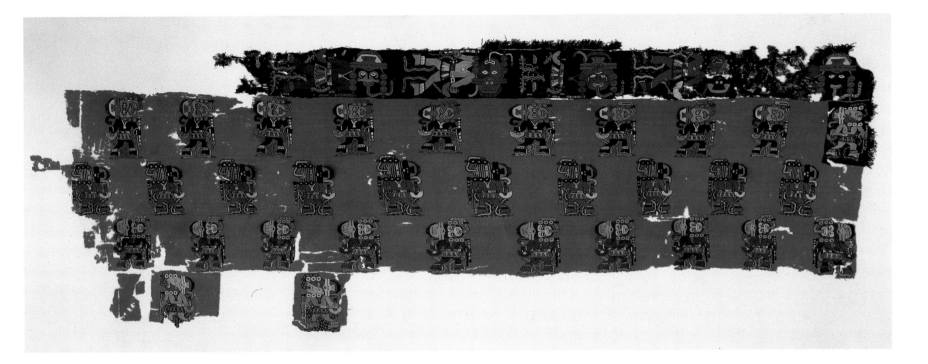

Plate 11
Embroidered Mantle with Shaman Figures
Cat. no. 191

Early Intermediate Period, Phase 1, Paracas, South Coast
0–A.D. 100
142 x 241 cm
Plain weave with stem-stitch embroidery
      plain weave
            warp: camelid fiber, ∧, 9/cm
            weft: camelid fiber, ∧, 9/cm
      embroidery: camelid fiber, ∧
William A. Paine Fund
31.501

Exhibitions: 25 Centuries; Paracas and Nasca; Textile Masterpieces.
Publications: Dwyer 1973: no. 8; MFA 1961: no. 267; Reeves 1949:105, figs. 3 and 5; Stafford 1941:18, fig. 5, pl. XV; 31; 48–49; 50, fig. 31; 78–79.
Related textiles: Part of garment set with MFA 31.502 (cat. no. 192); MFA 21.2559 (cat. no. 87); American Museum of Natural History 14907K (Dockstader 1967: no 99); Museum für Völkerkunde-Munich 34-41-7 (Lommel 1977:170, cat. no. 834, pl. 98; 224–225). For other shaman figure mantles see Paul and Turpin 1986.

Discussion: pp. 11, 25, 27–29, 32, 33; figs. II.7, II.12.

The great visual dynamism of this Paracas mantle was apparently accomplished by the team of embroiderers both intentionally and unintentionally (see pp. 27, 32). In the top web the rows of "ecstatic shaman" figures (see Paul and Turpin 1986) are oriented so that their thrown-back heads form a line, while their arched bodies alternately fall above and below the head line. In turn, every other row alternates the direction of the bodies (left- and right-facing), so that all four figural positions are present. Considering the complex curves making up each figure, which have been described as "a synthesis of contrasts" made up of "violent curves" (Stafford 1941:18), this arrangement makes for a very exciting, visually complicated pattern that is difficult to maintain in perceptual order. Paul and Turpin argue that this bizarre, impossible position symbolizes the shaman in magical flight to the spirit world while in a trance state (1986:24).

    Irregularities in the patterning, probably unintentionally introduced by the various embroiderers, further subvert a systematic understanding of the composition and add dynamism (see figs. II.7, II.12; see also Paul and Turpin 1986:48–50). Extra figures are added to columns on the right side of the piece, which interrupts the regular patterning of figure orientations and color repeats. Ruth Reeves, writing as an appreciative fabric designer, implies this irregularity was conscious, that the embroiderers "knew all there is to know about straight repeats and dropped repeats. . . . Their remarkable ingenuity in planning stripe repetitions, border patterns, checkerboard arrangements and contiguous interlocking motifs, show the Paracas embroiderers were not unmindful of the stellar role that spacial [sic] concepts must play in all fine textile design" (1949:105). Keeping in mind that our aesthetic response to ancient textiles is a subjective one —bearing no real relation to the original intent of the makers— we can nevertheless find beauty in both regular and irregu-

lar arrangements, whatever the causes. Certainly, this was not rejected during its time as a "defective" mantle; on the contrary, such images of shamans were among the most popular and repeated themes on Paracas embroideries (Paul and Turpin 1986:21). It is tempting to conclude that the shaman image, representing an intermediary with the supernatural realm who breaks the rules of everyday life, was to be illustrated with an equally rule-breaking composition.

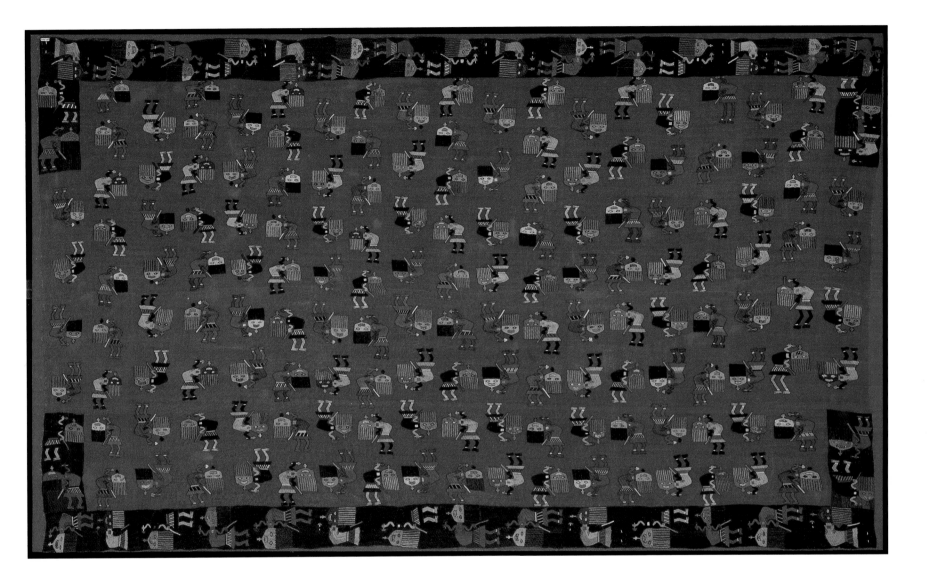

Plate 12
Embroidered Mantle with Shark Impersonators
Cat. no. 68

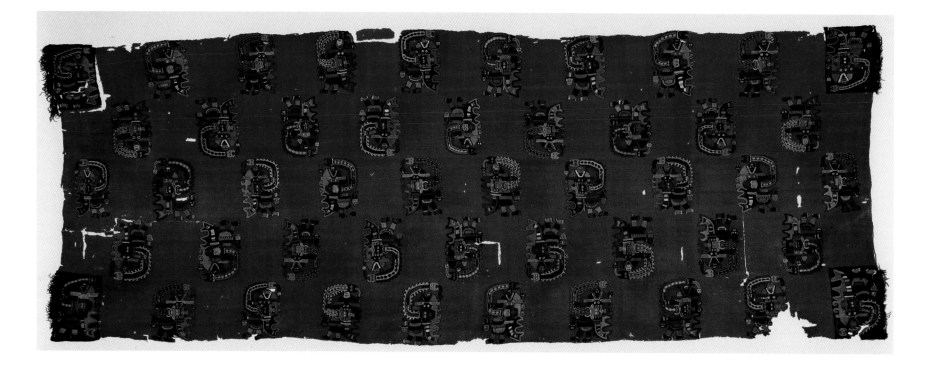

Early Intermediate Period, Phase 2, Paracas, South Coast
A.D. 100–200
92.7 x 264.2 cm
Plain weave with stem-stitch embroidery
    plain weave
        warp: camelid fiber, ∧, 12/cm
        weft: camelid fiber, ∧, 12/cm
      embroidery: camelid fiber, ∧
Denman Waldo Ross Collection
16.31

Exhibitions: 25 Centuries; Paracas and Nasca; 2500 Years.
Publications: Dwyer 1973: no. 2; Flint 1916:41; MFA 1961: no. 261; MFA 1976:396–397; MFA 1984:396–397; A. Rowe 1972:75, fig. 11; Stafford 1941:48, fig. 30; pl. XIV.
Related textiles: Museo Nacional 378-34 (Paul 1990a:124–125, figs. I.8, I.9); Museo Nacional 378-19 (Paul 1990a:74, pl. 21; 85, fig. 7.13).

Discussion: pp. 11, 25, 29, 30, 32, 33; fig. II.11a,b.

The remarkably talented creators of the Paracas block-color style took full advantage of the freedom inherent in the superstructural technique of embroidery. Because patterning is stitched to the surface of a completed plain-weave ground cloth, embroidery avoids the strictures of loom-bound structural methods. Thus, curves are naturally explored, as can be seen here in a repeated shark-impersonator figure consisting almost en-tirely of complex curves. The two-pronged flip of the tail and characteristic dorsal fins are counterposed by the near circle of a fantastical tongue emanation (the main figure's serrated-edged tongue transforms into the hair of a trophy head, whose tongue, in turn, becomes a snake). The resulting loose S curve of the figure as a whole alternates by row direction as the figures' orientations vary, which gives the composition a wonderfully free, lilting quality.

This composition belongs to the most innovative of the three Paracas embroidery styles (e.g., compare the linear style of cat. no. 303, color pl. 4a,b). Different block-color compositions may share major identifying features, such as the shark iconography (see related textiles listed above) and certain minor conceits, such as the elements in the mouth emanation; however, "there may be as many versions of a single iconographic type as there were artists working" (Paul 1990a:66). Versions also exist in other media: there is a remarkably similar shark impersonator made as a ceramic vessel (ibid.:90, fig. 7.21).

Artists also expressed themselves through a range of choices within an extremely colorful palette: in this composition alone it is possible to count nineteen distinct shades (six golds and tans, four reds and pinks, four blues, two greens, two browns, and white). In addition, formal idiosyncrasies are often found, as in the irregular positioning of two of the corner figures on green square backgrounds. Those on the right side are upside down in relation to the other figures in their row, in contrast to those on the left. Exploiting the great freedom of embroidery, the Paracas block-color embroiderers expressed their own unique interpretations.

Plate 13
Embroidered Mantle with Composite Figures
Cat. no. 70

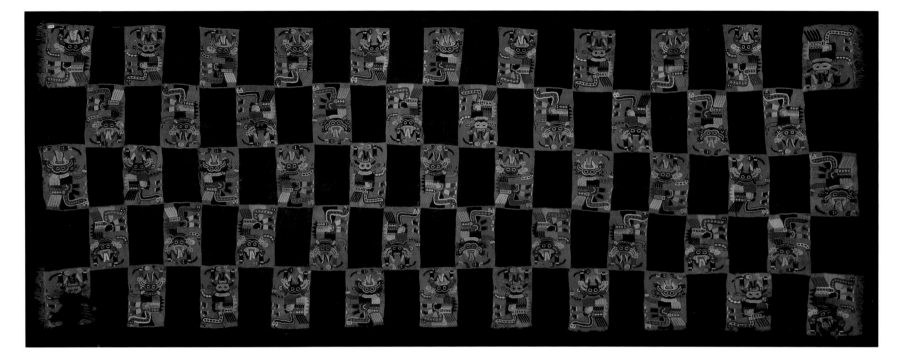

Early Intermediate Period, Phase 2, Paracas, South Coast
A.D. 100–200
111.7 x 274 cm
Plain weave with stem-stitch embroidery; fringe
    plain weave
        warp: camelid fiber, ∧, 11/cm
        weft: camelid fiber, ∧, 11/cm
    embroidery: camelid fiber, ∧
    fringe: camelid fiber, ∨
Denman Waldo Ross Collection
16.33

Exhibitions: 25 Centuries; Paracas and Nasca.
Publications: Dwyer 1973: no. 3; Flint 1916:40–41 (illus. top p. 40); Means 1932:56–57, specimen 30, figs. 50, 51; MFA 1961: no. 262 (illus.).
Related textiles: Said to have been in same bundle as MFA 16.31 (cat. no. 68, color pl. 12); Museo Nacional 319-110 and 253-8.

Discussion: pp. 11, 25, 32.

The spectacular Paracas mantle was the crowning element of a multilay-ered series of lavishly embroidered garments. Like the mummy bundle in which the individual was later buried, the living body was wrapped in many textiles. "The mantle was draped lengthwise around the neck and over the shoulders and arms as a cloak, completely and majestically con-cealing the body of the person who wore it" (Paul 1990a:52). Underneath the mantle, the person might be clad in a combination of poncho, loin-cloth, skirt, and tunic, while on the head wear a turban or headband. An extremely close identification of the person and cloth through the various stages of life is found in all Andean traditions: ancient, Colonial, and modern. In addition, the concealment of inner layers that are completed, though unseen, represents the consistent Andean focus on essence over appearance (see cat. no. 288, color pl. 62; Lechtman 1984).

This mantle, like cat. no. 69 (color pl. 5), is embroidered in a checkerboard pattern. It is immediately apparent that more than half the surface of the cloth is filled with embroidery, since each of the yellow rectangles containing a figure was stitched on top of the purple ground cloth, representing the expenditure of an extraordinary amount of time and effort. A rough estimate of the amount of time necessary to produce this mantle comes to about 1,342 hours (118 hours for the weaving and 1,224 hours for the embroidering stages), using calculations summarized by Paul (1990a:32, note 14). Astonishingly, all the textiles in an entire large mummy bundle might have taken between 11,000 and 29,000 hours to produce (ibid.). The total creation time for the corpus of Paracas textiles as a whole becomes astronomical; it must be figured in many thousands of hours. Thus, the personal, as well as societal, dedication to cloth creation in the Andes cannot be underestimated.

Plate 14a,b
Fragments of a Hanging
Cat. no. 295

Early Intermediate Period, Paracas-Nasca Transition, South Coast
About A.D. 200
a: 69.9 x 113.6 cm
b: 58.5 x 19 cm
c: 21.5 x 29 cm
d: 45 x 18.5 cm
Plain-weave discontinuous interlocked warp and weft
      warp: camelid fiber, V, 35/cm
      weft: camelid fiber, ∧, 35/cm
Edwin E. Jack Fund
67.313a–d

Exhibitions: 2500 Years.
Publications: Paul 1991:255, fig. 7.6; A. Rowe 1972:68, figs. 1, 2; 71, fig. 5.
Related textiles: MFA 65.599 (cat. no. 290, color pl. 44); MFA 64.2044 (cat. no. 289, color pl. 17); Brooklyn Museum 34.15.79 (A. Rowe, 1972:69, fig. 3).

Discussion: pp. 17, 25.

This hanging is by far the most elaborate example of discontinuous warp and weft technique in the Museum's collections; there is only one strikingly similar piece known: a more complete and better preserved but slightly less densely patterned hanging converted into a poncho in the Brooklyn Museum (34.15.79; see A. Rowe 1972:69, fig. 3). This remarkably difficult technique of producing sheer but colorful cloth, explained in the entry for cat. no. 289 (color pl. 17), has been refined here to an unparalleled degree. Not only the sheer number of interlocked shapes but also the achievement of so many curves (such as the flower held by the main figure in the large top fragment; see color pl. 14b) make it nearly impossible to calculate the number of scaffold threads necessary to build the pattern. Moreover, only four fragments (one large and three small) still exist of what was originally a much larger hanging. The Brooklyn hanging may have been as long as 245 centimeters (8 feet) before its conversion to a poncho, and the Boston piece is wider than it by nearly 41 centimeters (16 inches). Thus, if what remains represents less than one third of the composition, then the time and effort invested in the total creation of 6,350 square centimeters (2,500 square inches) of such a complex pattern in this technique become even more mind-boggling. As in the creation of the Paracas embroideries, which share the imagery of this slightly later weaving, the Andean fiber artist gave precedence to the attainment of visual goals over all else.

    Although numerous people devoted great portions of their lives to embroidering mummy bundle cloths, perhaps only a very few had the specialized skills needed to weave such masterpieces. The fact that only two have been found may well reflect their rarity in antiquity rather than simply the vicissitudes of archaeological preservation (since thousands of the embroideries have survived). These weavings may have been more highly prized and probably considered more sacred, not only because of their quality and rarity but also because one of them was later converted; reuse, like imitation, was a high form of praise often given to textiles throughout the Andean past (for examples from later periods, see cat. no 12, color pl. 38, and cat. no. 48, color pl. 69a,b, respectively.

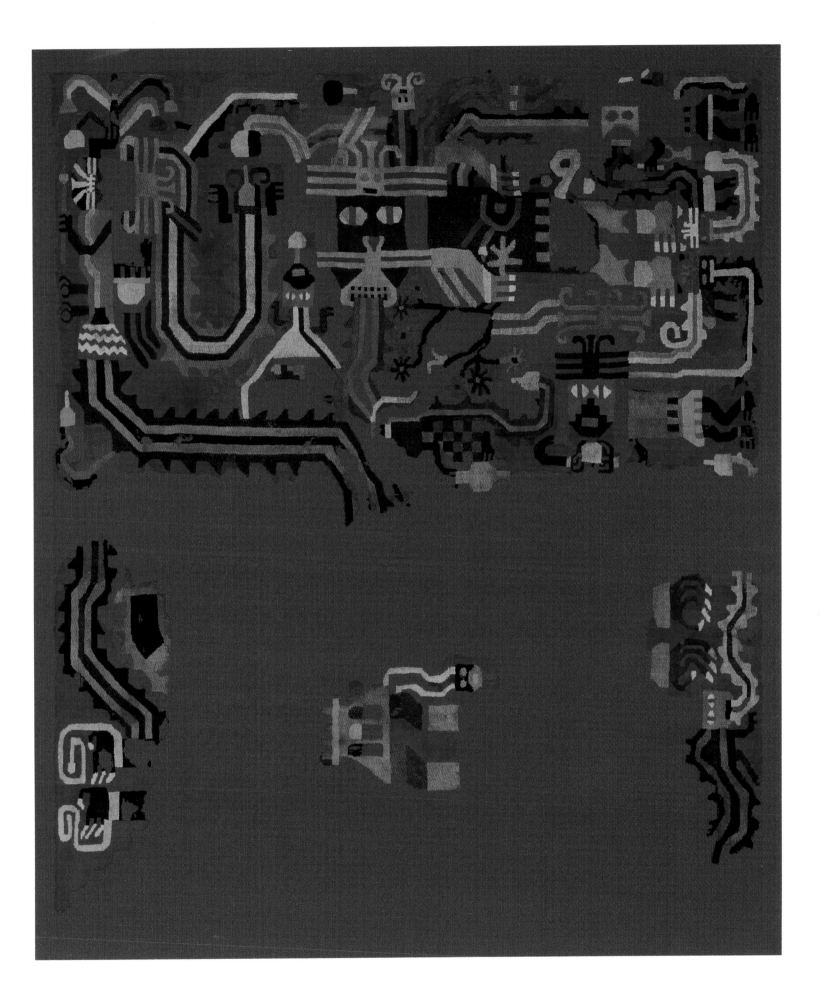

90 / To Weave for the Sun (plate 14b)

Plate 15
Fragment of a Tabbed and Fringed Border
Cat. no. 190

Early Intermediate Period, Phase 2 (?), Nasca, South Coast
About A.D. 300
17.5 x 61 cm
Plain weave with stem-stitch embroidery; fringe; cross looping (upper tabs)

       plain weave
              warp: camelid fiber, /\, 16/cm
              weft: camelid fiber, /\, 16/cm
       embroidery and looping: camelid fiber, /\
       fringe: camelid fiber, /V
Mary Woodman Fund
31.500

Exhibitions: Paracas and Nasca.
Publications: Dwyer 1973: no. 14.
Related textiles: "Schmidt Collection, Paris" (Harcourt 1962:184; pl. 107a); Textile Museum 91.473 and 91.38 (Bird and Bellinger 1954: pl. XCII; see also p. 75).

Discussion: p. 20.

The late Paracas style of embroidery overlaps with early Nasca style; there is a gradual and not always clear transition between the two South Coast styles during the Early Intermediate Period. Nasca style retains some "Paracoid" traits throughout its later development, hence this fragmentary border could represent either a transitional Paracas-Nasca style or possibly a later archaizing Nasca border, much like cat. no. 295 (color pl. 14a,b). Though somewhat of a stylistic hybrid, the design was nonetheless coordinated to achieve visual unity: the color sequence of the fringe at the bottom almost exactly mirrors that of the small cross-looped tabs at the top.

    Paracas features include the complete coverage of the dark green ground cloth by stem-stitch embroidery, the general appearance of the face masks worn by the figures (e.g., see Tushingham 1976: 106–107, cat. no. 123), the overall color scheme, and the multicolor fringe (see cat. no. 303, color pl. 4a,b). Yet, although the motifs include a mixture of recognizable figure parts from Paracas impersonators and supernaturals, they do not add up to a coherent figure; such a characteristic piecemeal approach signals the strong influence of Paracas compositions, not Paracas production itself. Diagnostic Nasca features are evident in the profusion of floral and vegetal motifs and the dark outlining of all shapes (here accomplished, strikingly, in dark purple). Strict attention to detail and to the finishing of an uncut yet multipartite cloth is a hallmark of the dedicated, meticulous Andean textile artist.

Plate 16
Head Tie with Pendants
Cat. no. 169

Early Intermediate Period, Nasca, South Coast
About A.D. 300 (?)
a (left): 26 x 18 cm
b (right): 26.5 x 18 cm
cord: 653 x 0.4 cm
Oblique double-twined double cloth (in sprang technique) with cross looping (pendants); warp-faced double cloth (cord)
        camelid fiber, /\
Gift of Edward Jackson Holmes
30.248a,b

Exhibitions: 25 Centuries.
Publications: MFA 1961: no. 276.
Related textiles: Art Institute of Chicago 1955.1792a,b (Cahlander and Baizerman 1985: color pl. 14); Dumbarton Oaks B509 (Lothrop et al. 1957: cat. no. 345, pl. CXLII); original pair made up of Museum of Mankind 1931.11-23-15 (Cahlander and Baizerman 1985: color pl. 15) and Dumbarton Oaks B510 (Lothrop et al. 1957: cat. no. 346, pl. CXLII); Musée de l'Homme 34-145-2 (Harcourt 1962:81; 82, fig. 54; pl. 58); Ohara Museum 0328 (Kajitani 1982:48–49, pl. 61); "Collection Fritz Iklé" 13024 (Harcourt 1962:82; 161, pl. 57).

Discussion: p. 20.

This enigmatic ensemble, consisting of two large bell-shaped pendants connected by a cord over 6 meters (20 feet) long, probably represents a head tie and pendant ornaments. Kajitani proposes that it was worn with the cord wrapped many times around the head covering and the bell-shaped elements hanging down to the sides (1982:36). On the other hand, Harcourt, an early pioneer in the description of ancient Andean textile techniques, called a similar piece a neck covering (1962:81–82). Since no depictions of it are known, its exact use may remain a mystery. Similarly, the extreme abstraction of the motifs and the very close tones of gold and tan make subject identification speculative; however the antlerlike head projections may denote a deer. As in Paracas textiles (e.g., cat. no. 85, color pl. 6), three different abstract interpretations of the animal motif appear in various parts of the piece (pendant body, looped top, and cord).

　　Technically, this ensemble, and most of the related pieces mentioned above, are absolutely unsurpassed. To explain the technique fully is impossible here; however, it is important to point out that each of the bell-shaped pendants is a single, shaped textile that was worked from both wide ends (now at the bottom) toward the middle (the narrow neck now at the top) as in sprang (see Emery 1966:64–66). In oblique double-twining, "pairs of elements moving on an oblique course enclose elements moving on the opposite diagonal as they twine about each other" (ibid.:64, fig. 79). If this were not already complicated enough, two layers of cloth were twined at once, their threads changing layers to form the pattern, as in double cloth. One layer in each color can be distinguished along the bottom edges of the pendants.

　　Thus, three separate techniques are blended together (sprang, twining, and double cloth) in a completely unique, innovative, and extra-

ordinarily challenging way. Kajitani comments: "there is . . . no parallel [culture] in the world that achieved such complex patterning in sprang technique, here based on the concept of double cloth" (1982:36). An idiosyncratic fiber expression such as this shows the facility with which Andean weavers —never inhibited by difficulty of execution or complacent in the sufficiency of traditional methods— conceptually transformed various techniques into one.

Plate 17
Cloth with Stepped-Fret Band
Cat. no. 289

Early Intermediate Period, Nasca, South Coast
About A.D. 300–500 (?)
111 x 175 cm (approx.)
Plain weave; plain-weave discontinuous interlocked warp and weft (center strip); slit tapestry (border)

> plain weave and discontinuous warp and weft
>> warp: camelid fiber, /, 10/cm (approx.)
>> weft: camelid fiber, /, 10/cm (approx.)
> tapestry
>> warp: cotton, /\, [less than 1 cm wide]
>> weft: camelid fiber, /\, 56/cm

J. H. and E. A. Payne Fund
64.2044

Exhibitions: 2500 Years.
Related textiles: Similar technique: MFA 69.599 (cat. no. 290, color pl. 44), MFA 67.313 (cat. no. 295, color pl. 14a,b). Similar ground cloth: "Collection of Heinrich Hardt, Berlin" 1076 (Harcourt 1962:150; pl. 4).

Discussion: p. 45.

Three important, exquisite examples of the discontinuous warp and weft technique are held by the Museum (see also cat. no. 290, color pl. 44, and cat. no. 295, color pl. 14a,b). This one, however, is unique in its gossamer-thin threads and unusual tones of maroon, powder blue, and light purple. Single-ply threads give the piece its lightness, and the use of camelid fiber allowed the dyeing of such jewel-tone colors. Yet it was the choice of technique that allowed the elusive aesthetic goal of strong colors in a feathery cloth to be achieved. Andean fiber artists often went to great technical lengths to maximize color, whether in high-thread-count tapestry (such as cat. no. 322, color pl. 67a,b) or densely packed embroidery (such as cat. no. 85, color pl. 6).

The particular challenges posed by discontinuous warp and weft necessitate explanation, since the outward appearance of a simple plain weave is deceptive. As the name implies, neither warp nor weft elements span the entire piece but rather are made up of many differently colored threads interlocked to form a pattern (such as the stepped frets in the center panel). The pattern is set down first in the warp, then the matching wefts are woven in to intersect exactly each color area. In other words, same-color threads cross in both directions to form individual shapes. Obviously a great deal of preplanning is necessary. In addition, what really distinguishes this method and makes it so arduous is that the irregularly shaped sections of warp must be kept taut while they are being threaded to the next color area's warps. The warp is the load-bearing element, therefore it is usually made of the strongest fiber available (typically cotton), and threads are kept as continuous as possible. Since none of these conditions apply here, other measures are necessitated, specifically, the use of scaffold threads. Scaffolds, as in architectural construction, are affixed tightly across the loom (perpendicular to the warp) to hold the various colors of warp thread in place as they are being inter-

locked with one another. Only after the complete pattern is in place, with the many discontinuous warps now acting as continuous, can the scaffolds be removed. Every line along which the colors change (the vertical direction in this photograph) had a scaffold thread holding its place as the piece was being warped. To give an idea of how many scaffolds were utilized in the center band, the first "warp" changes color twenty-four times. In order to limit the number of scaffolds, such stepped designs are generated naturally (see also cat. no. 290, color pl. 44); however, curves are also found (see cat. no. 295, color pl. 14a,b). Labor economy was never uppermost in Andean textile artists' minds.

Discontinuous warp and weft can be seen as an intriguing extension of the Andean predilection for weaving finished shaped textiles as opposed to cutting and assembling cloth. Each color area is treated as its own finished textile, simultaneously being woven with and attached to tens or even hundreds of other tiny webs. It is understandable that this technique was invented only once in world history and by the relentlessly innovative Andean weaver. Beyond technical considerations, the haunting, spider-web beauty of this piece stands out, even among the many textile masterpieces represented in the Museum's collection. The survival of such a supremely delicate cloth is also rare and quite remarkable.

Plate 18
Bag with Abstract Interlocked Birds (?)
Cat. no. 274

Early Intermediate Period, Phase 9, Nasca, South Coast
About A.D. 500
27 x 22 cm
Plain-weave ground cloth with embroidery in running stitch; plaited
fringe; needle-knit edging
       plain weave
              warp: camelid fiber, ∧, 14/cm
              weft: camelid fiber, ∧, 14/cm
         embroidery, fringe, and edging: camelid fiber, ∧
Samuel Putnam Avery Fund
52.481

Related textiles: Museo Nacional 01662 (Kajitani 1982:46–47, pl. 55).

Discussion: p. 14.

In spite of its only fair state of preservation, this bag retains a design with
a great deal of visual impact and sophistication. To form the pattern the
dark brown plain-weave ground was left undecorated, or "reserved," between and within the square motifs. This creates a dark brown grid embroidered with highly abstracted interlocked designs. The motifs probably refer to birds (with diamond-shaped heads, dots for the eyes, fretlike
necks and bodies). The two parts of each square, one right side up and
the other upside down, compete for perceptual ownership of the inner-
most dark brown diagonal (see cat. no. 240, color pl. 53, on contour rivalry). The viewer flips between the two image orientations and notes an
overall checkerboard pattern of blue/gold and red/white color combinations. An additional visual undercurrent, the color olive green appears
only in the edging between the bag and the fringe. Thus, typically, apparent design simplicity gives way to aesthetic elaboration.

      The function of this bag, in all probability, was to carry and con-
tain coca leaves. When chewed with lime, these leaves helped the ancient highlanders to maintain stamina and suppress hunger on long
mountain treks (see also cat. no. 265, color pl. 66). Obviously, the bag
has lost its strap, which might have been plaited like the fringe tops. The
use of textiles for practical purposes did not contradict the artistic approach with which they were designed and produced; the function of
works of art is individually determined by each culture.

Plate 19
Tapestry Band Fragment with Abstracted Animals
Cat. no. 79

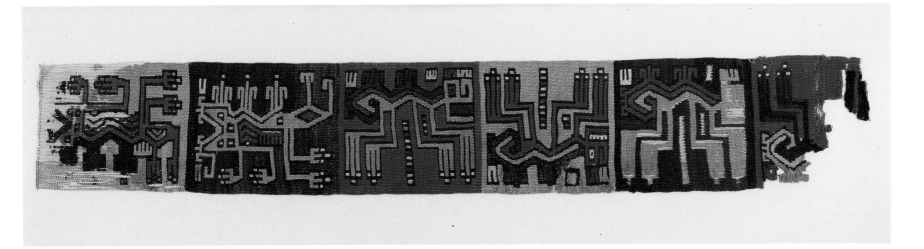

Middle Horizon, Nasca-Wari Transition, South Coast
About A.D. 500–600
13.7 x 95.3 cm
Slit tapestry
       warp: cotton, /\/, 6.3/cm
       weft: camelid fiber, /\, 39/cm
Denman Waldo Ross Collection
16.42

Exhibitions: 25 Centuries; 2500 Years.
Publications: MFA 1961: no. 275.
Related textiles: Metropolitan 59.135.3 (Kajitani 1982:37, 50–51, pl. 64); Museo Na-
cional 01425 (Kajitani 1982:36–37, 50, pl. 62, top right); Museo Nacional (Lavalle and
Lang 1980:92).

Discussion: p. 23

Weft losses, though unquestionably tragic, allow certain structural information to become visible. Toward the left edge one can see clearly the
heading cords, that is, threads woven in at the very beginning of the
weaving process to secure the warp threads and anchor the weaving to
the loom. Some of the warps threads are noticeably bichrome: a light
brown thread has been plied (twisted) with a natural white thread. This is
a characteristic of many tapestries of the Middle Horizon (which makes
it very easy to note the direction of the plying as Z [/] or counter-clock-
wise). Other multicolor threads can be seen in the two left-most squares:
brown and white fibers were spun together to create a mottled tan. This
method of generating a new color with existing colors of thread is seen
occasionally in ancient Andean textiles (cat. no. 62, color pl. 37) and
more frequently in Colonial examples (e.g., cat. no. 293, color pl. 73). It
can be understood as part of a culture-wide dedication to the maximiza-
tion of color possibilities.

Another formal opportunity that has been embraced in a typically intense fashion is the striking abstraction of the two animals depicted.
One of the animals, found in the two left-hand squares, appears reptilian
while the other, found in the four right-hand squares, appears feline.
Identification is based primarily on the direction of the legs, which are
more horizontal in the former and more vertical in the latter. However,
the degree of shape abstraction makes it difficult even to distinguish
which end is the reptile's head. The feline lacks the usual fangs, which
tend to be diagnostic, but retains a curled nose that is found in many later feline images. Rather than emphasizing clearly identifiable subjects,
the artists were obviously interested in the elaboration of pattern for its
own sake. The inversion of every other figure adds to the magnificent visual variety created by the fiber artist using only two repeated images.

Plate 20
Bag with Human and Vegetal Motif
Cat. no. 174

Early Middle Horizon, Nasca, South Coast
About A.D. 500–600
36.8 x 18.4 cm
Slit tapestry; fringe
     tapestry
            warp: cotton, multiple Λ, 3 groups/cm
            weft: camelid fiber, Λ, 38/cm
     fringe: camelid fiber, /\/
Gift of Edward Jackson Holmes
30.253

Related textiles: Matching, except in background color: Museo Nacional (Lavalle and Lang 1980:87, lower fig.).

Discussion: p. 14, 23.

In startlingly vivid shades of yellow, red, and blue, this front face of a fringed bag sums up the Museum's representation of Nasca textiles. Nasca style spans from the beginning of the Early Intermediate Period to that of the Middle Horizon; it overlapped both earlier Paracas style, from which it continuously drew inspiration (see cat. no. 295, color pl. 14a,b), and that of the later Wari, which it influenced while being conquered politically (see cat. no. 319, color pl. 21a,b). Paracas holdovers remain visible even in this late Nasca work: the corner motifs refer to the mouth masks seen on Paracas cult figures (e.g., cat. no. 70, color pl. 13). However, Nasca retained its own recognizable set of features, many of which are represented here and serve to interrelate all the Nasca textiles in the Museum's collection. These include the bag as a dominant object, particularly the type with long fringes (see cat. no. 274, color pl. 18); the color scheme, dark outlining, and high level of abstraction (see cat. no. 79, color pl. 19); and the profusion of plant forms (see cat. no. 190, color pl. 15). The motif here can be seen as an inverted human figure (predominantly in blue), with its head in the lower center, hands to either side, and feet at the very top. Sprouting from the body are plant forms; in Nasca ceramics and painted textiles agricultural abundance and vegetal motifs are common (see Sawyer 1979).

    The extremely bold design, another hallmark of the style, is accentuated by an equally bold technical choice: the use of multiple warps together in bundles creates visibly pronounced vertical ridges, causing the wefts to resemble a sort of long running stitch (as in cat. no. 274, color pl. 18). Various techniques are employed to create the same effect throughout Nasca textiles, and very large-scale, extraordinarily graphic designs are consistently found (e.g., see Harcourt 1962: pl. 4). Although this is quite a small bag, its composition is characteristically monumental. It is no wonder that the Wari found in the Nasca style aesthetic visual power and sophistication suitable to adopt as their own (such as in cat. no. 213, color pl. 25). As in other cultures, Andean textile artists no doubt were influenced by one another in complex ways difficult to reconstruct archaeologically.

Plate 21a,b
Sleeveless Tunic (?) with Tie-dyed Stepped Triangles
Cat. no. 319

Plate 22a,b (overleaf)

Tapestry Tunic with Stepped-Diamond and Double-Headed Animal Motifs

Cat. no. 313

Middle Horizon, Wari-related, Nasca Area, South Coast
A.D. 500–800
114 x 187 cm
Tie-dyed plain-weave discontinuous warp and weft pieces reassembled with warps dovetailed and weft slits sewn
warp: camelid fiber, ∧, 18/cm
weft: camelid fiber, ∧, 8/cm
Textile Fund and Helen and Alice Colburn Fund
1983.252

Related textiles: MFA 24.323 (cat. no. 147); MFA 44.176 (cat. no. 235); MFA 52.479 (cat. no. 272); Amano (Tsunoyama 1977:23, color pl. 8); Museo Nacional 53406 (Kajitani 1982: pl. 89); Museum für Völkerkunde-Munich X.176 (Lommel 1977:157; 218–219, cat. no. 723, pl. 94); Textile Museum (Reeves 1949:104).

Discussion: pp. 17, 20, 21, 23, 35, 37.

The exuberantly colorful geometry, several subtly different readings of which have been masterfully balanced by the textile artist, make this piece extremely interesting on an aesthetic level. Each stepped-triangle color area has been tie-dyed with an asymmetrical arrangement of vertical lines and diagonal series of circles. Where four triangles intersect, the vertical lines form squares and the diagonals shadowy diamonds. Simultaneously, since each of the four triangular pieces are dyed differently, overall diagonal lines of same-color triangles also vie for attention. Yet, if we trace a single one of these color diagonals, such as the yellow-background shapes, the characteristic Wari emphasis on variation is immediately apparent: all the stepped outlines face to the right in one and should all face left in the next, but several break the pattern. Thus, the virtuoso textile artist has melded into a single composition a number of simultaneous readings, some regular and others not, some determined by shape (the diamonds) and others by color (the overall diagonals).

Understanding how the composition was physically woven, decorated, and assembled only increases our appreciation of the technical ingenuity of the Andean weaver. Each stepped-triangle shape of cloth was woven as a separate natural-colored textile, with its threads in both directions turning back rather than interlocking with any those of the adjacent triangle. Scaffold threads temporarily held together a series of these shaped pieces, a strip of which was all tie-dyed in the same colors. When the scaffolds were pulled out, the variously colored individual parts were reassembled with warps dovetailed and weft slits sewn. Thus, the commonly used term "patchwork" does not do justice to the intricacy of the creative process. To my knowledge, the process used here is unique in world fiber history (like the closely related discontinuous warp and weft seen in cat nos. 289, 290, and 295 [color pls. 17, 44, 14a,b]. A technical discovery of this kind underscores how important it was to the ancient Andeans not to cut fabric, how much labor was expended to obtain a particular visual effect, and how central innovation was to the aesthetic system.

Middle Horizon, Wari, probably South Coast
A.D. 500–800
100 x 103.5 cm
Interlocked tapestry with eccentric wefts
warp: cotton, ∧, 11.8/cm
weft: camelid fiber, ∧, 44.1/cm
Charles Potter Kling Fund
1978.124

Exhibitions: Textile Masterpieces.
Related textiles: MFA 1978.46 (cat. no. 313, color pl. 23a,b; American Museum of Natural History 41.0/1086, 1118, 1142, 1144, 1161, and unnumbered (Stone 1987: vol. 3:124–125, cat. no. 156a–f; vol. 4: color pl. 106).

Discussion: pp. 13, 20, 23, 35, 36, 38–40.

This and the other magnificent Wari tunic, cat. no. 312 (color pl. 23a,b), provide an opportunity to examine the contributions of the weavers to design. Deviant color choices in Wari tunics seem to show where the artists put their own personal interpretations into the composition (Stone 1986, 1987). Although this piece is more formally regular than the other Museum tunic, there are numerous intentional irregularities, such as striping of different colors in a single shape (color pl. 22b). These details add dynamism to the repetitive alternation of motifs that apparently was prescribed for such an official uniform.

The weaving process, literally involving as many as a million individual color changes per tunic (Stone 1987, vol. 1:76–77), certainly necessitated unique skills and must have been extremely time-consuming on its own. However, besides conveying important messages about the Middle Horizon weavers, these textiles illuminate the virtuosity of Wari spinners, dyers, and embroiderers. Many people were involved both before the weaving began (the camelid herders, spinners, and dyers) and after the weaving was finished (the assemblers or embroiderers). Herders bred, raised, tended, and sheared thousands of camelids (the New World camels: the llama, alpaca, guanaco, and vicuña) to produce the fiber for the wefts. Spinners then produced between six and nine miles of gossamer-thin thread to be woven in each one. Next came the dyeing of the camelid fiber thread in almost every color seen (even naturally occuring browns were dyed to enrich their saturation). A great deal of esoteric knowledge was necessary to prepare and dye the thread evenly and brightly; certain colors, especially greens and blues from the indigo plant, were very difficult to obtain (see cat. no. 214, color pl. 29). After weaving was complete, the two pieces were joined, and approximately 3.5 meters (nearly 12 feet) of embroidery were added over the seams. These stitches blend in with the surrounding colors and make the tunic look continuous rather than assembled. The overriding concern for completeness, physical and conceptual, is typical of Andean textile artistry. When the tunic was finally finished, the wearer displayed the "seamless" accomplishment of the many people who contributed their time and skill to the complex creative process.

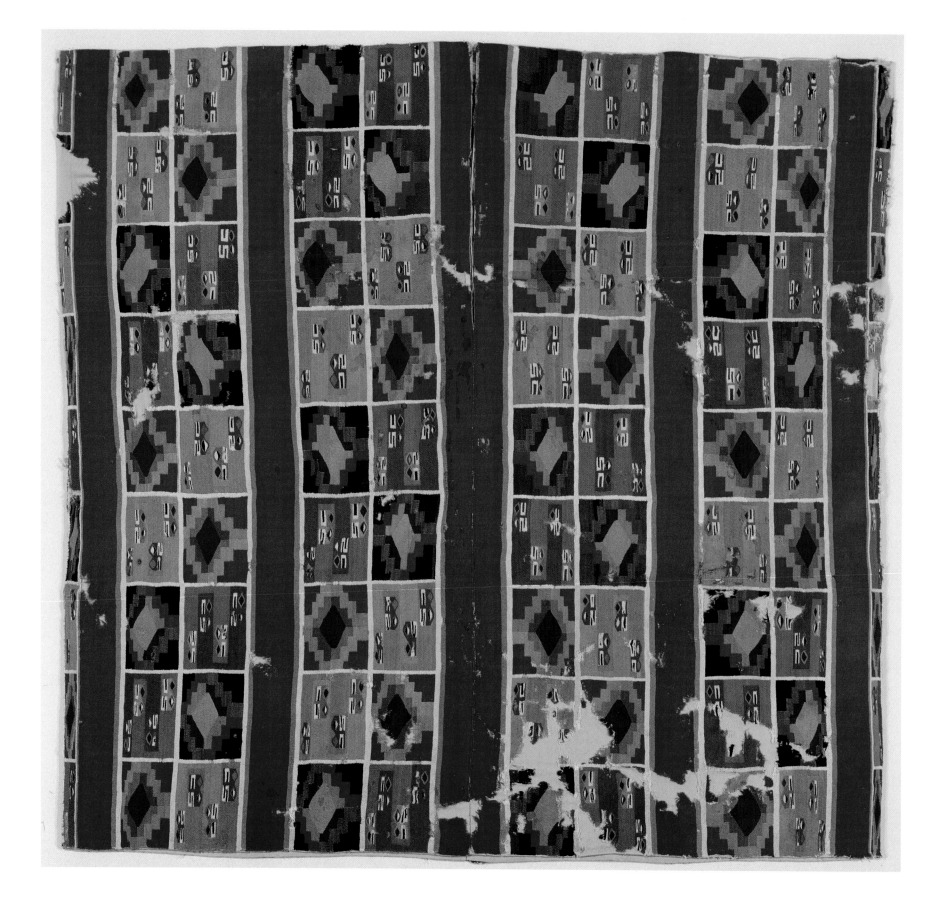

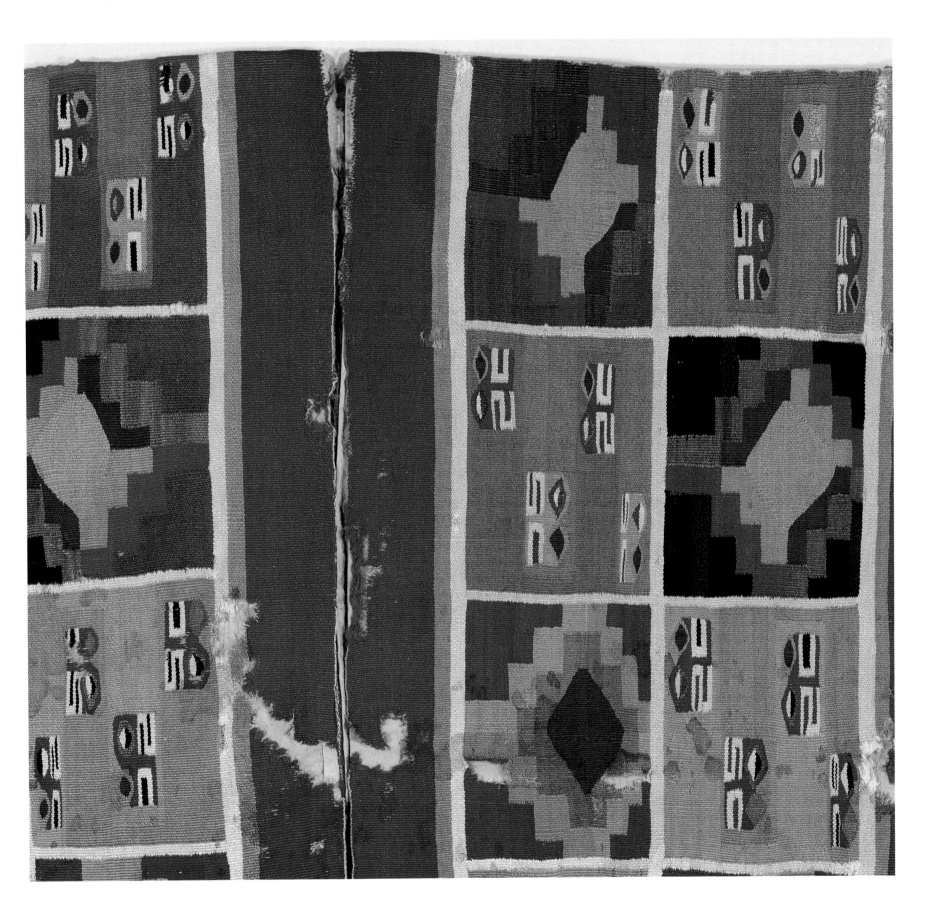

Plate 23a,b

Tapestry Tunic with Face, Stepped Fret, and Double-Headed Animals

Cat. no. 312

Middle Horizon, Wari, probably South Coast
A.D. 500–800
101 x 103.8 cm
Interlocked tapestry
        warp: cotton, $\wedge$, 10.2/cm
        weft: camelid fiber, $\wedge$, 37.8/cm
Charles Potter Kling Fund
1978.46

Exhibitions: 2500 Years.
Publications: Stone 1987, vol. 2: figs. 3-56, 3-71, 3-99, 3-132; vol. 3:97–98, cat. no. 121; vol. 4: color pl. 84.
Related textiles: MFA 1978.124 (cat. no. 313, color pl. 22a,b); Cleveland Museum 56.84 (Stone 1987, vol. 3:99, cat. no. 123; vol. 4: color pl. 85); Dumbarton Oaks B. 500 (Lothrop et al. 1957: cat. no. 351, pl. CXLVII); Lowie Museum 7771 (Stone 1987: vol. 2, figs. 3-55, 3-65a–c, 3-85, 3-110, 3-141; vol. 3:97, cat. no. 120; vol. 4: color pl. 84).

Discussion: pp. 23, 35, 38–40, 49; fig. III.11a,b.

Wari tunics were woven collaboratively by groups of highly skilled artists, each of whom contributed an individual interpretation of set repeated motifs. Upon close observation, it is possible to differentiate three distinct motifs in the grid-based composition of this well-preserved tunic. One square contains a stepped fret (a curlicue with a stepped outline) and a profile face (a triangle dominated by a vertically bisected eye below a wide headband). Another square consists of two interlocked U-shaped animals, with heads at each end (again dominated by a subdivided eye and usually containing two small mouths each). The degree of abstraction is particularly high in this example (making its motifs admittedly hard to read), which is a characteristic of the Wari style in general and of tunic designs in particular. Abstraction follows the forms out to their most essential shapes without regard for the easy legibility of subject matter.

      Close comparison of the various repetitions of a particular motif, such as the double-headed animal, reveals many variations on a theme. Some double-animal motifs include heads with only eyes, others have some heads with squares for mouths and some heads without mouths, still others have heads with various numbers and positions of U-shaped mouths. Altogether, there are sixteen different types of this motif, as well as four types of profile faces and two types of stepped frets in this dramatic composition. A striking formal anomaly, in the form of a single dark indigo blue animal head, can be seen in color pl. 23b (see also fig. III.11b). Although such variation in design details may appear of little consequence, it shows that a rather surprising amount of leeway was given to the weavers as they carried out a set design. Repetitive motif alternation itself does not signal the rote reproduction of design elements that tends to be characteristic of craft. Instead, underlying visual variety consciously adds artistic dynamism to an otherwise regular composition. It can be argued that the interspersing of various motif types throughout the composition reveals the creative contribution of individual collaborating weavers themselves.

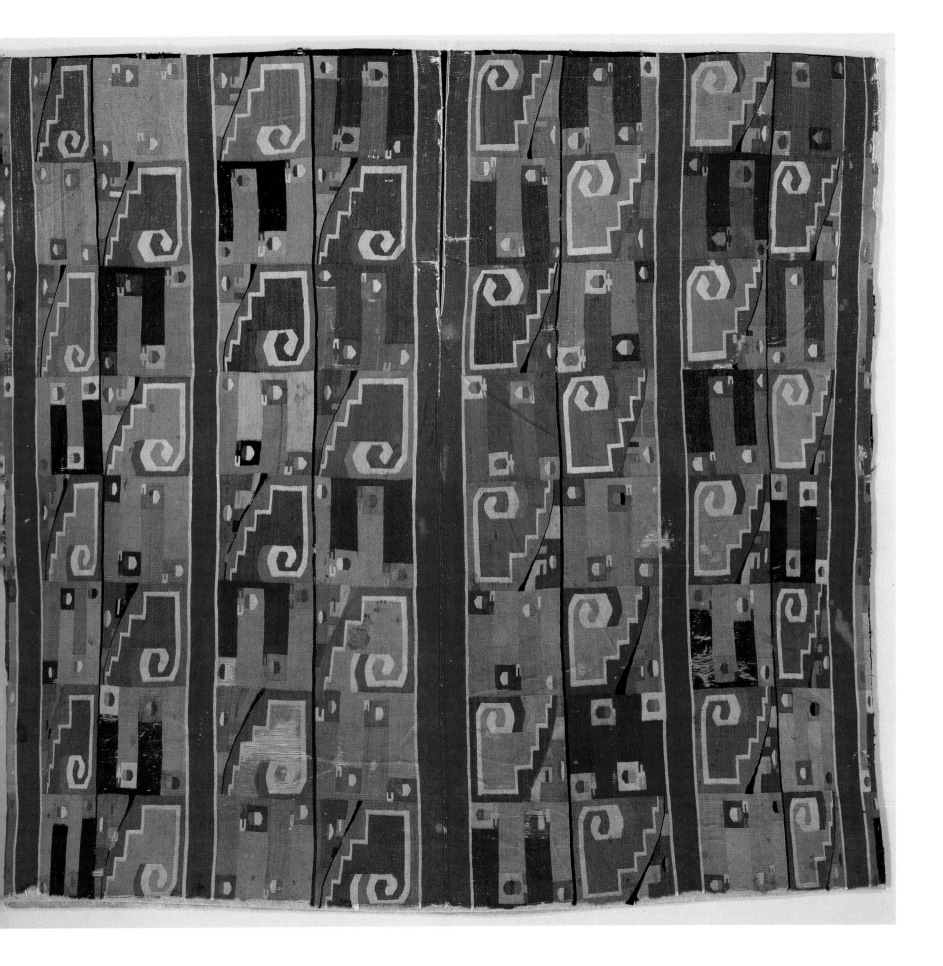

Plate 24 (overleaf)
Tunic Fragments with Human Skulls
Cat. no. 316 A,B

Middle Horizon, Wari, probably South Coast
A.D. 500–800
1980.448 (above): 84 x 106 cm
1980.660 (below): 89 x 107 cm
Interlocked tapestry
      warp: cotton, ∧, 14/cm
      weft: camelid fiber, ∧, 49/cm
A. 1980.448: Charles Potter Kling Fund
B. 1980.660: Gift of Vivian Merrin

Related textiles: Private collection (Taullard 1949: pl. 39); Paul 1985b:34, top;
0Reid 1985:71.

Discussion: pp. 20, 23, 35.

The reunited halves of this magnificent tunic have been mounted so as to
approximate their original arrangement, leaving space for the lost center
area around the neck slit (apparently deteriorated from organic staining
by the mummy). The tunic is now opened out; that is, its side seams were
cut before the Museum's acquisition of its halves. According to similar
tunics (see related textiles above), the center would have had the subtle,
gold-on-gold, long zigzag ("tuning fork") of the background pattern. The
groups of eight oversized motifs are oriented so as to appear upright
when the tunic was being worn. These abstracted skulls feature enlarged
concentric circles as gaping eye sockets and enigmatic appendages below, which could symbolize tassels, hair, or streams of blood. The representation of trophy heads is found elsewhere in Wari art (see cat. nos.
200A and 200C, color pl. 26, lower right and upper left), but the bare
skull is rarely shown. The intimidating effect of an official wearing sixteen giant skulls must have been calculated by the bellicose Wari state.

      A sophisticated play between representationalism and abstrac-
tion characterizes the design. The whiteness of bone and the bulging
quality of the skull is realistically retained, yet the overall shape and dark
outlining exaggerates a stylized hourglass symmetry. The scalloped
edges of the teeth succinctly typify molars but, at the same time, set up a
pattern with a pronounced figure-ground reversal: the dark spaces between top and bottom rows of teeth create a line of dark circles that read
as "figure" in competition with the teeth themselves. Another accurately
stylized feature is the indention at the back of the human mandible (jaw-
bone) captured with a bent line. Besides overall abstraction, creative interpretation is seen in the purposeful inclusion of four bright red anomalies in an otherwise gold, white, brown, and pink design. In the upper
piece, red anomalies consist of the center of the bead in front of the teeth
in the top-left corner skull and the center of the circle at the bottom of the
outermost "tassel" in the top-right corner skull. In the lower piece, they
are the central molar in the top-right corner skull and the circle and areas in front of the mouth of the second skull from the lower right corner.
Formal deviations and anomalies are characteristic of all Wari tunics (see

cat. nos. 312 and 313, color pls. 23a,b and 22a,b; see also Stone 1987, vol.
1:148–178). These dynamic aesthetic choices underscore how abstraction
as a process extracts the essential from the observed and places the inter-
ests of pattern —and its interruption— above superficial verisimilitude.
The prodigious artistic mentality responsible for such a probing style
makes its presence felt, although we will never know a single weaver's
name.

Plate 25
Tunic Fragment with Face Motifs
Cat. no. 213

Middle Horizon, Wari, probably South Coast
A.D. 500–800
45 x 20.8 cm
Interlocked tapestry; darning
       warp: cotton, ∧, 11/cm
       weft: camelid fiber, ∧, 44/cm
Gift of Mrs. John C. Spring in Memory of Mrs. A. Craige Spring
36.582

Exhibitions: 2500 Years.
Publications: Stone 1987, vol. 3:93–94, cat. no. 115; vol. 4: color pl. 81.
Related textiles: Museo Nacional 01166 (Lumbreras [1979?]:33; Stone 1987, vol. 2:
figs. 3-23, 3-105; vol. 3:90–91, cat. no. 112; vol. 4, color pl. 78); original made up of
fragments from Museo Nacional 32-436 and 02359 and Rietberg RPB 1302 (Anton
1984:128, no. 98; 223 [Rietberg]; Stone 1987, vol. 3:92–93, cat. no. 114a–c; vol. 4, color
pls. 80–81); original made up of fragments from Museum of Mankind
1954.W.Am.5.533, Metropolitan 32.32.1 and 33.149.57, and Dumbarton Oaks B.517
(Stone 1987, vol. 3:91–92, cat. no. 113a–d; vol. 4, color pls. 78–80).

Discussion: pp. 22, 35, 38, 39, 41; fig. III.12a,b.

This boldly graphic tapestry fragment comes from along the side seam of
a Wari tunic, one half from the front of the tunic and the other from the
back (see cat. no. 313, color pl. 22a,b and cat. no. 312, color pl. 23a,b).
Two of the characteristically narrow side columns meet, and figure-8-
stitch embroidery covers the seam. A great deal of care was taken to
mask this join, by varying the color of the embroidery thread according to
the motifs over which it passed (see also cat. no. 290, color pl. 44).

The fragment contains slightly more than two repetitions of the
face motif (counting a repetition as two complete frontal faces, one right
side up and the other upside down). Each frontal face is itself made up of
two mirror-image half-faces in different color combinations. A gold and
red motif repetition at the top is followed by a blue-green and red one,
with the top part of another gold and red one repeated at the lower edge.
From this evidence, and that of more complete tunics with this type of
motif, it is safe to assume that the original alternated these two color
combinations (see related textiles above). However, the design is not as
simple as this; the use of contrasting colors perceptually splits the two
halves of each face, which draws attention away from its coherent meaning as a face. This is part of a pervasive Wari design system in which
artistic elaboration of pattern overwhelms and subverts subject matter
(Stone 1987, vol. 1:187–188). Abstraction, another key Wari aesthetic
choice, is here taken to an extreme: below the face a "body" may be indicated by the series of triangular serrations. Since this is a side column,
the motif is even more truncated than it would have appeared in the
wider central columns of the original tunic. The great reduction in shape
is balanced by the elaborated perceptual ambiguities in coloration, creating a strong, dynamic visual statement.

The patterning of color, even in so small a fragment, shows a diagnostic Wari characteristic that brings us closer to the artists responsible for these spectacular tapestries. Two color deviations can be seen.

The first is an orange area next to the face in the top right upside-down gold face. Again using other more complete compositions as evidence, this tends to be a "wild card" area in the face motif, that is, where a variant color is most often assigned. A second deviation is more unusual, and remains slightly problematic, but is still in keeping with the Wari aesthetic system. It appears in the form of darning in the motif quarter directly below that containing the orange deviation. (It is extremely typical for formal deviations to cluster together in this way.) The lower point of the body has been rewoven partly with red and partly with blue-green ancient thread. Although it is difficult to prove conclusively that this took place in the Middle Horizon, modern reconstruction tends to try to match adjacent colors (no repairs were made to the other small areas of weft loss seen in the fragment). Wari or Wari-influenced peoples would tend to choose a visually salient deviation such as this in the form of red and blue-green (Stone 1987, vol. 1:149–178). The inclusion of two such deviations in a small fragment shows how central variation was to the creative Wari textile designers.

Middle Horizon, Wari, probably South Coast
A.D. 500–800
A. 31.701 (lower right): 11.1 x 11.2 cm
B. 31.702 (lower left): 10.9 x 12.1 cm
C. 31.703 (upper left): 10.8 x 10.8 cm
D. 31.704 (upper right): 11 x 12.9 cm
Interlocked tapestry with eccentric wefts
      warp: cotton, $\wedge$, 14/cm
      weft: camelid fiber, $\wedge$, 52/cm
Harriet Otis Cruft Fund
31.701–704

Related textiles: Brooklyn Museum 34.559.1, 34.559.2 (2 faces); Detroit 36.24, 36.25 (1 face, 1 diamond; Weibel 1936:13); Metropolitan 33.149.85a,b (1 face, 1 diamond); Museum für Völkerkunde-Berlin AAM 5882 T21, T22 (2 faces); Museum für Völkerkunde-Munich 78-300477 (1 face); Museum of Mankind (2 faces); Rhode Island School of Design 50.383, 50.384 (1 face, 1 diamond); Rietberg RPB 1303a–d (4 faces; Haberland 1971:331, top [2 of the 4]); Textile Museum 91.119 (2 faces, 2 diamonds; Lapiner 1976:238, no. 547); Victoria and Albert T75.1933 (1 face). See also Peabody-Harvard 42-12-30/3378.

Discussion: pp. 22, 35.

Numerous examples of these frontal faces and diamond squares exist in various collections, all apparently cut from larger compositions by unscrupulous dealers. Their uniform technical characteristics, iconography, and measurements suggest they came from a limited number of original pieces. A more complete piece (see related textiles, above), now in the collection of the Peabody Museum of Archaeology and Ethnology at Harvard University, suggests a possible reconstruction; it shows stripes and rows of sideways S-shapes flanking a row of alternated diamonds and faces. However, differences in the scale and exact appearance of the motifs between the Harvard piece and the other fragments, as well as the fact that some of the fragments retain side selvages (as here), makes it difficult to be certain that all face and diamond panels belonged to such a continuous piece. Perhaps there were large textiles as well as bands containing this same imagery.

In all cases the diamond-pattern backgrounds match those of the faces, reinforcing their roles as parts of a larger composition. Most of the known faces are predominantly gold or blue, as here, but some are green or pink. As in other Wari tapestries, particularly the tunics (cat. no. 313, color pl. 22a,b; cat. no. 312, color pl. 23a,b), minor formal variations are characteristic. In these two faces, for example, minor differences occur in the dark brown outlining around the outermost eye. In other fragments (see related textiles, above), more striking deviations have been included, such as a gold face heavily striped with green (Rietberg RPB 1303b [Haberland 1971:331, top left]). These design details help reveal the hand of individual weavers.

Whom these heads represent remains conjectural; however, they may symbolize the trophy heads of high-status enemies of the Wari state. Large, round earspools usually connote elite status, and the use of con-

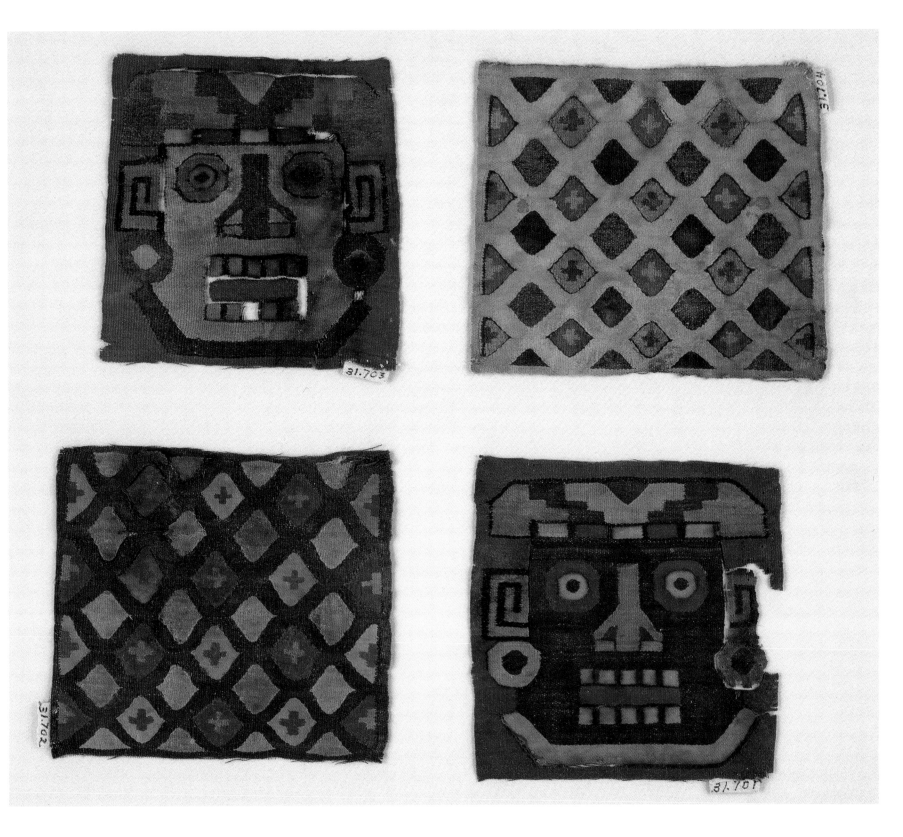

centric rather than vertically bisected eyes may represent the death state (see the skulls in cat. no. 316, color pl. 24, and the profile faces in cat. no. 312, color pl. 23a,b). Since the Wari conquest state spread over the coastal regions, these trophy heads could possibly symbolize conquered local leaders. The fact that high-thread-count tapestry, with its concommitant lavish effort and skill, was chosen for their images would have further reinforced the prestige of the conquered and therefore of the conqueror.

Middle Horizon, Wari, probably South Coast
A.D. 500–800
11.4 cm (height) x 47.5 cm (circumference)
Larkshead knotted ground with supplementary cut pile
        ground: camelid fiber, ∧; cotton (green top area), ∧
        supplementary pile: camelid fiber, ∧
Mrs. Cabot's Special Fund
47.1096

Exhibitions: 25 Centuries; 2500 Years.
Publications: Cavallo 1960:3–4, fig. 1; MFA 1961: no. 285; Lapiner 1976: fig. 574.
Related textiles: MFA 09.128 (cat. no. 55); MFA 47.1088 (cat. no. 241, color pl. 28); MFA 47.1089 (cat. no. 242); Museo Nacional (Lavalle and Lang 1980:100); Museum of the American Indian 23/7082 (Dockstader 1967: fig. 141); Bullowa Collection in general (Frame 1990: back cover, pls. 1, 3, 4, 7, 8).

Discussion: pp. 35–37; fig. III.8.

A recent exhibition of Wari four-cornered hats at the Metropolitan Museum of Art finally brought these splendid works to public attention (Frame 1990). Colorfully dyed cut-pile checkerboard patterns of animals, faces, and geometric motifs fill these rather small adult hats. According to ceramic effigy vessels depicting the tapestry-tunic wearers, the hats were worn rather high on the head (fig. III.8). The evident wear on this piece, the loss of some of the pile especially along the creased edges, is typical of most examples. Pile headbands are also known (see cat. no. 241, color pl. 28; cat. no. 242), indicating a range of headgear types. Through the textiles in his elaborate ritual ensemble, the wearer was transformed into a dynamic geometric pattern.

Here the design features a composite animal, predominantly avian (beak and three-toed feet) but also camelid (long tail, neck, and hunched back). Various similar, yet not identical, creatures are found on other pile hats (see related textiles, above). Composite figures are characteristic of all pre-Columbian art, part of the creative possibilities within a symbolic rather than a perceptual art system. The four corner peaks may have represented animal ears originally (Frame 1990:6); in a sense, this would have made a human-animal composite of the wearer.

The pile hat also represents one of the many unusual techniques invented by the ancient Andean fiber artists. The ground or base for the decoration is made from a continuous yarn that has been square-knotted probably with the aid of a needle (the variation is known as a larkshead knot; see Emery 1966:36–37). The colored threads —whose loops are later cut to form the pile— are introduced simultaneously with the knotting, rather than sewn in after the ground has been completed. Although the pile threads remain supplemental (i.e., they could be removed and the hat would remain intact), the process of working them along with the ground knotting is typically Andean in its emphasis on structural integrity and in its balancing of two different motions at once.

Plate 28
Pile Headband with Diamond Motifs
Cat. no. 241

Plate 29 (overleaf)
Tapestry Fragment with Jaguar
Cat. no. 214

Middle Horizon, Wari-related, probably South or Central Coast
A.D. 500–800
11.6 cm (height) x 60.3 cm (circumference)
Larkshead knotted ground with supplementary cut pile
　　　ground: cotton, multiple \ threads plied /
　　　supplementary pile: camelid fiber, ∧
Mrs. Cabot's Special Fund
47.1088

Exhibitions: 25 Centuries; 2500 Years.
Publications: MFA 1961: no. 278.
Related textiles: MFA 09.128 (cat. no. 55); MFA 47.1096 (cat. no. 249, color pl. 27); MFA 47.1089 (cat no. 242); Museum für Völkerkunde-Berlin VA 65459 (Eisleb 1980:140, pl. 345); Museum für Völkerkunde-Berlin VA 65458a,b (Eisleb 1980:140–141, pl. 346), VA 7468 (Eisleb 1980:141, pl. 347); Museum für Völkerkunde-Berlin VA 20922 (Eisleb 1980:141, pl. 348).

Discussion: pp. 35–37.

This strikingly well preserved pile headband was created in the same technique as the pile hat: knotting with supplemental threads looped and cut to form pile (cat. no. 249, color pl. 27). However, like headbands in other techniques (cat. no. 278, color pl. 31), it was made first vertically as a band then sewn together to form a ring (according to the sideways direction of the cut pile). A longer row of cut loops hides the back seam. The headband features one of the many variations of the diamond motif, a favorite during this period (see cat. no. 313, color pl. 22a,b) and later (cat. no. 234, color pl. 64).

　　　Because of its three-dimensionality and the way it has been mounted, the inside face of the headband can be glimpsed in this photograph. It is possible to see just how evenly the ground was knotted, completely by hand, and to recognize once again how important finish was in Andean textile traditions. In almost every textile discussed in this catalogue, particularly Wari and related pieces, no dangling thread ends can be seen on the back; in fact, rarely can the front and back faces of a tapestry from this period be distinguished. Not only a dedication to perfect technical execution and the virtuosity it entails, this represents also a conceptual emphasis on what has been called "essence": all faces are complete whether or not they would ever have been seen (see cat. no. 288, color pl. 62; see also p. 22). Thus, although the front face shows the beautifully dyed and patterned cut pile, the reverse is equally essential to the object and therefore received equal care.

Middle Horizon, Wari-related, Atarco Style
About A.D. 700
21.2 x 35.4 cm
Interlocked tapestry
　　　warp: camelid fiber, ∧, 18.1/cm
　　　weft: camelid fiber, ∧, 48.8/cm
Otis Norcross Fund
36.625

Exhibition: 2500 Years.

Discussion: pp. 35, 40.

The extensive use of the dye indigo for the feline's body points up the great importance of dyeing processes and of blue in particular as a symbol of prestige in the Andean fiber arts and society. Although the ancient and Colonial weavers are renowned for their prodigious talent, the dyers were no less skilled in obscure, time-consuming, and difficult techniques. Dyeing with indigo, as with other dyes, requires a deep understanding of the environment, plants, fibers, and chemistry (in the sense of reactions of materials on one another). However, unlike most other dyes, indigo is remarkably elusive, unpredictable, and indirect; therefore the control over it would represent not only a technical feat but also an almost magical power of transformation on the part of the dye specialist. In the case of this textile, the lavish amount of blue serves to elevate the jaguar, whose rulership of the animal world is proclaimed in many ways throughout Andean art (see Lapiner 1976). Typically, color is being used symbolically (blue equals importance) rather than descriptively (the feline itself is not blue).

　　　A brief review of the process of indigo dyeing will help reveal why blue consistently played a special, prestigious role. Polakoff explains that indigo exists in two states: as a "white," that is, clear or slightly yellowish glycoside (an organic compound found especially in plants that when hydrated produces sugars and related substances); and as an oxidized blue pigment (activated in air) (1980:29–31). The problem of dyeing fiber with indigo lies in the fact that the colorless form is water soluble and can therefore be absorbed by fibers, while the blue form is insoluble and nonabsorbent. The solution is found in a complex alternation of the two forms, beginning with the steeping of the indigofera plant for twelve to eighteen hours to extrude the white glycoside. Then oxygen is introduced to turn the white form into the blue, typically by violently agitating the solution. Because it is now insoluble, blue indigo falls as a sediment to the bottom of the solution and can be drained off. It is usually dried in balls to be stored, traded, or transported. However, to dye fiber indigo blue, the dried material must be returned to its white state by being deoxidized and dissolved; most cultures use a bath of ammonia produced by fermented human urine. Fibers immersed in the bath will not display the blue color until oxygen is added. As if by magic, the blue color "develops" before the dyer's eyes as the fiber is drawn out into the air

and dried. Obviously, it is of the utmost difficulty to end up with a strong, evenly colored blue thread when the process is conducted completely "blind." The textile artists' developed powers of visualization apply to dyers as well as to weavers.

The implications of such a convoluted process are far-reaching. At the outset, one wonders how such an "invisible" dye could have been discovered independently by so many cultures around the world, from West Africa to Indonesia to the Americas. Given that the esoteric knowledge and techniques *were* developed and passed down, the amount of time and high failure rate involved make the successful accomplishment of blue gain even more in power and status. And, most important, the se-

ries of transformations from colorless to colorful states would have associated the color blue with magical transformation, that is, the supernatural. As a result, whoever wore blue or whatever image was assigned blue shared in that special, powerful, possibly sacred status. The enhanced standing of the dye process also helps account for the widespread use of blue and blue-green, one of the variations of indigo, as color anomalies (e.g., see cat. no. 312, color pl. 23b; see also Stone 1986; 1987, vol. 1:64–66, 170, 173–174). The culture-wide involvement in fiber allows a dye process to communicate and enhance special status, emphasizing that noniconographic levels of meaning based on the properties of textiles played an important part in Andean aesthetic messages.

Plate 30
Tapestry Border Fragments with Staff Bearers
Cat. no. 125

Middle Horizon, Wari-related, probably Central-North Coast
A.D. 500–800
24.300a (right): 19.4 x 18.4 cm
24.300b (left): 18.7 x 18.1 cm
Interlocked tapestry with eccentric wefts
      warp: cotton, three ∧, 10 groups of 3/cm
      weft: camelid fiber, ∧, 44/cm
Helen and Alice Colburn Fund
24.300a,b

Publications: Means 1932:43, specimen 1, fig. 16.
Related textiles: Private collections (Anton 1984:135, figs. 111, 112).

Discussion: pp. 34, 35, 41; fig. III.1a.

These two small fragments demonstrate the creative interpretation of a set Wari design by local, probably North Coast, peoples after the "classic" style had spread through much of the Central Andes. The staff-bearing figure, hallmark of the Wari and Tiwanaku states of the Middle Horizon period, is commonly seen in two forms: the winged profile attendant figure and the frontal deity (sometimes characterized as an early representation of Viracocha, the Inca creator god; Demarest 1981). Both are found on stone sculpture at the site of Tiwanaku in Bolivia (fig. III.7).

    Various changes in iconography, design, and technique have been made as the staff bearer is represented in a peripheral context. Here a simpler version, usually shown in profile, is oriented frontally as figures tend to be in North Coast styles. The bent knees of the Sun Gate attendant type are indicated by splaying the legs outward in a typical North Coast pose (see cat. no. 317, color pl. 60a,b). What would be the lower half of the staff is replaced by a jagged filler element, and the eye is concentric rather than split (compare with that of the profile face in cat. no. 312, color pl. 23a,b). The birds in the border are wholly local, and their arrangement around the rectangular background for the figure is not seen in classic Wari compositions. The style here is generally more curvilinear, owing to the use of eccentric wefts. The dark outlining of the figure and high color contrast with the ground make the figure uncharacteristically readable. Technically, the use of tripled warps and the presence of finished edges on the sides, probably indicating that strips were sewn together, are both diagnostic features of coastal traditions. The colors are muted in comparison to the jewel tones of a classic Wari tapestry (see cat. no. 313, color pl. 22a,b); for example, the background red is not

Plate 31
Tapestry Headband with Staff Bearers
Cat. no. 278

the cochineal scarlet but a rustier red-brown (cf. cat. no. 62, color pl. 37, and cat. no. 78, color pl. 36).

Yet the prestige of Wari imagery in a peripheral area was such that certain aspects were copied almost exactly. For instance, these staff bearers' feet are precisely those of the classic Wari tunic images. Some costume parts are similar, such as the headdress and the belt. The latter displays the familiar nested squares with a typical animal-head image; however, the combination of these particular Wari elements is unusual (the animal head generally appears as the staff ends or behind the profile figure's back foot). Thus, although the local textile artists were influenced by the dominant Wari style, they made distinctive choices in the presentation of sacred imagery according to their own textile tradition.

Middle Horizon, Wari-related, probably North Coast
A.D. 500–800
10.1 cm (height) x 49.7 cm (circumference)
Slit tapestry
      warp: cotton, pairs of $\wedge$, 9 pairs/cm
      weft: camelid fiber, $\wedge$, 32/cm
Samuel Putnam Avery Fund
52.485

Related textiles: MFA 51.578 (cat. no. 262); Museo Oro 3714 (Tushingham 1976:109, cat. no. 128); Seattle 76.50; Herscher 1983:61.

Discussion: pp. 34–36, 41; fig. III.1c.

This tapestry headband was woven as a thin, vertical strip, turned inside out then converted to its horizontal format at some point in antiquity, judging from the fact that the warp threads and the figures are oriented sideways and what was originally the back face of the fabric is placed on the exterior. The two faces are distinguishable in this case by a few visible wefts floating from one color area to the next (a shortcut to weaving back in the ends of each color of thread), seen on the present exterior, not on the interior. It has not been accidentally mounted with the wrong face out since the join area in the back, visible in the photograph as a tangle of threads, is finished on the present exterior. Conversion of fancy textiles from one type of garment to another is often found in the Andean textile tradition, particularly in the Late Intermediate Period along the North Coast (e.g., see cat. no. 12, color pl. 38). Another band in this same general style has had feathers and gold pendants added to its upper edge (Tushingham 1976:109, cat. no. 128). The style of these bands and their reuse constitute a sign of the great value assigned to the tapestry technique and to the reinterpretation of Wari imagery (see cat. no. 125, color pl. 30).

Abstraction taken to an extreme of intentional illegibility, so characteristic of the broad Wari style, is particularly evident here (fig. III.1c). This version of the staff bearer —a standing, frontal human with feet turned out, arms to the sides holding two upright staffs, and wearing an elaborate headdress— has been distilled almost entirely into series of nested squares. Scattered filler squares around the body further obscure the image, while in repeated figures (on the sides not shown in this photograph) the body becomes entirely vestigial; only columns of squares ultimately stand for the original motif. Rather than resulting from a misunderstanding of the staff bearer, this atomization represents the artistic mind following out visual possibilities to their logical extreme. Abstraction is one of the most sophisticated, universal, and cross-culturally fascinating aesthetic processes, and one amply explored in the Andean fiber tradition.

Plate 32
Featherwork Tunic Fragment with Figures, Heads, and Geometric Motifs
Cat. no. 282

Middle Horizon (?), Wari-related Culture (?)
A.D. 500–800 (?)
99.5 x 98.5 cm
Plain-weave ground cloth with sewn rows of cut feathers
      ground:
                  warp: cotton, /, 14/cm
                  weft: cotton, \, 10/cm
      feathers:
                  Scarlet Macaw or Red-and-Green Macaw (red); Blue-and-Yellow Macaw (turquoise, yellow); Razor-billed Curassow or Salvin's Curassow (dark brown-black); Great Egret or Snowy Egret (white)*
J. H. and E. A. Payne Fund
60.253

Exhibitions: 25 Centuries.
Publications: MFA 1961: no. 290, cover.
Related textiles: MFA 66.905 (cat. no. 292, color pl. 61); MFA 1971.76 (cat. no. 302); Amano (Bird et al. 1981:150); Milwaukee Public Museum (Anton 1984:34, fig. 23, top).

Discussion: pp. 13, 14, 17, 35, 36, 51.

Featherwork was held in the highest esteem by the ancient peoples of the mountains and the coast, who traded with the Amazonian jungle inhabitants for colorful iridescent feathers. To obtain the feathers or to transport finished featherwork items entailed the arduous traverse of the world's second highest mountains. In general, the emphasis on bright, solid color in all the Andean fiber techniques makes it understandable that the gorgeous feathers of the tropical birds were so strongly desired and so greatly valued. The most likely types of feathers used here were identified by John P. O'Neill as follows: the red-orange from either Scarlet Macaw (*Ara macao*) or Red-and-Green Macaw (*Ara chloroptera*); the turquoise and yellow from the Blue-and-Yellow Macaw (*Ara ararauna*); the black (faded to dark brown) from the Razor-billed Curassow (*Mitu tuberosa*) or Salvin's Curassow (*Mitu salvini*); and the white from the Great Egret (*Egretta alba*) or Snowy Egret (*Egretta thula*). He commented that the brightest feathers most likely come from a newly moulted bird and that after thousands of years most feathers appear lighter than they were originally. Thus, as with most woven textiles, we must imagine the tunic with even more jewel-like tones.

    The imagery on this piece shows that the relationship between featherwork and other prestige-fiber media, such as tapestry, was a close one. The standing figures are depicted here wearing simplified tapestry tunics (see cat. no. 312, color pl. 23a,b, and cat. no. 313, color pl. 22a,b), with their characteristic columns of rectangular motifs suggested by stacks of alternating color squares. The frontal faces below the tunic wearers correspond in a general sense to trophy heads found on other ta-

pestries (cat. nos. 200A and C, color pl. 26). The stepped triangles along the lower edge match the interlocking shapes of the tie-dyed mantle cat. no. 319 (color pl. 21a,b). According to these basic similiarities, the featherwork may be placed within the Wari style of the Middle Horizon, although it could be a later archaizing piece; it was not necessarily made where the tapestries were woven. Other well-known examples of featherwork from this period include a Tiwanaku-style hat (Bennett 1954:77, fig. 86) and a series of large, simple turquoise and yellow checkerboard banners (see Lavalle and Gonzalez 1988:153). However, this piece remains distinctive and may well be unique.

* I am indebted to John P. O'Neill (personal communication, 1991) for identifying the feathers.

Plate 33
Cap and Human Hair Braids
Cat. no. 187

Middle Horizon or later, Wari-related culture (?), South Coast
A.D. 500–800 or later
60 cm total length (cap: 15 cm; braids: 45 cm)
Cap: Simple looping
      cotton (white) \, camelid fiber (undyed) \
Braids: Oblique interlacing (plaiting), with wrapping at lower ends
      human hair; dyed camelid fiber, ∧, /
Mary Woodman Fund
31.497

Exhibitions: 25 Centuries.
Publications: MFA 1961: no. 306.
Related textiles: MFA 78.99 (cat. no. 35); MFA 31.709 (cat. no. 205); 52.483 (cat. no. 276); Brooklyn Museum 41.427 (Larsen 1986:237, fig. 255); Musée de l'Homme X33-271-1 (Harcourt 1962:166, pl. 78c); Museo Arqueologico Regional, Huaraz, 011 (Musées Royaux d'Art et d'Histoire 1990:209, cat. no. 262); Museo Nacional (Lavalle and Lang 1980:157).

Discussion: pp. 16, 17, 21, 35, 36.

Human hair wigs in various forms are known from the South Coast beginning in the Middle Horizon period. Although none of this particular type, with cap and wrapped braids, have been securely dated and may be from later pre-Hispanic periods (Ann Rowe, personal communication, 1991), the wig tradition and ideas behind it shed some light on this fine example. Wigs have been found in association with the mummy bundles of elite Wari state representatives buried along the desert coast (Reiss and Stübel 1880–1887, vol. 1: pl. 16, figs. 1, 2). The body of the deceased was encased in an elaborately layered construction found in various configurations throughout Andean history (see Paul 1990a:35–47). During the Middle Horizon, the seated corpse in fetal position was surrounded by unspun cotton fiber and sewn into a coarse cloth bag, over which was dressed the deceased's tapestry tunic (see cat. no. 312, color pl. 23a,b, and cat. no. 313, color pl. 22a,b; see also Stone 1987, vol. 2:fig. 1-1; A. Rowe 1986:154–155; 169, figs. 7–10). Attached to the top was a stuffed, decorated false head wearing the deceased's hair as a wig (see A. Rowe 1986:155–156, figs. 13, 14; 171). The result was an impressive "fiber sculpture," roughly 1.5 meters (5 feet) tall, of the person as an oversized torso and head (see fig. III.9). These bundles served to preserve the person and high-status items of dress while, at the same time, concealing the whereabouts of the body and head. Belief in the soul's needing both its identity and protection during an afterlife journey may be inferred. As part of the larger Andean "textile primacy," the wearer during life and after death was identified with and even transformed into a textile. Even the hair took part in this overall patterning, with the ends of over ninety braids painstakingly wrapped in bands of dyed camelid fiber thread.

The color patterns of these braid ends are characteristic of the Wari or Wari-influenced aesthetic, which features color combination repetitions, variations on a theme, and a hierarchy of dye colors. There are five basic color combinations, all of which begin with red and end with red then gold. In between are, in order of frequency: brown, white, brown; blue, white, brown; purple, white, purple; blue, white, blue; and brown, gold, brown. This hierarchy shows that blue and purple, products of the rarer dyes (indigo, plain and overdyed with cochineal), appear less often than the other colors. The substitution of gold for white in the last group and the asymmetry of one combination (blue, white, brown) are typical variations that add visual dynamism.

Plate 34
Fragment of Four-color Complementary Warp Weave
Cat. no. 218

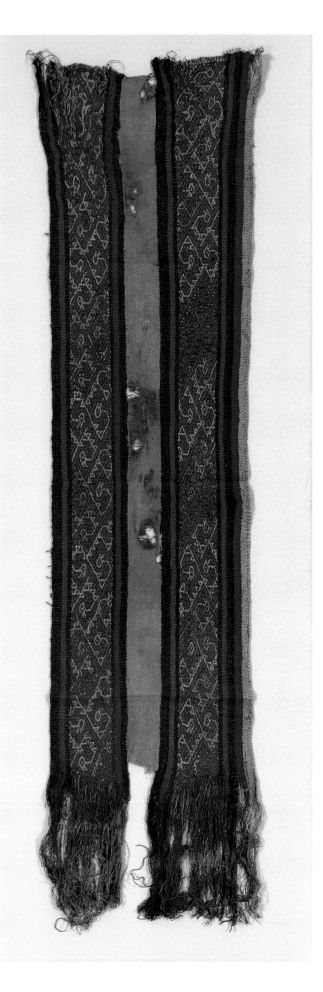

Middle Horizon or Late Intermediate Period, Central or South Coast
A.D. 900–1200
103 x 24.7 cm
Plain weave; four-color complementary warp weave with outlining
    plain weave
          warp: cotton, ∧, 23/cm
          weft: cotton, ∧, 11/cm
    complementary warp
          warp: camelid fiber and cotton (white), ∧, 12/cm
          weft: camelid fiber, pairs of ∧, 5 pairs /cm
Arthur Mason Knapp Fund
42.440

Related textiles: MFA 42.452 (cat. no. 230); Amano (Tsunoyama 1977:41, color pl. 28); Textile Museum 91.323 (A. Rowe 1977:91, note 6); Textile Museum 91.593 (A. Rowe 1977:82, 92, color pl. V); Textile Museum 91.605 (A. Rowe 1977:48, fig. 48).

Discussion: pp. 17, 20.

This fairly modest fragment has been singled out for special attention because it exemplifies a technique of particular importance in the Andes. Warp patterning is found in many pre-Conquest and especially post-Conquest pieces because the Spanish took over tapestry production but left this separate technical tradition to continue as the popular mode (see A. Rowe 1977:12). Complementary warp weave belongs to a conceptual scheme fundamental to Andean thinking and social practice. As the name implies, in warp patterning the weaver sets down the available colors in a sequence of stripes as the load-bearing warps are threaded onto the loom. In this technique the wefts are invisible, serving only to hold the warps on one face of the cloth or the other as they create the pattern. (By contrast, weft patterning has the crosswise threads carry the design, which can be varied at any time by introducing new colors of wefts; warps are the purely structural, unseen element [e.g., see cat. no. 308, color pl. 50]). Thus, warp patterning is the more rigidly structured approach, but the challenging actualization of its possibilities involves the vitally important idea of reciprocity, which appealed strongly to the Andean fiber artist.

    Here one can see two applications of warp patterning: the solid red and brown stripes are elementary warp striping, while the complex designs of interlocking birds are four-color complementary warp weave with outlining (A. Rowe 1977:81–93). The solid light orange area is a strip of plain weave to which the two warp-patterned strips are sewn. Complementary warp usually involves two colors of warps that substitute for each other on the two faces, playing reciprocal and equivalent roles (when one passes over a weft, the other passes under it, etc.). Certain more complex pieces add in a third color that serves as an outline to the motif while the original two colors continue to complement one another. Rowe has commented that "the warp-patterned weaves in which the imagination and skill of Andean weavers are most clearly manifest are those involving more than two sets of warps" (ibid.:81). Here, three col-

Plate 35
Fragment of a Strip with Mother and Child Figures
Cat. no. 217

ors substitute for one another, and a fourth outlines the figures; only one more level of the technique, five-color, was achieved (cat. no. 230; see also A. Rowe 1977:48, fig. 48). In this piece the white, now mostly lost, appears less often than the gold and red, while medium brown serves as the outlining color throughout. On the back face the positions of white, red, and gold are different.

Certainly, the challenge of such weaving is easily apparent, even in a brief description such as this. However, it is the underlying idea of the threads as reciprocal —if one moves, another must move in a mirror-image fashion— that is so characteristically Andean. In nearly all aspects of pre-Columbian and modern indigenous Andean social organization, two complementary roles are juxtaposed. Reciprocity forms the basis for survival in the supremely difficult climate. The kind of thinking in which interdependent parts form the whole encouraged the development of warp-patterned weaving to the heights of complexity seen here.

Late Intermediate Period, Lambayeque, North Coast
A.D. 1000–1476
5.8 x 5.4 cm
Slit tapestry with eccentric wefts; supplemental wefts (belt)
      warp: cotton, V, Λ, 12/cm
      weft: camelid fiber, Λ, cotton (white and light brown), \, 60/cm
Gift of Miss Gertrude Townsend
41.719

Exhibitions: 2500 Years.
Related textiles: MFA 50.657 (cat. no. 254); Museum für Völkerkunde-Berlin (Schmidt 1929:493); Museum für Völkerkunde-Munich 34-41-39 (Lommel 1977:130, fig. 74, cat. no. 386).

Discussion: pp. 14, 43.

The photograph belies the diminutive size of this tapestry patch, which measures only about 5.5 centimeters (slightly over 2 inches) square. Extremely fine details of a woman carrying a child in a cloth sling are captured in tapestry containing 60 wefts per centimeter (over 150 wefts per inch). Note, for example, the pattern of minute green and gold cross shapes in the carrying cloth (known in modern times as a *llicla* in Quechua and still used to carry children; see Medlin 1986:275). Both figures have fingernails and toenails indicated by one white weft thread only. Further attention to detail is seen in the woman's belt, embellished with a three-dimensional, twisted red and green thread added during the weaving process. "Eccentric" wefts, which trace curves rather than follow the strict rectilinear arrangement of warp and weft, allow many rounded edges to be formed in a tiny space. Artistic virtuosity is emphasized in the creation of such a miniaturized but complex composition (compare, for example, cat. no. 33, color pl. 56).

There is reason to believe this was one of many matching small patches, possibly cut from strips (since there are side selvages but the top and bottom edges are cut). A photograph from the Museum's correspondence surrounding this piece shows, albeit rather indistinctly, at least twenty-three of these patches appliquéd onto a loosely woven plain-weave textile that might have been a mantle or poncho. The current whereabouts of this composition or of its other component patches remain unknown. The use of appliqués as well as the combination of cotton and camelid fiber for the wefts are characteristic of Lambayeque textiles (see cat. no. 206, color pl. 58) but are unusual in most other ancient Andean fiber traditions.

Plate 36 (overleaf)
Border with Bird-headed Figures
Cat. no. 78

Late Intermediate Period, Lambayeque, North Coast
A.D. 1000–1476
75 x 10 cm
Interlocked and slit tapestry; intermittent weft-loop fringe (left side);
edge binding
      warp: cotton, V, 13/cm
      weft: camelid fiber, ∧, 60/cm
Denman Waldo Ross Collection
16.41

Exhibitions: 25 Centuries; 2500 Years.
Publications: Means 1932:45, specimen 5, figs. 21a,b; MFA 1961: no. 291 (illus.);
Townsend 1932:64–65 (illus.).
Related textiles: Museum für Völkerkunde-Berlin (Schmidt 1929: pl. XI); Museum für
Völkerkunde-Berlin (Schmidt 1929:488).

Discussion: pp. 22, 43.

The presence of Z-plied warps, the somewhat muted color scheme, and
the figures in bent-knee pose wearing crescent-shaped headdresses —all
signal this piece as a North Coast composition. Stylistically it can be assigned to the far north Lambayeque culture, which was conquered
around 1325 by the Chimu state to the south. Two bird-headed figures,
one large to indicate importance and one small to show subservience,
grasp a staff or agricultural implement. A large fish is fitted into the
scene above the smaller figure. One may conjecture that the meaning of
the combination of motifs —perhaps symbolizing earth (implement), sea
(fish), and air (bird head)— is linked to a ritual for fertility.

      Technically speaking, the tapestry is of the highest quality, with
a weft count of 60 threads per centimeter (over 150 threads per inch).
Originally, the gold weft-loop fringe seen in places along the left side
would have appeared at regular intervals, as on other Lambayeque-style
bands (see Schmidt 1929: pl. XI; 488). The ability to create detail in tapestry has been exploited to the utmost; notice the figures' complex tunic
designs and the little lines on the fishes' fins —all captured in only a few
weft threads. There is a marked liveliness in the composition despite the
repetition of the scene. The alternation of background colors and figure
orientation is regular; however, the assignment of individual colors within each block varies. This is typical of Andean textile design, in which
the artists took all afforded opportunities to make repeated motifs distinctive.

Plate 37
Tapestry Strip with Figures and Large Birds
Cat. no. 62

Late Intermediate Period, Lambayeque, North Coast
A.D. 1000–1476
76 x 23.7 cm
Slit tapestry with underfloated wefts
      warp: cotton, V, 8/cm
      weft: camelid fiber, Λ, 46/cm
Denman Waldo Ross Collection
10.267

Exhibitions: 25 Centuries; 2500 Years.
Publications: MFA 1961: no. 302.
Related textiles: Four parts of the same original composition or an exactly matched one: Art Institute of Chicago 1955.1706a–c (see Taullard 1949: fig. 121); probable two more parts of the same: Amano R.0197 (Tsunoyama 1977:37, color pl. 24); "Gaffron Collection, Berlin" (Lehmann 1924: pl. X); Lavalle and Gonzalez 1988:256.

Discussion: pp. 17, 22, 38, 43.

Four additional panels of the same or an identical composition are located in the Art Institute of Chicago, and two more are now in Berlin (see related textiles, above). If all seven known webs were sewn together side by side, as are two of the Chicago pieces, the original piece would have been wider than 140 centimeters (approx. 55 inches). (Since all panels are cut at the top, it is impossible to reconstruct the original height.) The assembling of multiple strips, often to create very large cloths, is common in the Late Intermediate Period (see cat. no. 12, color pl. 38; cat. no. 161, color pl. 52; cat. no. 315, color pl. 39).

    The extraordinarily bright colors of this tapestry give us a closer idea of the hues achieved by Andean dyers over six hundred years ago. Andeans went to extreme lengths to attain the strongest, most lasting colors, as demonstrated here by the overall range of colors and particularly by the use of cochineal for the scarlet red (although the dye has not been chemically tested, its hue and saturation are characteristic of cochineal). A number of more unusual colors are also preserved in this example, most notably two shades each of green and purple. These more fugitive hues tend to be harder to produce and shorter lived, lending to the overall Andean textile palette we experience today a misleading emphasis on brown, gold, and red. Another unusual color, a yellow-orange, is generated by plying together a gold and an orange thread to create an intermediate tone (a practice seen occasionally in various periods; e.g., cat. no. 79, color pl. 19, and cat. no. 293, color pl. 73). Virtuoso dyeing and threadmaking, with their concomitant effort, were part of the emphasis placed on color variety in textiles.

    The intense scarlet red of the background was produced from the cochineal beetle, whose bodily fluid (carminic acid) produces the most brilliant, permanent, natural red dye known. This insect (*genus dactylopius*) lives as a parasite on the prickly pear cactus (Spanish: *nopal* [*genus opuntia*]). When cultivated, as they were in the pre-Columbian era, these insects grow to double the size of uncultivated beetles and require twice as much time to complete the life cycle (Ciesla 1988:14–15). They must be protected from the elements, then painstakingly harvested, their bodies dried and pulverized. Hundreds of insects are needed to make a few ounces of the dye; about a cup of powdered cochineal beetles is needed to color only one pound of yarn (Ross 1988:19). However, despite the arduous nature of its production, cochineal was the preferred red dye in ancient and Colonial textile traditions and is still used today both in Peru and abroad. (In fact, the Spanish made a second fortune, after that from precious metals, selling cochineal to Europeans hungry for a red source superior to madder, until some cacti and insects were smuggled to Europe [Ciesla 1988:15]). An expanse of red such as seen in this textile indicates the important contributions of many workers other than the weavers and underscores the society-wide dedication to textile production.

Plate 38
Fragment of a Sleeve (?) with Standing Figures
Cat. no. 12

Plate 39 (overleaf)
Openwork Mantle Fragment with "Moon Animal" Motifs
Cat. no. 315

Late Intermediate Period, Lambayeque, North Coast
A.D. 1000–1476
34 x 28 cm
Slit tapestry
        warp: cotton, ∧, 10/cm
        weft: camelid fiber, ∧, 66/cm
Gift of Edward W. Hooper
78.75

Publications: Means 1932:45, specimen 4, fig. 20; MFA 1907:213; MFA 1908:204;
MFA 1911:206; MFA 1913:208; MFA 1914:208; MFA 1915:214; MFA 1916:231; MFA
1919:231; MFA 1920:231; MFA 1922:231.
Related textiles: MFA 50.656 (cat. no. 253); Museo Nacional (Lavalle and Lang
1980:117); Museum für Völkerkunde-Berlin (Reiss and Stübel 1880–1887: pl. 46).

Discussion: pp. 14, 43.

The typically muted, brownish colors of many Lambayeque-style textiles
are seen here in this composite of two panels. It is impossible to say with
complete certainty that the two were joined in this configuration in antiquity (both are cut above and below, with the viewer's right panel inverted
and the left coarsely edged). The whip stitching that joins the parts appears to be done with ancient thread, although the color match is not exact. At some point in time, the two bands were converted to another function, probably a sleeve to a tunic (see A. Rowe 1984:137, fig. 139; Means
1932:45). This type of reuse, quite widespread, emphasizes the great value ascribed to decorative textiles (see cat. no. 48, color pl. 69a,b). The extremely high thread count, 66 wefts per centimeter (more than165 wefts
per inch), independently verifies the status of the piece and underlines
why it would have been chosen for reuse; great technical achievement
held its value over time in such a textile-conscious culture.

In addition, the design of large, crescent-headdressed figures
with smaller, subsidiary ones indicates a power relationship: the pose
represents a version of the traditional Andean captor-captive scene, in
which the dominant figure grasps the hair of his captive (Donnan
1978:151, fig. 228). The superiority of two of the oversized figures (on the
right and the lower left) is emphasized further by their tunics being covered with gold-colored squares, perhaps representing the extraordinary
tunics with thousands of appliquéd beaten gold plaques (see Bird et al.
1981:108–109). The third figure (upper left) has a tunic with a zigzag pattern that also resembles the composition of actual tunics of the time
(Margaret Young-Sánchez, personal communication, 1991). The self-referential nature of depicting a high-status textile in a weaving is common
in Andean fiber arts and reinforces the significance of both image and
vehicle.

Late Intermediate Period, Chimu, North Coast
A.D. 1000–1476
209 x 133 cm
Brocaded plain weave with spaced warps and wefts, supplemental
threads wrapped around woven squares; weft-faced plain weave with
supplemental weft patterning (lower border); tapestry (side borders); layered fringe
        plain weave
                warp: cotton, \, 12/cm
                weft: cotton, \, 12/cm
        brocading, borders, fringe: camelid fiber, ∧
Arthur Tracy Cabot Fund
1980.211

Exhibitions: Chimu Textiles.
Publications: A. Rowe 1984:89–90, fig. 67; 93, note 16; MFA 1980:33.
Related textiles: Amano R.0082 (Tsunoyama 1977:111, color pl. 120; VanStan 1966:16,
fig. 59) [closely related but not part of same original, as suggested by A. Rowe 1984:93,
note 16]; Peabody-Harvard (A. Rowe 1984:91, fig. 69). For the Moon Animal motif
alone, see Lavalle and Gonzalez 1988:241.

Discussion: pp. 44, 45; fig. IV.2.

In its present configuration, this textile in the "Toothed Crescent Headdress Style," probably a mantle, has been reconstructed to quite an extent. However, as Ann Rowe commented concerning this and several related pieces, "although they are sufficiently fragmentary that their
original form is in doubt, they are included here because they represent
Chimu weaving at its best." (1984:89). Two of three original panels and
the woven lower border remain, while the thin red border along the right
side (which overlaps the motifs in an uncharacteristic fashion) most likely has been added after antiquity [ibid.:90]). The mantle would have
been at least 30 percent larger, and consequently even more impressive,
when it was first fabricated as much as a thousand years ago.

A very similar fragment showing the same figure (albeit with a
frontal instead of a profile face and a thicker body) has a provenance of
Pisquillo Chico in the Central Coast Chancay Valley (see Tsunoyama
1977:111, color pl. 120; VanStan 1966:16, fig. 59). Since these two fragments are definitely Chimu in character, they may represent another example of the interaction between the various local coastal peoples during
this period (see cat. no. 306, color pl. 42). Both pieces feature the long-
tailed animal wearing a headdress known as the "Moon Animal," found
in much earlier North Coast traditions beginning as early as 300–100
B.C. In the Moche style (about A.D. 300–600), it sits on a crescent shape,
thought to symbolize the moon, among radiating circles, interpreted as
stars. Since the moon was apparently an important deity in Chimu religion, it has been assumed the meaning remained fairly constant among
later North Coast cultures (A. Rowe 1984:69). Sacred subject matter, the
use of many different colored supplemental threads to brocade the figures, and the great size of the original mantle —all indicate the importance of this piece to the Chimu.

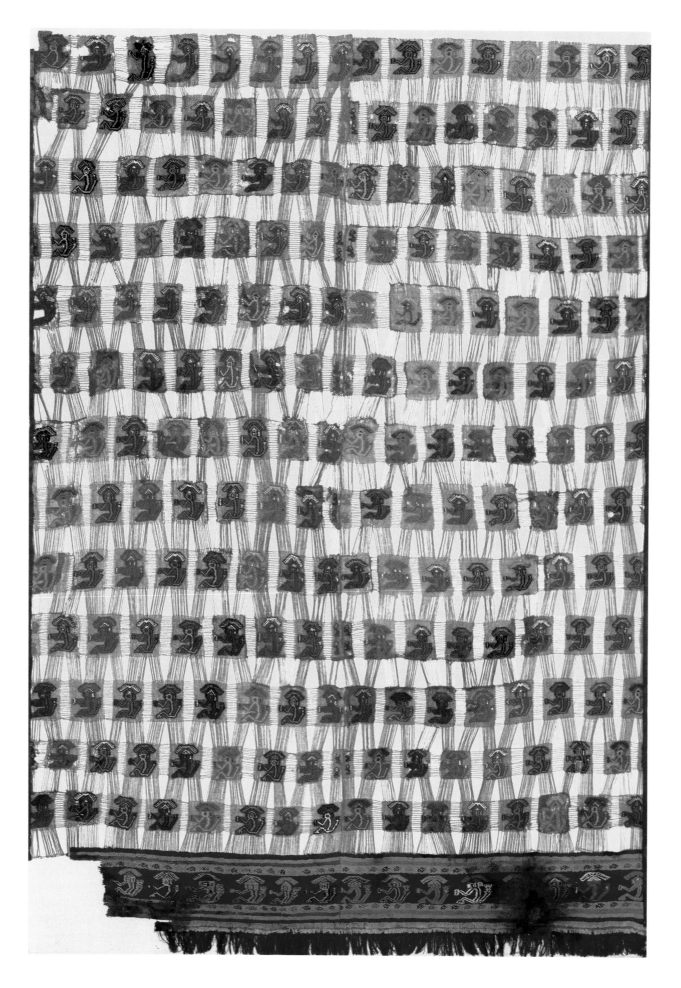

130 / To Weave for the Sun (plate 39)

Plate 40
Tasseled Tapestry Band with Birds
Cat. no. 284

Late Intermediate Period, Chimu, North Coast
A.D. 1000–1476
217 x 3.7 cm
Slit tapestry with underfloated wefts; tiered fringe
      warp: cotton, ∨, 9/cm
      weft: camelid fiber, cotton (white), ∧, 30/cm
Gift of Mrs. Samuel Cabot
60.1132

Exhibitions: 25 Centuries.
Publications: MFA 1961: no. 311.
Related textiles: Art Institute of Chicago 1955.1640 (A. Rowe 1984:70, fig. 46; the piece
is matched with Art Institute of Chicago 1955.1730, A. Rowe 1984:66, color pl. 8);
American Museum of Natural History (Lehmann 1924:125, lower photograph, second
band from the top). On this style generally see A. Rowe 1984:66–93.

Discussion: p. 45.

In vivid stripes of scarlet, pink, gold, and two shades of olive green, this
long tapestry band combines typical Chimu-style motifs of birds with
stepped frets. Probably a belt, it is most closely related to pieces in what
Rowe has termed the "Toothed Crescent Headdress Style" (1984:66–93).
Although the birds do not wear headdresses themselves, originally the
band most likely formed part of a garment set with a closely matched,
more elaborate loincloth or tunic with figures wearing this characteristic
North Coast headdress (see cat. no. 315, color pl. 39; see also Rowe
1984:70, fig. 46; 66, color pl. 8). Like similar bands, this piece ends in the
multitiered tassels found throughout later Chimu textiles. These tassels
"are made starting at the bottom with a heavy foundation cord tied
around the center of each bunch of yarns that will form the tiers. These
yarns are then folded down and the tops wound with another fine yarn,
usually of a matching color. The foundation cord knots itself in the intervals between tiers" (ibid.:72).
      The weavers went to some effort to develop a three-dimensional,
multicolored, layered fringe that would continue the overall striping pattern of the band. A notable variation within the striping color repetition
occurs just above the fringe on one end: two stripes are woven in an
anomalous blue-green color. The closely related loincloth end in the Art
Institute of Chicago (1955.1730; A. Rowe 1984:66, color pl. 8) also contains a blue-green anomaly, as do other Chimu textiles (see cat. no. 317,
color pl. 60a,b). Blue-green color anomalies have been found to be especially characteristic of earlier Wari tapestries (e.g., see cat. no. 312, color
pl. 23a,b; see also Stone 1986; 1987, vol. 1:167–171), and later Inca tapestries also have some strong color deviations (see cat. no. 234, color pl.
64). The fairly widespread Chimu anomalies may have been in imitation
of the Wari or could have been developed independently for similar reasons (blue-green produced by the indigo dye being particularly rare and
the color itself symbolically important; see cat. no. 214, color pl. 29;
Stone 1987, vol.1:64–65). In either case, artists purposely introduced
anomalies into relatively stable compositions to add visual liveliness and

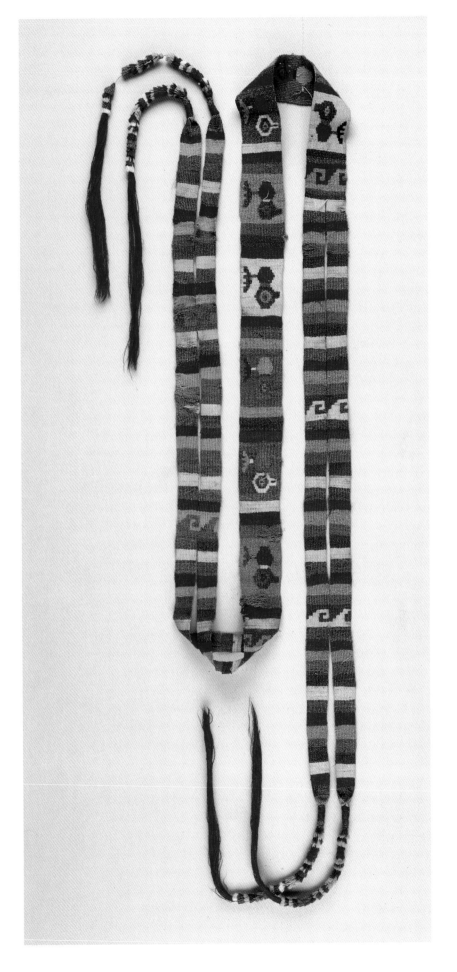

to express the wearer's high status via the understood special importance of the color. This wide appreciation of textile technology (such as the esoteric nature of indigo dyeing) ensured that an aesthetic device like the blue anomaly could reinforce social status. The ability of the fiber medium to create its own meaning system, often independent of iconographic symbolism, proves once again its great power and centrality within Andean thought

Plate 41
Tunic or Poncho with Abstract Bird and Geometric Motifs
Cat. no. 246

Late Intermediate Period, Chimu, North Coast
A.D. 1000–1476
54 x 96.9 cm
Slit and dovetailed tapestry
      warp: camelid fiber, pairs of ∧, 6–8 pairs/cm
      weft: camelid fiber, ∧, 26.7/cm
William Francis Warden Fund
47.1093

Discussion: pp. 23, 46.

The lively design of this tapestry features a bold checkerboard arrangement, the effect of which is enhanced by the piece's near-perfect state of preservation. High contrast between bright gold and dark brown squares creates a first impression of design simplicity; however, a number of subtle compensations have been made by the artist(s) for potential imbalances in the composition. For instance, the differences between the principal colors in hue, value, and intensity are resolved in various sophisticated ways. The darkness of the brown is relieved by the superimposition of rows of small hooked motifs (which may be birds abstracted to an extreme or simply related geometric shapes). The yellow hooks create perceptual holes in the squares, as if to reveal bits of the continuous gold ground running below (Arnheim 1974:228). This effect of capturing some of the ground color in the figure is known as "transparency" (seen particularly in Paracas linear-style embroideries, see p. 25); here it serves to lighten the potentially weighty brown portions. The red hooks, through the perceptual effect called assimilation (Arnheim 1974:363), visually match the similar colors of the borders above and below, thereby linking together the entire composition. Together the red and gold hooks restate the overall design by their checkerboard coloration.

    The interlockable hook shapes echo the interlocked birds and stepped frets of the borders. Two possible readings of the border design are visually inseparable, so that the viewer's eye continuously shifts between the two: light pink birds come forward as figure, facing one direction, then recede for dark pink frets to assume that role facing the opposite direction. Again, a form of transparency is exploited in that a small amount of one color is introduced into the other motif (the red dots in the bird's "tail" and pink dots in the base of the fret), here creating the impossible impression that each color runs below the other. A sophisticated aesthetic achievement by the artist, such perceptual ambiguity establishes a fascinating visual situation for the viewer (see also cat. no. 240, color pl. 53).

    In this case, as with most Andean textiles, one should properly use the word "artists," since there are indications of collaborative production here. The two webs that form the two garment halves are quite different from each other, suggesting their manufacture by separate individuals. The one on the viewer's left is larger in overall dimensions (54 x 49.4 centimeters [21 1/4 x 19 1/2 inches] versus 52.8 x 47.5 centimeters

[20¾ x 18¾ inches]) and therefore in the size of the checkerboard squares. It also has a higher thread count for both warp and weft elements. Although both introduce a lighter brown for some of the stripes in the border, the left one does it twice, but the right only once. The weaver of the right-hand web may not have planned the checkerboard design as carefully, leaving a gap of yellow below the lower brown squares.

Overall, the execution of the tapestry weave is not of the very highest quality in comparison with other contemporaneous examples (e.g., cat. no. 308, color pl. 50; Margaret Young-Sánchez, personal communication, 1991). Warps can be seen between the wefts, especially in the gold areas, indicating loose packing of the wefts. Conservation of the precious highland trade commodity, camelid fiber, would seem a likely reason; however, unlike most coastal pieces, camelid fiber was used here

for the warps instead of cotton. Camelid fiber warps are neither an economical nor a particularly practical choice of fiber for the load-bearing element. Technical coarseness and the unusual hooked motifs may indicate that this is a local or peripheral Late Intermediate Period interpretation. The range of textile expressions at this time remains wide and difficult to define. Yet close observation of the many beautiful pieces from this period consistently reveals aesthetic complexity employed in the service of visual unity and dynamism.

Plate 42
Pair of Miniature Shoes with Metal Plaques and Soles
Cat. no. 306

Late Intermediate Period, North Coast
A.D. 1000–1476
a: 10.2 x 6.7 cm (across toes)
b: 10.2 x 6.5 cm (across toes)
Tapestry; plain weave (lining); appliqué metal plaques; metal soles
    tapestry
        warp: cotton, V, 6/cm
        weft: camelid fiber, ∧, 28/cm
    plain weave
        warp: cotton, pairs of \ and /, 12 pairs/cm
        weft: cotton, \, 10/cm
    plaques: approx. 75 percent silver, 25 percent copper, trace lead
    (one exception, approx. 60 percent silver, 40 percent copper,
    more lead)
    soles: approx. 55 percent silver, 45 percent copper, trace arsenic
Gift of Landon T. Clay
1975.662a,b

Exhibitions: Chimu Textiles.
Publications: A. Rowe 1984:155; 158; 163, notes 10, 11, 160, fig. 169.
Related textiles: Shoes: Metropolitan (Loan from Goldberg Collection) L1978.25.503
(A. Rowe 1984:160, fig. 168); Museo Oro 4143, 4144 (Tushingham 1976: cat. nos. 248,
249). For other objects with metal plaques: Museo Oro (Bird et al. 1981:108–109); A.
Rowe 1984: figs. 148, 150, 152, 167, and pl. 23.

Discussion: pp. 18, 20, 43, 51.

These fascinating miniature silver-plated shoes are completely nonfunc-
tional, in the sense of their actually being worn. Rather than being used
as apparel for an infant or "doll," they served to symbolize shoes among
other tiny, high-status, sculpted and woven tomb offerings in silver, fiber,
and featherwork (A. Rowe 1984:150–160). Along with such pairs of shoes
found in Central Coast tombs were diminutive representations of trees,
musical instruments, tools, and bags, some of which were executed in
Chancay and some in North Coast style. Such a stylistic mixture is understandable during the Late Intermediate Period, which is characterized
by its regionalism. These varied groups of offerings also indicate at least
an active trading relationship between the North Coast and Central
Coast peoples (ibid.:160).

    North Coast characteristics are present in the woven portions of
the shoes (for example, the lining has the typical Z-plied paired warp
structure). The use of small, square metal plaques is found in other
miniature and full-size garments associated generally with the Chimu
(see related textiles, above), the most stunning example being a large tunic covered with thousands of thin gold plaques (Bird et al.
1981:108–109). In Chimu culture, the precious metals were restricted to
the royal and noble classes; these shoes would therefore represent an offering made for a person of very high rank. Considering the effort involved in the weaving of shoe and lining (including dyeing with
cochineal for the brilliant scarlet color), the assembling of the parts,

sewing of the many individual plaques, in addition to the entire metal-
working procedure, these shoes display the labor intensity characteristic
of Andean arts destined for elite burials.

    Some intriguing discoveries were made about the creative
process involved in fabricating these shoes when they were subjected to
material analysis by the Research Laboratory of the Museum. All but one
of the tiny squares in both shoes were found to be so similar in metallur-
gical composition as to have been cut from a single sheet. (The exceptional plaque may have been a replacement, probably made in ancient
times.) Under the microscope it was possible to see the ruling lines
drawn to guide the cutting of the squares. The sheets had been ham-
mered to the extraordinary thinness of 0.15 to 0.40 millimeters and then
decorated in the repoussé technique with a large central circle and many
small surrounding circles. To reconstruct their original effect as they
were laid in a grave nearly a thousand years ago, the modern viewer
must visualize these shoes as untarnished, shining silver plaques and
soles against the brilliant red cloth.

Tunic with Stripes and Interlocked Animal Motifs
Cat. no. 285

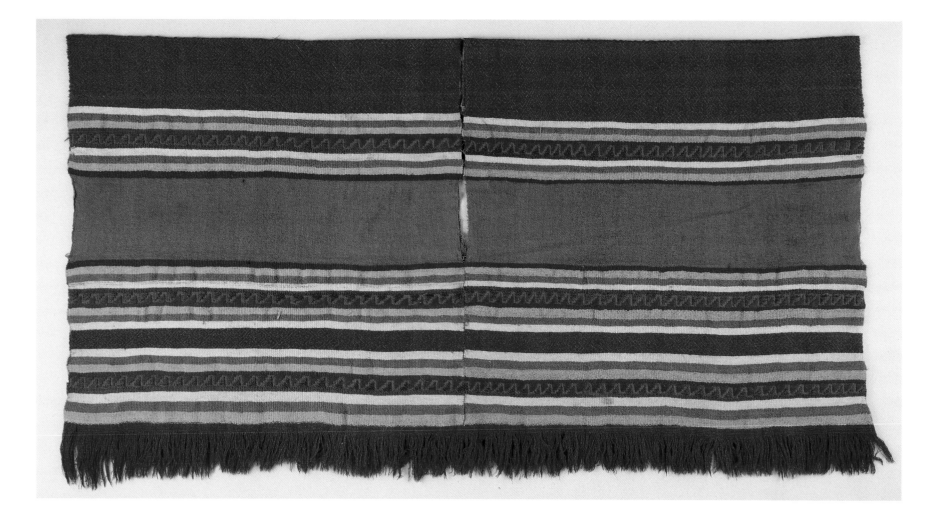

Late Intermediate Period, North Coast
A.D. 1000–1476
48 x 91 cm
Plain weave; weft-faced bands; reserved line supplemental weft patterning; cut fringe

      plain weave

               warp: cotton, pairs of \, 20 pairs/cm

               weft: cotton, /, 18/cm

          supplemental wefts and fringe: camelid fiber, ∧

Gift of Mrs. Samuel Cabot
60.1133

Exhibitions: 25 Centuries.
Publications: MFA 1961: no. 312; A. Rowe 1984:62–64, fig. 41.
Related textiles: Textile Museum 1983.41.5a,b (A. Rowe 1984:62, fig. 38); Textile Museum 1983.41.6 (A. Rowe 1984:62, fig. 39); Textile Museum 1961.3.1A (A. Rowe 1984:63, color pl. 7).

Discussion: pp. 23, 45.

Subtle geometry played out in a brilliant palette of red, gold, olive greens, white, and natural light brown cotton sets apart this deceptively simple waist-length sleeveless tunic. Judging from other garment sets in this general North Coast style (some of which were excavated in the "Las Avispas" burial platform in the Chimu capital city of Chan Chan [A. Rowe 1972, 1984]), the tunic originally would have been worn with a matching turban and loincloth. From the archaeological evidence Ann Rowe has elucidated the diagnostic technical features of North Coast textiles, the following of which are found in this piece: cotton fiber, plain weave made up of tightly spun but unplied threads, warps combined in pairs, additional camelid fiber for patterning, and a separate, plain-color fringe with cut ends.

      The Museum's example seems to belong in a group of closely related pieces, some of which come from the site of Cao Viejo, displaying

what Rowe terms "reserve-line" supplemental weft patterning (Rowe 1984:57). This materially economical but aesthetically complex approach floats the red, camelid-fiber nonstructural wefts over most of the light brown ground cloth (see color pl. 43b). Thus, the supplemental wefts are effectively "tacked down" under a single warp; this served to maximize visually the precious imported camelid fiber. Aesthetically the technique outlines a figure in the "reserved" (uncovered) ground cloth color, giving the impression of a red ground with light brown lines delineating figures. Further complicating the reading of the pattern, the motif interlocks a series of extremely abstracted snakes (with diamond-shaped eyes and mouth in a notched diamond-shaped head affixed to a thin diagonal line) that can also be read as felines (the notches seen as ears in a frontal face). Upside-down and right-side-up motifs share the reserved brown line between them in another example of the ambiguous perceptual effect known as "contour rivalry" (see cat. no. 240, color pl. 53). As so often

in Andean fiber arts, apparent geometric simplicity gives way under close observation to embedded multiple readings.

Plate 44
Hanging with Two Large Figures
Cat. no. 290

Late Intermediate Period, North Coast
A.D. 1000–1476
147 x 214 cm
Plain-weave discontinuous (interlocked) warps and (interlocked and dovetailed) wefts

> warp: cotton, pairs of \, 14 pairs/cm
> weft: cotton, \, 9/cm

Textile Income Purchase Fund
65.599

Exhibitions: 2500 Years; Chimu Textiles; Textile Masterpieces.
Publications: A. Rowe 1984:55, fig. 30; MFA 1965b: cover.
Related textiles: MFA 67.313a–d (cat. no. 295, color pl. 14a,b); MFA 64.2044 (cat. no. 289, color pl. 17); Metropolitan 1979.206.601 (A. Rowe 1984:53, color pl. 4); Textile Museum 91.849 (A. Rowe 1984:54, fig. 27); Textile Museum 91.850 (A. Rowe 1984:54, fig. 28); Textile Museum 91.854 (A. Rowe 1984:54, fig. 29).

Discussion: pp. 18, 23, 45.

One of the most visually powerful compositions in the Museum's collection, this large-scale cotton hanging, featuring two standing frontal figures, is among a group of only five known Chimu textiles in this exact style and technique (A. Rowe 1984: color pl. 4, figs. 27–29). These five represent a subset of what Rowe terms the "Bird Lot Style," named for Junius B. Bird, Andean textile pioneer, who researched an important series of North Coast garment sets (ibid.:37). According to archaeological information from Chan Chan (see cat. no. 285, color pl. 43a,b), such sets were found folded or rolled as burial offerings with sacrificial victims (ibid.:23). Interestingly, this piece also shows evidence of having been folded in fourths (Jane Hutchins, personal communication, 1988). The colors in these strikingly graphic pieces represent those naturally occurring in Andean cotton (*gossypium barbadense*) —white, tan, light and dark brown, and a purplish gray not seen here— as well as an indigo-dyed blue more difficult to achieve with cotton fiber (see cat. no. 206, color pl. 58).

The unique visual effect of a very sheer yet colorful cloth results from another of the arduous techniques so favored by the Andean textile artist: discontinuous warp and weft (on the technique, see entry for cat. no. 289, color pl. 17; cat. no. 295, color pl. 14a,b). Not only have the threads in both directions been planned so as to overlap, forming two figures, but in addition this has been accomplished in four separate panels that match exactly. (Because the stepped shapes below the figures' feet match their headdresses, it is possible that originally two additional panels were sewn to the lower edge of the hanging, making it very large indeed [Margaret Young-Sánchez, personal communication, 1991]). To join the panels with the left and right halves of a figure, separate thread colors were used to match the figure's body, face, headdress, and so on. Great care in collaborative weaving certainly reached new heights in the Late Intermediate Period.

Upon close comparison of the four panels, distinct artists' hands among the collaborators may be suggested. The second panel from the right alone has light brown instead of white heading cords, and its execution is generally more haphazard. Additionally, it includes an outright mistake in the lower left stepped-triangle shape. The dyelot differences in the dark browns are more noticeable as well. Despite the varying parts, however, a visually seamless —though physically discontinuous— composition is achieved through skill, effort, and planning.

Plate 45
Fringed Border Fragment with Headdress Motifs
Cat. no. 266

Color plate 46 (overleaf)
Openwork Tunic with Tie-dyed Circles
Cat. no. 1

Late Intermediate Period, North Coast
A.D. 1000–1476
25.2 x 21.8 cm
Slit tapestry with spaced warps, looped pile, looped fringe, embroidery,
and compound tassels
       tapestry
              warp: cotton, \/, 8/cm
              weft: camelid fiber, /\, 40/cm
       other threads: camelid fiber, /\
Elizabeth Day McCormick Collection
51.2453

Related textiles: MFA 78.102 (cat. no. 38); Amano R.0207; Amano R.0272. See also A.
Rowe 1984: figs. 35, 36, 47, 64, 69; color pls. 5, 11.

Discussion: p. 45.

Although the Museum's collection includes many remarkably well preserved textiles, this diminutive fringe fragment, nearly one thousand
years old, may be the single most brilliantly colored piece of all. All of its
varied colors —scarlet and pink, light and dark purple, gold and light orange, light green and blue green— seem as bright as those made by
modern chemical dyes. Like all pre-Hispanic and many post-Hispanic
examples, however, all the colors were created using only natural veg-
etable and animal dyes (on cochineal see cat. no. 62, color pl. 37; on indigo see cat. no. 214, color pl. 29). Having a sense of the original intensity
of hues here can help us to imagine the entire corpus of Andean textiles
in its pristine glory.

    Another striking aspect of this piece is its three-dimensionality,
achieved through a variety of techniques. Negative space and textural
contrast were created in the border portion by spacing the warp threads
and trailing unsecured wefts across some of the gaps. Looped pile and
embroidery make the tiny headdress motifs project from the border surface. Equally balanced open spaces and three-dimensional projections
continue as a theme in the elaborate compound fringe below: the top
section leaves open areas between the long tasseled strands. The red col-
or and relative density of the woven border are echoed in the fringe below. Andean textile artists did not limit their vision of fiber to flat surfaces
but explored its sculptural possibilities (see also cat. nos. 39, 42, 41, color
pls. 55a–c).

Late Intermediate Period, North or North-Central Coast
A.D. 1000–1476
70 x 99.5 cm
Plain weave with spaced warps and wefts, tie-dyed; interlocked tapestry
with weft loop fringe (sleeves); slit tapestry, plain weave with warp substitution, and complementary warp weave (lower borders)
       plain weave
              warp: cotton, \ and \/, 19/cm
              weft: cotton, \, 19/cm
       interlocked tapestry
              warp: cotton, \/, 8/cm
              weft: camelid fiber, /\, 36/cm
       slit tapestry
              warp: cotton, paired \, 12 pairs/cm
              weft: camelid fiber, \, 12/cm
       plain weave with warp substitution
              warp: cotton, paired \, 14 pairs/cm
              weft: cotton, \, 9/cm
       complementary warp
              warp: cotton, paired \, 6 pairs/cm
              weft: cotton, \, 16/cm
Gift of Edward W. Hooper
78.64

Exhibitions: 25 Centuries; 2500 Years.
Publications: MFA 1961: no. 297; Means 1932:68–69, specimen 57, figs. 79 and 80.
Related textiles: MFA 1980.211 (cat. no. 315, color pl. 39); Peabody-Harvard (A. Rowe
1984:91, fig. 69).

Discussion: p. 17.

This lightweight, openwork tunic exemplifies several uniquely Andean
approaches to textile creation. On first glance, the body of the tunic appears rather simple and monochromatic; the borders add only a little
splash of color to the cream and light brown of the tunic body. However,
a great deal of special effort went into its overall elaboration. Simple
plain-weave construction was enlivened by leaving spaces between the
1-centimeter-square woven areas. Each of the approximately eighteen
hundred woven intersections was stitched around its edges to keep the
weaving concentrated. Then each was individually tied with thread to re-
serve a minute circle of the cream-colored natural cotton ground while
the entire piece was dipped in light brown dye. The widespread occurrence of such laborious processes throughout the Andean textile tradition
shows us the premium placed on the unique, final visual effect, without
regard to labor expenditure.

    Another characteristic Andean practice clearly evident here is
the combination of many different techniques in a single piece. Besides
the tie-dyed, spaced, stitched plain weave, itself a combination of techniques, the borders around the hem and sleeves include two types of weft
patterning (interlocked and slit tapestry) and two of warp patterning

Plate 47 (overleaf)
Double-Cloth Bag with Animal and Geometric Motifs
Cat. no. 275

(warp substitution and complementary warp). During the Late Intermediate Period many such distinct parts were cut and sewn together, as here, or varying techniques were worked on the same threads. The sewing thread appears to be ancient, which strongly suggests —without proving— that this additive composition represents the original configuration of the tunic.

Upon close observation, the textile is a contrast between muted color and brightness, openwork and density. However, it is important to remember that this was a garment: the wearer's movement would have added the swish of fringe and revealed another, possibly brightly colored garment beneath, showing through the spaced openings of the tunic. This dynamic three-dimensional composition would have transformed its wearer into a kind of kinetic fiber sculpture.

Late Intermediate Period, Chancay, Central Coast
A.D. 1000–1476
35.5 x 26 cm
Plain-weave double cloth
        warp: cotton ⋀, 11/cm
        weft: cotton ⋀, 10/cm
Samuel Putnam Avery Fund
52.482

Related textiles: MFA 21.2569 (cat. no. 97); MFA 30.236 (cat. no. 159); MFA 30.237 (cat. no. 160); MFA 35.1126 (cat. no. 210, color pl. 57); MFA 42.444a,b (cat. no. 222); Amano (Maeyama 1976:55, fig. 73, center); American Museum of Natural History (Crawford 1916:296).

Discussion: pp. 18, 22, 46, 48.

This complex double-cloth bag stands out in technique, design, and iconographic complexity. The fabric was created as a single hourglass-shaped web, then folded and sewn up the sides to form a bag. Shaped textiles, especially bags, are found in the ancient Andes during many periods (e.g., cat. no. 266, color pl. 45; see also Bird 1964). The desire to weave an object with all four finished selvages —to avoid cutting or piecing parts, even when its shape is complex— represents the characteristic Andean emphasis on entirety. Made as double cloth (see cat. no. 210, color pl. 57, on technique), it is intricately worked in a great many different patterns. Obviously, display of technical virtuosity was a primary consideration.

The bag acts as a sampler, its twenty-one distinct pattern areas arrayed in an irregular layout. Each pattern was worked only long enough to ensure that the weaver had a complete version (Margaret Young-Sánchez, personal communication, 1991). The visual effect is one of interrupted, continuous diagonals of motifs, giving the impression of patchwork, although it was woven as a single unit. This not only represents a sophisticated *trompe l'oeil* but also makes two sides that feature quite different formats and motifs. The more perfectly preserved side (seen in the photograph) features frontal faces, birds, several interlocked snake patterns, and fretted zigzags. The other side (not seen in the photograph), more iconographically varied, contains images of monkeys, birds, snakes, and deer. Whether its weaver actually used the bag as a mnemonic device to reproduce single patterns in other pieces, or whether it was simply an expression of the many patterns known to the maker, this bag quite consciously reveals the creativity of the Andean fiber artist.

144 / To Weave for the Sun (plate 47)

Plate 48 (preceding page)
Loincloth End with Long-tailed Birds
Cat. no. 61

Late Intermediate Period, Chancay, Central Coast
A.D. 1000–1476
77.2 x 40 cm
Slit tapestry with wrapped warps and woven fringe
warp: cotton, ∧, 8/cm
weft: camelid fiber, ∧, 32/cm
Denman Waldo Ross Collection
10.266

Exhibitions: 25 Centuries; 2500 Years.
Publications: Means 1932:47, specimen 9, fig. 25; MFA 1961: no. 301.
Related textiles: Amano R.0204 (Tsunoyama 1977:36, color pl. 23).

Discussion: p. 46.

The traditional emphasis on openwork in coastal textiles (cat. no. 286, color pl. 49) is recognizable here in this elaborate variation on slit tapestry. Two warp threads flanking each bird's tail were left uncovered by the wefts during weaving, then individually wrapped with the white and dark purple threads that served to outline the figure as a whole. The resultant three-dimensional effect blurs the usually separate categories of slit and outline, a typically Andean innovation. The wrapping is also reminiscent of the Chancay figural sculptures whose limbs, including fingers and toes, are covered in the same way (cat. nos. 39, 42, 41, color pls. 55a–c). Wrapping of various elements has a long history in the ancient Andean textile tradition, beginning with the very early Chavín style (see Conklin 1971). Here the "wrapped slits" create double shadows, which add visual interest to a repetitive motif.

   Other design features that contribute visual dynamism are the wide range of colors —golds, red, white, light and dark purple, blue, and dark green— as well as their somewhat irregular patterning. The diagonals of red birds are alternated with those of purple, green, and blue, in that order. Exceptions occur in the lower right corner: a darker gold is substituted for half of the purple diagonal, and the single corner bird is gold instead of blue. Such color substitutions, found in many Andean styles and periods, are almost always intentional rather than the result of running out of the "correct" color of thread (Stone 1987, vol.1:160–163). Here, there might well have been a scarcity of the rarer purple and blue thread; however, since weaving usually begins at the bottom of the piece, these substitutions most likely occurred at the start rather than the end of the process. Artistic choice and technical innovation consistently remain the dominant forces in the Andean fiber arts.

Plate 49
Openwork Headcloth with Feline-Snake Motifs
Cat. no. 286

Late Intermediate Period, Chancay, Central Coast
A.D. 1000–1476
81.3 x 114.3 cm (approx.)
Embroidered square mesh openwork
cotton, ∧
Gift of Mrs. Samuel Cabot
60.1134

Exhibitions: 2500 Years; Connections: Brice Marden.
Publications: Fairbrother 1991: [7].
Related textiles: MFA 60.1135 (cat. no. 287); Amano R.015 (Tsunoyama, 1977:142, pl. 156); Amano R.0160 (Tsunoyama, 1977:144, pl. 161); Amano R.0127 (Tsunoyama, 1977:145, pl. 162); Amano R.1591 (Tsunoyama, 1977:146, pl. 164); Amano R.2787 (Tsunoyama, 1977:150, pl. 170); Carlos Museum 1989.8.163; Rietberg RPB 1425a (Haberland 1971:339, cat. no. 163); Lavalle and Gonzalez 1988:278, 280, 281.

Discussion: p. 46.

Coastal South American culture was and still is based on fishing from the rich Humboldt Current and from the rivers that flow down from the Andes, and thus its textile tradition developed out of net-making needs and practices. Using the available wild —and later domesticated— cotton, coastal weavers emphasized textural effects in their textiles by varying density and movement of threads. (In general, this is in contrast to the highland textile tradition of patterning through color effects in solid, "textureless" weft- and warp-patterned cloth; see, for example, cat. no. 316, color pl. 24, and cat. no. 218, color pl. 34.) Monochrome cotton openwork, as seen in this headcloth, represents one of several very elaborate fiber-working developments to come out of the coastal environmental and cultural context (see O'Neale and Clark 1948).

   The shadowy pattern seen in this very delicate piece was created by setting up an open grid of warps and wefts, then embroidering in a crisscross fashion to fill in certain squares more than others. Extra groups of threads fill in more heavily the eyes (large X-shapes) and teeth (series of verticals) of a very abstracted feline-snake motif. Right side up, the diamond-shaped areas represent the feline heads, with two pointed ears, eyes, and mouth. Upside down the ears can be read as a snake's open mouth. The two versions interlock, which makes the pattern, admittedly already difficult to see, even trickier to maintain perceptually because of the "contour rivalry" between the various orientations of the motif (see cat. no. 240, color pl. 53).

   In fact, one of the most interesting features of this headcloth is that when it was worn the pattern would have collapsed with the very elastic cloth to become virtually invisible. Only when it was being woven could the feline-snake motifs even be discerned (and they are only visible now that the piece is mounted stretched out). This represents another example of the concept of essence over appearance (see cat. no. 288, color pl. 62); it was more important that the textile should have the pattern than that the pattern be displayed. Human perception is not necessarily privileged in Andean artistic traditions (for example, the giant Nasca

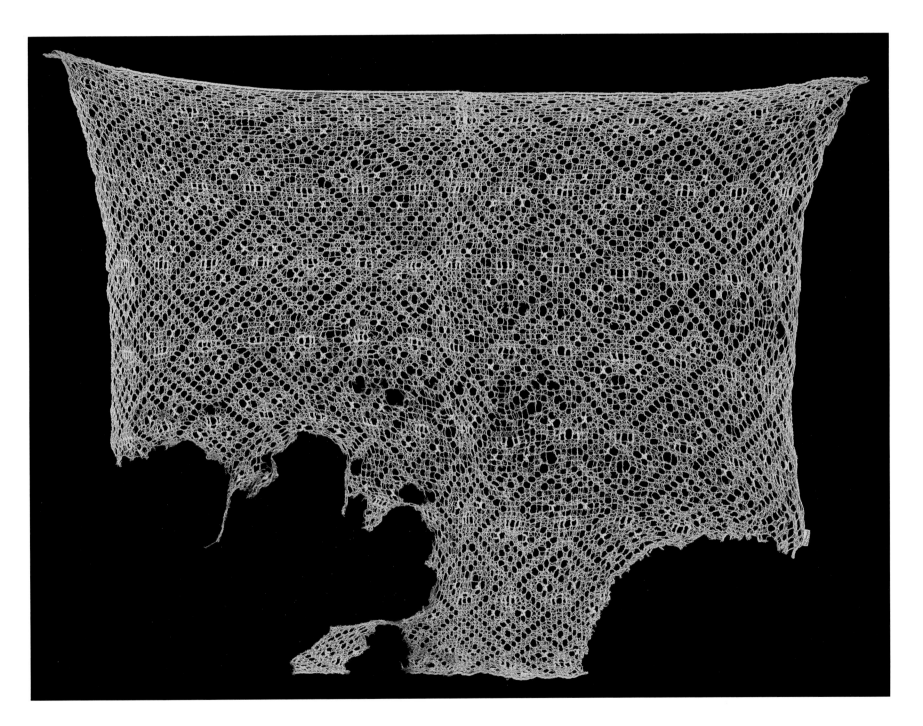

Lines drawn in the plains were too large to be visible to their makers; their meaning concerned the deities and the earth itself, requiring no validation by a human audience). In Andean textiles, levels of meaning are encoded in the materials, creative effort, pattern, and the act of wearing, as well as in the visible communication of subject matter.

Plate 50
Loincloth End Panel with Fish-eating Birds
Cat. no. 308

Late Intermediate Period, Chancay, Central Coast
A.D. 1000–1476
61 x 66 cm
Plain weave, slit tapestry with some underfloated wefts, looped fringe
    plain weave
          warp: cotton, \, 11/cm
          weft: cotton, /, 11/cm
    tapestry
          warp: cotton, ∧, 10/cm
          weft: camelid fiber, cotton (white), ∧, 56/cm
Gift of Landon T. Clay
1977.130

Exhibitions: 2500 Years.
Related textiles: Amano R2310 (Tsunoyama 1977:51, color pl. 41).

Discussion: pp. 22, 23, 43, 44, 46.

Typically Chancay in technique, design, and iconography, this beautiful end of a loincloth features sea birds holding fish in their beaks. Originally the creamy, natural cotton plain-weave portion visible above the tapestry section would have extended for a meter or more (several feet) to serve as the wrapping part of the loincloth. The very finely woven, decorative slit tapestry end, containing 56 wefts per centimeter (over 140 wefts per inch), would have hung down to the wearer's knees. Such a long, thick weft-loop fringe is common to Chancay garments.

The design in which a sequence of stripes and fretlike patterns flanks a central area of repeated motifs, particularly featuring birds, is perhaps the most characteristic arrangement in this style (Margaret Young-Sánchez, personal communication, 1991). Beaked birds appear not only in the wide band but also in a more abstracted form, heads upward, in both flanking bands. As in other textile depictions of avians in the Late Intermediate Period, the feathers are carefully delineated, albeit in an abstract fashion. Four tail feathers and one wing feather of the large birds are shown as bicolor ovals with a white line down the middle. Related woven textiles imitating featherwork also show abstract individual feathers in the same way (see cat no. 62, color pl. 37; cat. no. 302; Lavalle and Lang 1980:165–167; Kajitani 1982:74–75, pl. 105; Tsunoyama 1977:102, color pl. 109).

The extraordinary colors achieved and preserved in this piece should also be noted. Glowing golds offset brilliant scarlet and the softer shades of pink and maroon, while, most unusually, light and dark purple are well-preserved tones as well. This composition gives us a true sense of the original color scheme favored by the ancient Andean peoples: a high-contrast juxtaposition of solid, jewel-like colors. The sophistication with which strong colors are harmonized and the fine details (such as the separate claws delineated in each bird's foot) demonstrate why Chancay weavers are renowned for their high technical and aesthetic achievement.

Plate 51 (overleaf)
Painted and Resist Hanging with Fish Motifs
Cat. no. 300

Late Intermediate Period, Chancay (?), Central or North-Central Coast
A.D. 1000–1476
142 x 239 cm
Plain-weave panels sewn together, tie-dyed and painted
          warp: cotton, \, 8–14/cm
          weft: cotton, \, 8–14/cm
Textile Income Purchase Fund
1970.30

Related textiles: Museo Nacional (Lavalle and Lang 1980:154).

Discussion: pp. 21, 46.

This impressive hanging features a grid containing lively large-scale fish enclosing, emanating, and surrounded by smaller fish. In all probability it was even larger originally, since the addition of at least a fourth panel along the top would complete the squares in the uppermost register. Were the piece unmounted, its color scheme would appear considerably lighter and the cloth sheerer in texture (it is now seen against black, which darkens the tones and visually fills in the spaces between threads). The threads used to create this extraordinarily lightweight fabric are single ply (one thread instead of two twisted together) and very thin in diameter, an unusual characteristic it shares with cat. no. 289 (color pl. 17). Although the latter was created in a discontinuous structural technique, both plain-weave textiles were made painstakingly in order to achieve a difficult goal: the combination of a strong design with a gauzy cloth. The creative process consisted of weaving and assembling the panels of ground cloth, which then were painted with the black lines and then finally tie-dyed (by tying off the white fabric in small circles and immersing the cloth in a reddish brown dye). (The same combination of steps, albeit in a different sequence, was employed to paint Chavín-style textiles from the South Coast as early as 1000 B.C.; see Cordy-Collins 1979; Stone 1983).

Painting is known as a relatively straightforward and less time-consuming technique and one that allows greater design freedom than many woven techniques. Nevertheless, here the more complicated combination of painting and a resist technique presented the artists with a profound challenge. The use of such a sheer cloth created problems of distortion; the ground cloth could have been pulled out of alignment very easily. Yet the design features a grid of evenly spaced straight lines and very similar repetitions of the motifs, showing that preplanning and execution were of the highest order. Thus, the relative advantages of painting, such as rapidity of production and freedom of design, were not exploited to a great degree. In this sense, the traditional Andean attitudes of labor intensity and the transcendence of technical conditions can be found even in nonstructural compositions.

Plate 52 (preceding page)
Double-Cloth Mantle Fragment with Birds and Fish
Cat. no. 161

Late Intermediate Period, Chancay, Central Coast
A.D. 1000–1476
133 x 181.5 cm
Plain-weave double cloth, plain weave, sewn with whip stitch
       double cloth
              warp: cotton, ∧, 11–14/cm
              weft: cotton, ∧, 19/cm
      plain weave
              warp: cotton, ∧, 10–15/cm
              weft: cotton, ∧, 10–15/cm
Gift of Edward Jackson Holmes
30.238

Exhibitions: 25 Centuries; 2500 Years.
Publications: MFA 1961: no. 303 (illus.); Means 1932:63, specimen 46, fig. 68.
Related textiles: MFA 21.2569 (cat. no. 97); MFA 30.236 (cat. no. 159); MFA 30.237
(cat. no. 160); MFA 35.1126 (cat. no. 210, color pl. 57); MFA 42.444a,b (cat. no. 222);
MFA 52.482 (cat. no. 275, color pl. 47); "Museo de Luján" (Taullard 1949: fig. 150);
Museo Nacional (Lavalle and Lang 1980:154).

Discussion: pp. 17, 23, 46, 49.

Extremely large textiles such as this can be created by sewing together
several separate strips, a practice characteristic of the Late Intermediate
Period in particular. Originally this textile may have been even larger: a
matching fragment (such as the one published in Taullard 1949) could
have been attached to either edge. Its size and shape indicate that it
probably functioned as a mantle.

     An additive creative process is especially conducive to the iden-
tification of individual artists' contributions to design. Indeed, two different weavers' hands can be inferred by comparing the two main brown
and white double-cloth strips. The top one of these, which displays more
areas of thread loss, repeated the nested bird-and-fish motif almost exactly each time, measuring out the alternating brown- and white-background blocks equally. The textile artist added tiny O shapes to the
white-background squares and introduced three unprecedented images,
frontal birds, in the right-most half-block. By contrast, the weaver responsible for the lower patterned strip varied the motif interpretation (for example, one white-background square has only two instead of four main
bird heads) and did not measure the blocks as consistently. Most obviously, there is one major mistake in this strip: three brown blocks appear
in a row instead of the proper brown-white alternation (see the lower
right edge). Further evidence of a different weaver's mentality is the
more predictable resolution of the right corner half-design block as a
two-headed bird and the back half of the fish, that is, as literally half of
the usual motif. Apparently the first weaver was both more technically
skilled and aesthetically innovative, while the second was somehat more
careless but conventional. Double cloth, particularly containing such a
complex motif embedding birds inside a fish inside a quadruple bird,

presents the weaver with great technical and design challenges (see cat.
no. 210, color pl. 57). Understanding the inherent difficulties of techniques such as double cloth increases our appreciation of the overall level of skill demonstrated by Andean textile artists.

Plate 53
Fringed Tunic with Interlocked Birds
Cat. no. 240

Plate 54
Painted Hanging with Birds and Geometric Motifs
Cat. no. 296

(see preceding page)
Late Intermediate Period, Chancay, Central Coast
A.D. 1000–1476
88 x 112 cm
Slit tapestry
     warp: cotton, ∧, ∨, /3\, 7/cm
     weft: camelid fiber, ∧, 26/cm
William Francis Warden Fund
47.1087

Exhibitions: 2500 Years.
Related textiles: Amano (Cahlander and Baizerman 1985: color pl. 1); Museo Nacional (Lavalle and Lang 1980:158, lower right; 159).

Discussion: pp. 23, 46.

The strikingly bold, graphic quality of this piece reveals the characteristic design sophistication of the Chancay weaver. Embedded in the stepped diamond-shaped central areas and wide horizontal borders are ingeniously interlocked birds in red, gold, and light tan, each outlined in dark brown. The abstract birds, constructed principally of diagonals, have long beaks, concentric circle eyes, triangular bodies and tails, and a single leg.

    The textile designer carefully planned these deceptively simple motifs so that the dark brown top outline of one bird also constitutes the bottom outline of the next bird. It is certainly a difficult task to design a figure whose upper and lower silhouettes fit together facing in different directions. The sharing of the dark brown outline by the adjacent motifs is known in perceptual theory as "contour rivalry" (see Arnheim 1974:223–227). Each of the two images —for instance, a red and a tan bird— simultaneously claims the outline as belonging to itself; hence the visual "rivalry" over a contour. Such a situation remains perceptually ambiguous and therefore exciting, since the viewer cannot separate the two distinct images but constantly wavers between them. Artists in many different times and places, working in various media, have exploited this effect; the Dutch graphic artist M. C. Escher (d. 1972) immediately comes to mind in this regard. Contour rivalry not only holds viewer interest and demonstrates design virtuosity, but it also can contain symbolic meaning. The Andes have a long aesthetic tradition of double readings; two or more very distinct images may be melded into one (see J. Rowe 1962a: figs. 7, 16, 29). At one level, this conflation of images may have conveyed the deeply held belief in the interconnectedness of nature.

Late Intermediate Period, Chancay, Central Coast
A.D. 1000–1476
82.5 x 54 cm
Plain weave with applied pigment
     plain weave
        warp: cotton, ∧, 5/cm
        weft: cotton, ∧, 14/cm
     pigment: iron
Gift of Landon T. Clay
69.1078

Related textiles: MFA 30.249 (cat. no. 170); MFA 47.1085 (cat. no. 238); Private collection (Anton 1984:171, pl. 143). See also Bird 1973:15.

Discussion: p. 46.

Like cat. no. 248 (color pl. 65), this fragment was decorated with iron oxide stains (rather than dyes, which penetrate the cloth). Even the remarkably bright yellow and orange colors were generated from various stages of iron oxidation (Smith 1986). However, like modern paintings, such as those of Helen Frankenthaler, these textiles are still generally referred to as "painted." Here, allied with the Western painting tradition, the plain-weave ground cloth serves merely as the base for applied decoration rather than as a work of art in its own right. Because of the greater dominance of structural textiles in the Andean fiber tradition, relatively fewer painted examples exist (although they may simply be under-represented in museum collections).

    The scarcity and lower popularity of painted compositions can be traced to the fact that it is possible to produce a painted textile considerably more rapidly than a complex woven piece. Thus, paintings may have been reserved for lower-status individuals; however, the more elaborate and multicolored examples, such as this fragment and cat. no. 300 (color pl. 51), were not as simple to make as a dichotomy between "difficult" structural and "easy" painted textiles implies. The predominantly diagonal design is not anchored to the grid of the cloth's threads at all, which poses a challenge for the artist to paint straight parallel lines at a consistent angle. Minor distortions of lines can be seen here, yet they are not obvious. The white ground cloth was woven relatively coarsely; however, since little of it is left unpainted, a great deal of time still went into the cloth's decoration. Although admittedly less time-consuming, painting is roughly analogous to embroidery, the other major superstructural technique that in the Andes covered the majority of the ground cloth (e.g., see cat. no. 303, color pl. 4a,b). These two techniques also share a natural tendency to explore curvilinear designs (compare the wave patterns here with the undulations in a Paracas piece such as cat. no. 68, color pl. 12). Thus, under no circumstances could a textile such as this be considered as everyday. Andean textile artists explored all possible decorative techniques in their long and intimate relationship with the fiber arts.

Figural Sculptures and Tapestry Face
Cat. nos. 39, 42, 41

Late Intermediate Period, Chancay and Rimac Cultures, Central Coast
A.D. 1000–1476
Chancay:
78.103 (cat. no. 39): 36 x 19 cm
>   Slit tapestry (face), plain weave (dress), wrapping over reeds
>   (limbs)
>>   tapestry
>>>   warp: cotton, ∧, 6/cm
>>>   weft: camelid fiber, cotton (white and lower face
>>>   tan), ∧, 32/cm
>>   plain weave
>>>   warp: cotton, ∧, 23/cm
>>>   weft: cotton, ∧, 23/cm
>>   wrapping: camelid fiber, ∧
78.106 (cat. no. 42): 40 (including hair) x 12.7 cm
>   Slit tapestry, looping (nose), attached fringe (hair)
>>   tapestry
>>>   warp: cotton, ∧, 9/cm
>>>   weft: camelid fiber (and cotton for white), ∧,
>>>   32/cm
>>   looping: camelid fiber, ∧
>>   fringe: hair (probably human), ∧
Rimac:
78.105 (cat. no. 41): 36 (including hair) x 11 cm
>   Slit tapestry (face), braid (belt), wrapping over reeds (limbs)
>>   tapestry
>>>   warp: cotton, ∧, 8/cm
>>>   weft: camelid fiber, cotton (white), ∧, 26/cm
>>   braid: camelid fiber, ∧; cotton (white), /
>>   wrapping: camelid fiber, ∧
Gifts of Edward W. Hooper
78.103, 105, 106

Exhibitions: 78.105: 25 Centuries; 78.103, 78.105, 78.106: 2500 Years.
Publications: 78.105: MFA 1961: no. 299.
Related textiles: 78.103, 78.106: MFA 78.104 (cat. no. 40); Amano R.4004 (Tsunoyama 1977:199, fig. 232); Amano R.4014; Amano R.4015 (Tsunoyama 1977:24, color pl. 9); Amano R.4017; Amano R.4025 (Kajitani 1982:72, pl. 100 right); Amano R.4028, R.4047. 78.105: American Museum of Natural History 41.2/5630 (Skinner 1975:75).

Discussion: pp. 17, 20, 44, 46.

Figural sculptures in fiber have been referred to universally as "muñecas" (Spanish for "dolls"), a misleading designation because there is no evidence that they were playthings. Rather, they were highly symbolic; some of them appear in elaborate ritual scenes placed in burials (see related textiles, above). These miniaturized vignettes, whose subjects include weaving, drinking, marriage ceremonies, and curing, are made up of many characters and even display architectural settings. Bent reeds form their underlying structures, which are covered in various ways by

thread: wrapping, braiding, looping, and weaving, among others. Enormous care has been taken to differentiate and individually wrap the fingers and toes. These tiny sculptures certainly represent one of the most innovative, freely three-dimensional ways of thinking and working in fiber known.

These three examples illustrate several different styles and sizes of such intriguing figures. Cat. no. 39 (facing page) represents the typical Chancay-style female, with stepped facial decoration and a simple dress made with a horizontal neck slit. Plain cotton shifts of this kind probably were the everyday dress of the Chancay woman, although they are poorly represented in museum collections, perhaps owing to their unspectacular appearance (Margaret Young-Sánchez, personal communication, 1991). The miniature garments woven for figural sculptures are allied with the tiny, correct versions of full-size wear also offered in tombs (see cat. no. 33, color pl. 56). Cat. no. 42 (page 158, left) represents the face, also female, of a larger figure of similar type. Typically, two such faces were woven simultaneously on the same warp threads of a miniature backstrap loom (Bird et al. 1981:123). The top fringe representing the hair is actually spun and plied hair, probably human; this certainly proves that verisimilitude was an artistic and symbolic priority. Cat. no. 41 (page 158, right) represents a different, more unusual style, probably from the Rimac Valley. Details of dress, such as the four-color braided belt, again show the faithful rendition of actual textiles on a minute scale. The close identification of fiber and the person in the ancient Andes is most keenly felt in these detailed sculptures.

Plate 56
Miniature Tunic with Bird Motifs
Cat. no. 33

Late Intermediate Period, Rimac Culture (?), Central Coast
A.D. 1000–1476
15 x 12 cm
Plain weave with supplementary weft patterning
  plain weave
    warp: cotton ∧, 10/cm
    weft: cotton ∧, 10/cm
  supplementary wefts: camelid fiber, pairs of /, and cotton (white,
  ∧, and blue, pairs of /)
Gift of Edward W. Hooper
78.97

Exhibitions: 2500 Years.
Related textiles: MFA 24.325 (cat. no. 149). See also Bruce 1986a:189–190; 199, fig. 5;
201, fig. 8.

Discussion: pp. 16, 18, 46.

Most miniature garments such as this, rather than being clothing for tiny
figures (see cat nos. 39, 42, 41, color pls. 55a–c), as one might expect,
were apparently made expressly as burial offerings. Well over a hundred
miniature textiles of the Late Intermediate Period have been found at the
North Coast site of Pacatnamú, including tiny tunics, ponchos, loincloths, and crowns (Bruce 1986a). These miniatures were modeled directly after full-size garments, although they are necessarily simpler in many
ways. Idiosyncratic details, such as the series of multiple wefts seen as
horizontal ridges just under the neck slit, are also characteristic of full-
size tunics (Susan Bruce, personal communication, 1991).
      Thus, diminutive offering versions of garments seem to have act-
ed as substitutes for the more time-consuming and materially "expen-
sive" full-size ones (Bruce 1986a:192). As stand-ins, these are assumed to
have been made for persons of intermediate rather than high social status. Elite objects are better preserved archaeologically and more frequently collected than middle- or lower-status textiles, and it is therefore
all the more unusual and fascinating to glimpse how fancy textiles were
adapted for the pre-Columbian commoner. Here, for example, camelid
fiber is used only for the dark brown in the strip of patterning above the
hem, probably because it was a rare material on the coast and reserved
for the higher-status items. Although size, quality, and opulence of materials may have been scaled down for the everyday burial, the close identification of the individual with cloth —through a copy correct in all its
features— remains a constant feature of Andean textile primacy (see
pp. 17–18).

Plate 57
Double-Cloth Fragment with Felines and Birds
Cat. no. 210

Plate 58 (overleaf)
Fish-Shaped Tapestry Appliqué
Cat. no. 206

Late Intermediate Period, Rimac, Central Coast
A.D. 1000–1476
28 x 20.3 cm
Plain-weave double cloth
      warp: cotton \, 7/cm
      weft: cotton \, 7/cm
Samuel Putnam Avery Fund
35.1126

Exhibitions: 2500 Years.
Related textiles: MFA 52.482 (cat. no. 275, color pl. 47); MFA 30.238 (cat. no. 161, color pl. 52); MFA 40.168 (cat. no. 215); MFA 40.169 (cat. no. 216); Textile Museum 1983.41.1 (A. Rowe 1984:56, fig. 31); Textile Museum 1983.41.2 (A. Rowe 1984:56, fig. 32).

Discussion: pp. 14, 17, 22, 46.

Double cloth exemplifies the creative Andean approach to fiber as labor intensive, multileveled, and eidetic (based on visual thinking). In a simple application of the double-cloth technique, two colors of warps (the vertical, load-bearing threads) are alternated (A–B–A–B) as they are stretched taut on the loom. One set (A) is pulled forward and woven as a separate textile with its own weft (the horizontal) threads, while the other set of warps (B) is pulled back and also woven independently. However, to create a pattern the A and B threads must change faces (B coming to the front and A to the back, or vice versa), to anchor the two layers together and create an identical design in reversed colors on the different faces. For instance, the other side of this fragment has light blue cats on dark blue squares. Because each tiny shape represents the exchange of a group of warps from one face to the other, it quickly becomes clear that a great deal of effort and three-dimensional visual thinking went into simultaneously weaving two patterned cloths as one. Andean weavers invented many such complex structural techniques to achieve color reversal on the two faces (see cat. no. 237, color pl. 2).

The very nature of the technique also points up the fundamental notion of complementarity, which pervades the aesthetic and social realms of pre-Hispanic South American culture (e.g., see cat. no. 218, color pl. 34). Two layers of cloth, exchange of threads, and color reversals are all aspects of the principle of complementarity, or the balanced interchange of dual elements. Andean fiber arts themselves abound with other applications of this concept, and much of indigenous social organization itself was also based on this principle. Interdependent and reciprocal relationships, in thread as in people, literally created the fabric of ancient Andean life.

Late Intermediate Period, Rimac, Central Coast
A.D. 1000–1476
17.7 x 49 cm
Slit tapestry
      warp: cotton, /\, 12/cm
      weft: cotton, /, \, 52/cm
Harriet Otis Cruft Fund
31.710

Exhibitions: 25 Centuries; 2500 years; From Fiber to Fine Art.
Publications: Jablonski 1976:71; MFA 1961, no. 307; Salmon 1980:59, no. 59.
Related textiles: Cleveland Museum of Art 33.392; Museo Nacional (Lavalle and Lang 1980:150, 162); Textile Museum 91.193 (Kelemen 1943, pl. 179a); Taullard 1949: pl. 144, 121, top; Lavalle and Gonzalez 1988:269.

Discussion: pp. 22, 48.

This fish-shaped tapestry, completely finished on all twenty-five edges, represents a stellar example of the time-honored Andean practice of weaving irregular shapes. Though more extreme, it relates technically to other discontinuous techniques that utilize temporary or scaffold threads (see cat. no. 289, color pl. 17; cat. no. 290, color pl. 44; cat. no. 295, color pl. 14a,b; cat. no. 319, color pl. 21a,b). However, here it was the warp threads (running the long direction, sideways in the photograph) that were interlocked to scaffolds in order to finish out the rectangle so that it could be kept under even tension on the loom. The cut threads visible along various edges are the remains either of these scaffolds or of the sewing threads used to attach the piece as an appliqué, probably to a hanging (Margaret Young-Sánchez, personal communication, 1991).

The Rimac style remains the least known, and in some ways the most distinctive, of the various Late Intermediate Period regional coastal styles. This all-cotton Rimac-style fish tapestry displays rare and virtuoso dyeing of the various browns, gold, and blue of its palette. (Cotton has a cellulose structure that makes it relatively impermeable to pigmentation, as opposed to camelid fiber, which, as a hair, is a protein and receptive to coloration.) The subject matter of a solitary fish is also atypical, since fish are usually depicted only as minor elements in Late Intermediate Period compositions, particularly as prey for birds (see cat. no. 308, color pl. 50). In addition, the "X-ray" view, making visible the backbone and the five baby fish inside the belly, is also unique to the Rimac style (Margaret Young-Sánchez, personal communication, 1991). The open slits (left where weft colors change without interlocking) cleverly serve to describe the subject by separating the gills, teeth, and vertebrae from each other just as they are in the fish itself. Thus, technique, as always in Andean traditions, is creatively chosen for and applied toward aesthetic ends. The overarching artistic goal demonstrated here is to communicate the essence of a fish as fertility symbol rather than its external appearance.

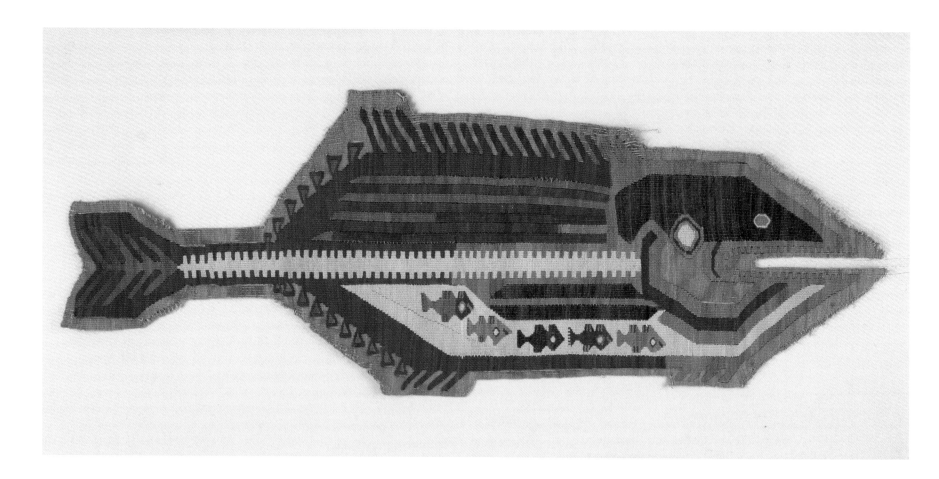

Plate 59
Garment Fragment with Double-Headed Birds
Cat. no. 268

(see preceding page)
Late Intermediate Period, Ica, South or Central Coast
A.D. 1000–1476
48.5 x 58 cm
Interlocked tapestry with underfloated wefts
 warp: cotton, pairs of /\, 11 pairs/cm
 weft: camelid fiber, /\, 36/cm
Elizabeth Day McCormick Collection
51.2455

Exhibitions: 25 Centuries; 2500 Years.
Publications: MFA 1961, no. 279; A. Rowe 1979:199, fig. 9.
Related textiles: MFA 51.2454 (cat. no. 267); Textile Museum 1966.7.37a (A. Rowe, 1979, fig 7, p. 195); "Garaño Collection" (Taullard 1949: fig. 136); Private collection, New York (A. Rowe 1979:199, fig 10); Private collection, New York (A. Rowe 1979:210, fig 20). See others in A. Rowe 1979.

Discussion: pp. 22, 48.

Twenty related examples of an undetermined garment type worked in this distinctive South Coast Ica style have been located by Ann Rowe (1979). Most are fragments of what were originally square garments consisting of tapestry areas, such as this fragment, on either side of a plain-weave cloth decorated with supplemental weft designs (ibid.:210, fig. 20). Although the plain-weave section is lost here, a tiny bit of cotton thread remaining on the top edge indicates it was probably light brown in color. A closely allied example retains the center portion decorated in a design of triangular fish worked in black thread; originally the complete version of this piece might have appeared similar. This fragment represents one of the corners, with the characteristic cross-knit, loop-stitch border covering two selvages. Although Rowe does not speculate on the use of the garment, modern Andean women wear a square textile known as a *llicla* folded into a triangle and pinned over their shoulders (see also cat. no. 48, color pl. 69a,b; Medlin 1986).

 Among the related Ica textiles, this piece displays a number of unique design innovations. In its application of the typical Ica-style color scheme (a clear red ground, darkly outlined motifs in bright yellow, as well as blue, green, violet, pink, and brown), it alone employs the red ground also as a motif color. For example, in the lower right-most motif the dark outlines surround a yellow linear contour, thus capturing the red ground inside the body of the double-headed bird motif. Perceptually this makes the background play roles as both "figure" and "ground." Such ambiguity between figure and ground is a hallmark of many Andean, particularly Late Intermediate Period, textile compositions (e.g., cat. no. 240, color pl. 53). To add further visual convolutions, there are at least two readings of the motif: as two birds facing each other (with upraised, diagonal open beaks and stepped curls for wings) and as a frontal face (with the birds' eyes for the eyes, the space between the birds as the nose, and the diamond in the joint bird body as the mouth). Rowe comments: "the elaboration of this visual pun also seems to be unique to this textile" (1979:198). She places this piece in the later part of her seriation of garment types, noting increased design variability as time went on. The innovations here and in later examples show the creative exploration of visual possibilities within a set design so often pursued by Andean fiber artists.

307

308

307.
Loincloth End
Late Intermediate Period, Central Coast
A.D. 1000–1476
126 x 70 cm (detail shown)
Plain weave; slit tapestry
Gift of Landon T. Clay
1977.129

308.
Loincloth End Panel with Fish-eating Birds
Late Intermediate Period, Chancay, Central Coast
A.D. 1000–1476
61 x 66 cm
Plain weave, slit tapestry with some underfloated wefts,
looped fringe
Gift of Landon T. Clay
1977.130
(Color pl. 50)

309.
Fragment of Tunic with Stepped-Block Yoke
Late Horizon–Early Colonial, Inca-related Culture
About A.D. 1500–1550
76.2 x 60.9 cm
Interlocked tapestry
Gift of Landon T. Clay
1977.131
(Color pl. 68)

310A, B.
A. Panel
Late Intermediate Period, Chancay, Central Coast
A.D. 1000–1476
47 x 16 cm
Slit tapestry
Gift of Landon T. Clay
1977.132
B. Panel
Late Intermediate Period, Chancay, Central Coast
A.D. 1000–1476
46.7 x 14 cm
Slit tapestry
Gift of Landon T. Clay
1977.133

311.
Fragments of Embroidered Figures
Early Intermediate Period, Phase 2, Paracas, South
Coast
A.D. 100–200
a (left): 12.3 x 6.5 cm
b (left center): 14.6 x 6.6 cm
c (right center): 14 x 6.8 cm
d (right): 13 x 6.6 cm
Plain weave with stem-stitch embroidery
Gift of Landon T. Clay
1977.134a–d

309

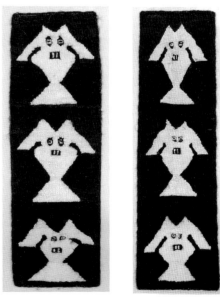

310A   310B

311

312

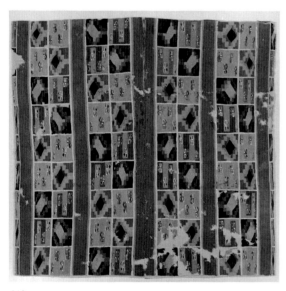

313

314

312.

Tapestry Tunic with Face, Stepped Fret, and Double-Headed Animals

Middle Horizon, Wari, probably South Coast
A.D. 500–800
101 x 103.8 cm
Interlocked tapestry
Charles Potter Kling Fund
1978.46
(Color pl. 23a,b; fig. III.11a,b)

313.

Tapestry Tunic with Stepped-Diamond and Double-Headed Animal Motifs

Middle Horizon, Wari, probably South Coast
A.D. 500–800
100 x 103.5 cm
Interlocked tapestry with eccentric wefts
Charles Potter Kling Fund
1978.124
(Color pl. 22a,b; fig. III.10a,b)

314.

Large Carpet

Colonial Period
17th–18th century
648 x 389 cm
Interlocked tapestry
Charles Potter Kling Fund
1978.182
(Fig. V.1)

315.

Openwork Mantle Fragment with "Moon Animal" Motifs

Late Intermediate Period, Chimu, North Coast
A.D. 1000–1476
209 x 133 cm
Brocaded plain weave with spaced warps and wefts, supplemental threads wrapped around woven squares; weft-faced plain weave with supplemental weft patterning (lower border); tapestry (side borders); layered fringe
Arthur Tracy Cabot Fund
1980.211
(Color pl. 39; fig. IV.2)

316A, B.

Tunic Fragments with Human Skulls

Middle Horizon, Wari, probably South Coast
A.D. 500–800
A. 1980.448 (above): 84 x 106 cm
B. 1980.660 (below): 89 x 107 cm
Interlocked tapestry
1980.448: Charles Potter Kling Fund
1980.660: Gift of Vivian Merrin
(Color pl. 24)

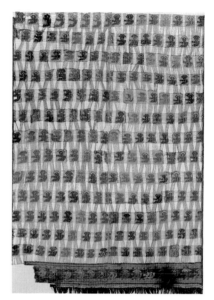

315

316A,B

317

318

317.
Mantle with Crescent Headdress Figures
Late Horizon, Chimu-Inca, North Coast (?)
A.D. 1476–1534
175.9 x 159.4 cm
Slit tapestry; fringe; tassels
Charles Potter Kling Fund
1981.284
(Color pl. 60a,b)

318.
Narrow Band
Probably Middle Horizon, South Coast, Nasca area
A.D. 500–800
a (right): 432 x 1 cm
b (left): 126 x 1 cm
Slit tapestry
Gift of Edward Merrin
1981.321a,b

319.
Sleeveless Tunic (?) with Tie-dyed Stepped Triangles
Middle Horizon, Wari-related, Nasca area, South Coast
A.D. 500–800
114 x 187 cm
Tie-dyed plain-weave discontinuous warp and weft
pieces reassembled with warps dovetailed and weft slits
sewn
Textile Fund and Helen and Alice Colburn Fund
1983.252
(Color pl. 21a,b)

320.
Fragment of a Tunic
Late Intermediate Period, probably North-Central Coast
A.D. 1000–1476
25 x 43 cm
Slit tapestry
Bequest of Betty Bartlett McAndrew
1986.503

321.
Fragment
Late Intermediate Period, probably North-Central Coast
A.D. 1000–1476
Slit tapestry
52 x 39 cm
Bequest of Betty Bartlett McAndrew
1986.504

319

320

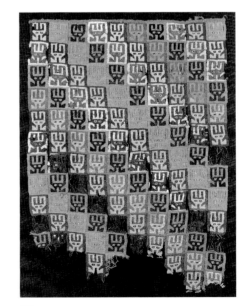

321

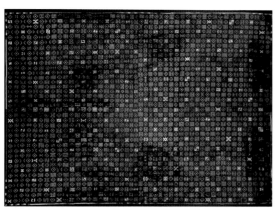

322

323

322.
Tapestry Mantle or Shroud with Tocapu Motifs
Early Colonial, Neo-Inca Culture
About A.D. 1550
119 x 171 cm
Interlocked tapestry; overstitched edging
Charles Potter Kling Fund
1988.325
(Color pl. 67a,b; figs. V.10–V.12, cover)

323.
Cover
Colonial Period
Late 17th century or later
186.7 x 153.6 cm
Interlocked tapestry
Gift of Landon T. Clay
1988.1085

324.
Cover with Guitar Players
Colonial Period
17th century or later
219 x 163.5 cm
Interlocked tapestry with eccentric wefts
Gift of Landon T. Clay
1990.624
(Color pl. 75)

324

GLOSSARY

For more extensive definitions of the following terms, the reader is referred to Emery, *The Primary Structures of Fabrics: An Illustrated Classification* (1966). Specific references are given in parentheses.

Appliqué. A small unit of cloth woven specifically to be sewn to a larger ground cloth; the technique of affixing small units to larger cloths.

Backstrap loom. The traditional loom of the Andes and elsewhere, consisting of a series of loom bars. The top bar is attached by a cord to a fixed object, such as a tree, and the bottom bar is attached to a belt that encircles the weaver, whose weight and backwards pressure against the loom serve to hold the warp threads taut.

Balanced plain weave. Plain weave in which both elements (warp and weft) have an equal count and thus are equally visible (Emery 1966:76).

Basting. A large, temporary, running stitch used to hold together two webs before final sewing or, here, to mark ground cloth for proper placement of embroidered figures.

Bichrome thread. A two-ply thread in which component single-ply threads are of different colors (typically, natural white and light brown).

Bobbin. A weaving tool used to pass wefts through a shed consisting of a thin, carved wooden stick wound with finished thread (Emery 1966:172).

Brocade. A general term for any woven technique in which supplementary decorative threads float over ground cloth; it may be difficult to distinguish from embroidery; see **Supplementary** (Emery 1966:171–173).

Camelid fiber. The silky hair of the native highland New World camelids, most probably of the alpaca, but possibly of the llama (pronounced y*ama*), guanaco (pronounced *gwah náh koh*), or vicuña (pronounced *vee kóon yah*). The term is employed here to distinguish it from sheep's wool used in some Colonial textiles.

Carding. The combing of raw fibers (cotton, camelid fiber) into parallelism to facilitate thread spinning.

Cochineal. The permanent, natural red dye made from the bodily fluid of the cochineal beetle, a parasite on the prickly pear cactus (*nopal*).

Complementary. A relationship between threads in weaving, either warps or wefts, that move in the same direction and are coequal; when one goes to one face, another goes to the other, and vice versa; see also **Complementary warp weave** (Emery 1966:150–154).

Complementary warp weave. Complementary warp usually involves two colors of warps that substitute for each other on the two faces, playing reciprocal and equivalent roles. For the use of three and four colors, see entry for cat. no. 218, color pl. 34 (Emery 1966:150–154).

Cotton. In the Andean region *gossypium barbadense,* a fiber growing wild and as a domesticate in the lower coastal altitudes; it was the basis for coastal fiber-art traditions and also was used extensively for the warp threads in highland-based textiles.

Cross-knit loop stitch. An embroidery and edge-finishing stitch that resembles a braid on the surface (Emery 1966:243).

Darning. A needle-woven mending technique used to fill in areas of warp and weft loss; may resemble tapestry (see entry for cat. 213, color pl. 25) (Emery 1966:233–234, 244).

Discontinuous warp and weft. A structural weaving technique unique to the Andes, usually plain weave, in which both elements are made up of interlocked threads so that color areas are solid although the fabric is gauzy (Emery 1966:79, 90).

Double cloth. A structural weaving technique, usually plain weave, in which alternate warps are pulled to the front and back faces to be woven with their own wefts as separate planes of cloth; warps trade faces to form a pattern (Emery 1966:156–158).

Double-faced. Front and back faces of a fabric that are identical in shape design, opposite in color assignment (Emery 1966:165).

Dovetail. A join in which both threads of the adjacent color areas turn back around a shared warp (Emery 1966:79–80).

Dye. A colorant that completely penetrates fibers; in the Andes these were natural dyes from plants and animals (such as indigo and cochineal).

Dyelot. A unit of fiber dyed in the same dyebath, having a unique color value and saturation in contrast to all other dyelots of the same hue. Slightly distinctive thread colors in a textile indicate that the weaver(s) took threads from more than one skein.

Eccentric. A thread movement that contrasts with the usual rectilinear relationship of elements, typically a weft bending around curves (Emery 1966:83).

Element. One set of threads, i.e., the weft as a whole and the warp as a whole. A single element is a single thread wound around to form a cloth; a double element is a cloth woven with warp and weft.

Embroidered square-mesh openwork. A form of openwork in which a mesh of warp and weft is set up. Threads are embroidered to fill in more or less completely the open squares in order to form a pattern (Emery 1966:216).

Embroidery. A superstructural technique in which threads are sewn onto a ground cloth; see **Figure-8 stitch; Running stitch; Stem stitch** (Emery 1966:229–249).

Featherwork. A textile-based technique in which the quills of feathers are bent down and affixed to a thread that in turn is sewn in a horizontal line to a ground cloth. A series of these overlapping lines creates a solid layer of feathers that can be patterned.

Fiber(s). The materials of textiles: in the traditional Andes these are cotton and camelid fiber (as well as sheep's wool, silk, and linen in Colonial and modern times).

Figure-8 stitch. An embroidery and joining stitch in which a continuous thread moves in a figure-8 pattern and forms two parallel ridges of closely packed stitches.

Floats. Any thread that passes over more than one of the other element (warps over wefts in warp patterning and vice versa) (Emery 1966:92).

Ground cloth. The base fabric, almost invariably woven in plain weave, for a superstructural technique (such as embroidery or painting).

Heading cords. Heavy threads at the top and bottom of a web that affix it to the loom bars and also serve as selvage reinforcement.

Heddle. A stick onto which loops of thread are wound, the loops entwining with warp threads to create a shed; for example, in plain weave the loops pick up every other warp.

Indigo. A natural blue dye from the *indigofera* plant that is extremely difficult to extract (see entry for cat. no. 214, color pl. 29).

Interlocked. A join in which threads of the adjacent color areas turn back after looping around each other between warps (Emery 1966:78–80).

Knotting. A single-element technique in which a series of knots form a fabric (Emery 1966:214–216).

Larkshead knot. A variant of a square knot (Frame 1990:29, note 13).

Lazy lines. Diagonal lines of noninterlocked wefts that indicate different work areas.

Loom product. Web; a unit of cloth with four selvages.

Looped fringe. Uncut wefts that are left longer than the side selvages to form a fringe.

Looped pile. Uncut pile; see **Pile** (Emery 1966:174).

Looping. A single-element technique in which a series of unknotted loops form a fabric (Emery 1966:31–33).

Mordant. Mineral treatment for fiber that aids in its absorption of dye and enriches the color (e.g., iron darkens).

Multiple warps. More than one warp thread used together as a unit.

Netting. A single-element mesh secured by knots (Emery 1966:46).

Oblique double twining. Two layers of a diagonal variant of twining worked simultaneously; see **Twining** (Emery 1966:64–65).

Oblique interlacing. Another term for braiding or plaiting (Emery 1966:60).

Openwork. A general term for techniques in which the elements are widely spaced. Textural rather than color differences create pattern.

Overcast stitch. A simple embroidery stitch that lays down a series of parallel stitches, typically over a selvage or seam (Emery 1966:233).

Paint. Pigment that does not penetrate fully the fibers of a ground cloth.

Paired warps. Two warp threads used together as a unit; particularly characteristic of Chimu weaving.

"Patchwork." Piecing of individual cloths as in quilting. The term is incorrectly applied to the scaffolded discontinuous warp and weft technique seen in cat. no. 319, color pl. 21a,b.

Pick. One passage of one element across the other (such as wefts across warps); also the tool used to lift certain (unheddled) threads to create a passage in a particularly complex pattern.

Pigment. Colorant of any kind. See **Dye; Paint;** and **Stain.**

Pile. Loops or cut ends of longer threads that project from the fabric surface and tend to obscure it (Emery 1966:148).

Plain weave. The most basic two-element weaving technique in which one element regularly crosses over and under the other (Emery 1966:76).

Plaiting. Braiding or oblique intertwining (Emery 1966:60).

Ply. To retwist single threads together, typically in the direction opposite to that in which the threads were spun; like the spin direction, the ply direction can be either S (counterclockwise) or Z (clockwise) (Emery 1966:13).

Resist. A cloth-dyeing technique in which some part of the cloth is covered (by a resin being painted on, as in batik, or by being tied off with a thread, as in tie-dye or plangi) so as to resist taking up the dye when the cloth is immersed in the dyebath; a "negative" technique, in relation to painting, which is a direct application or "positive" technique.

Running stitch. A simple line of over and under sewing or embroidery stitch, as in basting.

Scaffold threads. Temporary threads used to hold discontinuous areas of an element while they are being interlocked with others, as in discontinuous warp and weft; e.g., see cat. no. 289, color pl. 17 (Emery 1966:88, 90).

Selvage. The finished edge of the cloth, either at the weft ends or the warp ends.

Shed. "Temporary opening between two planes of warp threads selectively separated for passage of the weft" (Emery 1966:75).

Shed stick. A bar used to create a shed.

Single ply. Thread that is spun but not plied with another thread.

Skein. A wrapped ball of finished thread for storage or winding onto a bobbin.

Slit. A join in which threads of the adjacent color areas turn back without looping around each other between warps, creating a physical gap between adjacent color areas.

Spaced. When threads of one or both elements are held apart from one another to create spaces.

Spin. To twist fibers to create single-ply threads; the spin direction can be either S (counterclockwise) or Z (clockwise) (Emery 1966:9).

Spindle. A thin, carved, pointed stick that is used as a tool to spin thread; with its tip on a surface it can be turned to act as a weight and as a holder for the spun thread.

Spindle whorl. A small bead "strung" on a spindle to help hold the thread and act as a weight. In the traditional Andes a small bit of unspun cotton fiber wrapped around the shaft serves to wedge it on (Susan Bruce, personal communication, 1991).

Sprang. A general term for techniques worked from both ends of affixed threads toward the middle (Emery 1966:69).

Stain. A pigment that partially penetrates cloth fibers. Strictly speaking, this is what is commonly known as "painting" in Andean textiles.

Stem stitch. An embroidery stitch in which a forward stitch is followed by a backwards stitch half as long, then another forward stitch, etc., to create slightly overlapping diagonals; used to cover extensive areas of cloth in Paracas embroideries (Emery 1966:238–239).

Structural. A general type of technique in which the cloth and the patterning are built up simultaneously, as in tapestry or warp patterning; as opposed to superstructural techniques.

Superstructural. A general type of technique in which the cloth and the patterning are built up separately. The embellishment takes the form of embroidery, painting, or nonintegral (supplementary) threadwork and is added after the ground cloth has been woven; as opposed to structural techniques.

Supplementary. Any discontinuous patterning thread woven in while cloth is being built up but structurally nonintegral; characteristic of such techniques as brocade. Supplementary threadwork is sometimes indistinguishable from embroidery except that supplemental threads never cross from one weft passage to another since they are woven in with that passage (Emery 1966:140–148).

Tapestry. A weft-patterning variant of plain weave in which discontinuous patterning wefts are packed down, completely obscuring the warps; joins can be interlocked, slit, or dovetailed.

Thread count. The number of threads of each element in a given unit of measure (here centimeters); indicates whether the weave is balanced (warp and weft counts the same or very close), or warp- or weft-predominant (one count much higher than the other). Higher thread counts indicate thinner threads, more thread used, and imply great skill on the part of spinners and weavers. Andean thread counts are among the highest known.

Tie-dye. A type of resist technique in which portions of cloth are tied tightly with thread, most often in circles, so that when the entire cloth is immersed in the dyebath those areas resist, or fail to take up, the dye. It is considered a "negative" technique (designs are what remain after the rest is pigmented) in relation to a "positive" technique (direct application of pigment creates pattern) such as painting; see **Resist**.

Tiered tassel. "Tassel made up of heavy foundation cord tied around the center of each bunch of yarns that will form the tiers. These yarns are then folded down and the tops

wound with another fine yarn, usually of a matching color. The foundation cord knots itself in the intervals between tiers" (A. Rowe 1984:72).

Triple cloth. A weaving technique in which three planes of cloth, usually in plain weave, are woven simultaneously, the thread of different colors exchanging planes to create two to three different compositions; see **Double Cloth** (Emery 1966:158–159).

Twining. A nonloom technique in which two threads of one element spiral around the other element to secure it in place (Emery 1966:196–207).

Two-faced. Fabric in which the front and back faces are dissimilar in patterning, as opposed to double-faced, in which the two faces are structurally identical (Emery 1966:165).

Two-ply. Thread that is made up of two single-ply threads twisted together. It is the usual thread for all weaving purposes since it is stronger and more balanced (different spin and ply directions balance tensions to create a straight thread).

Underfloat. Any thread that passes under more than one of the other element. Not a patterning device but a practical, labor-saving one: threads of the same color trail from one small color area to the next so that their cut ends will not have to be woven back in each time (Emery 1966:122).

Vicuña. The smallest, wild camelid with the silkiest hair. The use of this camelid fiber was restricted to the Inca royalty.

Warp. The load-bearing vertical element strung onto the loom first, usually —but not always— the longer and stronger of the two elements; may carry patterning. See **Complementary warp weave; Warp patterning**.

Warp-faced. Cloth in which the warp threads predominate on the faces (versus balanced weave or weft-faced).

Warp patterning. A general category of techniques in which the warp threads carry the design (see **Complementary warp weave**); opposite of weft patterning, such as tapestry.

Web. Loom product; a unit of cloth with all four selvages.

Weft. The non-load-bearing horizontal element passed through the warps, usually —but not always— the shorter and less strong of the two elements; usually carries patterning. See **Tapestry**.

Weft-faced. Cloth in which the weft threads predominate on the faces (versus balanced weave or warp-faced).

Weft patterning. A general category of techniques in which the weft threads carry the design (see **Tapestry**); opposite of warp patterning, such as complementary warp weave.

Whip stitch. A diagonal sewing stitch used to join two webs (Emery 1966:245).

Wool. A general term for animal fiber; here used only to denote fibers that could be sheep's wool (Colonial Period only).

Wrapping. Winding of threads in a spiral; may be around another thread (see cat. no. 61, color pl. 48), or a braid (see cat. no. 187, color pl. 33), or a stick (see cat. no. 39, color pl. 55a).

BIBLIOGRAPHY

Adorno, Rolena
1982　*From Oral to Written Expression: Native Andean Chronicles of the Early Colonial Period.* Latin American Series, no. 4. Syracuse, N.Y.: Maxwell School of Citizenship and Public Affairs, Syracuse University.
1986　*Guaman Poma: Writing and Resistance in Colonial Peru.* Austin: University of Texas Press.

Adovasio, James, and Thomas F. Lynch
1973　"PreCeramic Textiles and Cordage from Guitarrero Cave, Peru." *American Antiquity* 38, no. 1, pp. 84–89.

Anton, Ferdinand
1984　*Altindianische Textilkunst aus Peru.* Munich: List.

Arnheim, Rudolf
1974　*Art and Visual Perception: A Psychology of the Creative Eye.* Rev. ed. Berkeley: University of California Press.

Bennett, Ian, ed.
1977　*Complete Illustrated Rugs and Carpets of the World.* New York: A & W Publishers.

Betanzos, Juan de
1987　*Suma y narración de los Incas.* Translated by María del Carmen Martín Rubio. Madrid: Ediciones Atlas. [Originally written in 1551.]

Bird, Junius B.
1963　"Pre-ceramic Art from Huaca Prieta, Chicama Valley." *Ñawpa Pacha* 1, pp. 29–34.
1964　"Shaped Tapestry Bags from the Nazca-Ica Area of Peru." *Textile Museum Journal* 1, no. 3, pp. 2–7.
1973　*Peruvian Paintings by Unknown Artists, 800 B.C. to 1700 A.D.* New York: Center for Inter-American Relations.

Bird, Junius B., and Louisa Bellinger
1954　*Paracas Fabrics and Nazca Needlework 3rd Century B.C.–3rd Century A.D.* Washington D.C.: National Publishing Co.

Bird, Junius B., Elizabeth P. Benson, and William J. Conklin
1981　*Museums of the Andes.* Great Museums of the World. New York: Newsweek.

Bonavia, Duccio
1985　*Mural Painting in Ancient Peru.* Translated by Patricia J. Lyon. Bloomington: Indiana University Press.

Browman, David L.
1974　"Pastoral Nomadism in the Andes." *Current Anthropology* 15, no. 2, pp. 188–196.

Bruce, Susan
1986a　"Textile Miniatures from Pacatnamu, Peru." In *The Junius B. Bird Conference on Andean Textiles,* 1984, edited by Anne Pollard Rowe, pp. 183–204. Washington, D.C.: Textile Museum.
1986b　"The Audiencia Room of the Huaca 1 Complex." In *The Pacatnamú Papers,* vol. 1, edited by Christopher B. Donnan and Guillermo A. Cook. Los Angeles: Museum of Cultural History, University of California.

Cahlander, Adele
1980　*Sling Braiding of the Andes.* Weaver's Journal Monograph IV. Boulder: Colorado Fiber Center.

Cahlander, Adele, and Suzanne Baizerman
1985　*Double-Woven Treasures from Old Peru.* St. Paul, Minn.: Dos Tejedoras.

Cammann, Schuyler
1964　"Chinese Influence in Colonial Peruvian Tapestries." *Textile Museum Journal* 1, no. 3, pp. 21–34.

Carcedo Muro, Paloma, and Izumi Shimada
1985　"Behind the Golden Mask: The Sicán Gold Artifacts from Batán Grande, Peru." In *The Art of Pre-Columbian Gold: The Jan Mitchell Collection,* pp. 60–75. New York: Metropolitan Museum of Art.

Carlisle, Richard
1990　"Amazon." In *The Illustrated Encyclopedia of Mankind,* vol. 1, pp. 56–60. Editor-in-chief, Richard Carlisle. New York: Marshall Cavendish.

Cavallo, Adolph S.
1960　"A Cap, a Shirt, and a Question Mark." *Bulletin of the Museum of Fine Arts, Boston* 58, no. 311, pp. 3–11.
1967　*Tapestries of Europe and of Colonial Peru in the Museum of Fine Arts, Boston.* 2 vols. Boston: Museum of Fine Arts.

Ciesla, William
1988　"Points about the Prickly Pear." *Américas* 40, no. 4, pp. 10–15.

Cobo, Bernabé
1979　*History of the Inca Empire.* Translated and edited by Roland B. Hamilton. Austin: University of Texas Press. [Translation of *Historia del Nuevo Mundo,* libs. 11 and 12, written in 1653.]
1990　*Inca Religion and Customs.* Translated and edited by Roland B. Hamilton. Austin: University of Texas Press. [Translation of *Historia del Nuevo Mundo,* libs. 13 and 14, written in 1653.]

Conklin, William J.
1971　"Chavín Textiles and the Origins of Peruvian Weaving." *Textile Museum Journal* 3, no. 2, pp. 13–19.
1986　"The Mythic Geometry of the Ancient Southern Sierra." In *The Junius B. Bird Conference on Andean Textiles,* 1984, edited by Ann Pollard Rowe, pp. 123–136. Washington D.C.: Textile Museum.

Conrad, Geoffrey W.
1982　"The Burial Platforms of Chan Chan: Some Social and Political Implications." In *Chan Chan: Andean Desert City,* edited by Michael E. Moseley and Kent C. Day. School of American Research Advanced Seminar Series. Albuquerque: University of New Mexico Press.

Cordy-Collins, Alana
1979　"Cotton and the Staff God: Analysis of an Ancient Chavín Textile." In *The Junius B. Bird Pre-Columbian Textile Conference,* 1973, edited by Ann Pollard Rowe, Elizabeth P. Benson, and Anne-Louise Schaffer, pp. 51–60. Washington D.C.: Textile Museum and Dumbarton Oaks, Trustees for Harvard University.

Crawford, M.D.C.
1916　"The Master Weavers of the Desert Empire." *Harper's Magazine* 133, no. 794, pp. 287–297.

Daggett, Richard E.
1991　"Paracas: Discovery and Controversy." In *Paracas Art and Architecture: Object and Culture in South Coastal Peru,* edited by Anne Paul, pp. 35–60. Iowa City: University of Iowa Press.

Demarest, Arthur A.
1981　*Viracocha: The Nature and Antiquity of the Andean High God.* Peabody Museum Monographs, no. 6. Cambridge: Peabody Museum of Archaeology and Ethnology, Harvard University

De Mesa, José, and Teresa Gisbert
1962　*Historia de la pintura cuzqueña.* Buenos Aires: Universidad de Buenos Aires, Facultad de Arquitectura y Urbanismo.

Diez de San Miguel, Garci
1964　*Visita hecha a la provincia de Chucuito por Garci Diez de San Miguel en el año 1567,* edited by Waldemar Espinoza Soriano. Lima: Ediciones de la Casa de la Cultura del Perú. [Originally written in 1567.]

Disselhoff, H.D.
1961　"Berliner Museum für Völkerkunde: Neuerwerbungen peruanischer Altertümer." *Baessler-Archiv,* n.F. 9, no. 2, pp. 199–216.

Dockstader, Frederick J.
1967   *Indian Art in South America.* Greenwich, Conn.: New York Graphic Society.

Donnan, Christopher B.
1978   *Moche Art of Peru: Pre-Columbian Symbolic Communication.* Los Angeles: Museum of Cultural History, University of California.
1984   "Ancient Murals from Chornancap, Peru." *Archaeology* 37, no. 3, pp. 32–37.
1986   "An Elaborate Textile Fragment from the Major Quadrangle." In *The Pacatnamú Papers,* vol. 1, edited by Christopher B. Donnan and Guillermo A. Cock. Los Angeles: Museum of Cultural History, University of California.

Dwyer, Jane P.
1973   *Paracas and Nasca Textiles, 500–200 B.C.* (Gallery Guide). Department of Textiles and Costumes, Museum of Fine Arts, Boston.

Eisleb, Dieter, and Renate Strelow
1980   *Altperuanische Kulturen: Tiahuanaco III.* Berlin: Museum für Völkerkunde.

Emery, Irene
1966   *The Primary Structures of Fabrics: An Illustrated Classification.* Washington, D.C.: Textile Museum.

Emmerich, André
1969   *Art of Ancient Peru.* New York: André Emmerich Gallery.

Fairbrother, Trevor
1991   *Connections: Brice Marden* (Exhibition Brochure). Boston: Museum of Fine Arts.

Flint, S.G.
1916   "Peruvian Textiles." *Bulletin of the Museum of Fine Arts, Boston* 14, no. 85, pp. 40–41.

Frame, Mary
1986   "The Visual Images of Fabric Structures in Ancient Peruvian Art." In *The Junius B. Bird Conference on Andean Textiles,* 1984, edited by Ann Pollard Rowe, pp. 47–80. Washington, D.C.: Textile Museum.
1989   "Research-in-Progress Report, Orientation and Symmetry: The Structuring of Pattern Repeats in the Paracas Necropolis Embroideries." In *Textiles as Primary Sources: Proceedings of the First Symposium of the Textile Society of America,* 1988, compiled by John E. Vollmer, pp. 136–138. St. Paul, Minn.: Textile Society of America.
1990   *Andean Four-Cornered Hats: Ancient Volumes.* From the Collection of Arthur M. Bullowa. New York: Metropolitan Museum of Art.

1991   "Structure, Image, and Abstraction: Paracas Necrópolis Headbands as System Templates." In *Paracas Art and Architecture: Object and Context in South Coastal Peru,* edited by Anne Paul, pp. 110–171. Iowa City: University of Iowa Press.

Fung Piñeda, Rosa
1978   "Analisis tecnológico de encajes del antiguo Peru: Periodo Tardío." In *Tecnológia Andina,* edited by Roger Ravines. Lima: Instituto de Investigación Tecnológica Industrial y de Normas Tecnicas.

Garaventa, Donna Marie
1979   "Chincha Textiles of the Late Intermediate Period, Epoch 8." *The Junius B. Bird Pre-Columbian Textile Conference,* 1973, edited by Ann Pollard Rowe, Elizabeth P. Benson, and Anne-Louise Schaffer, pp. 219–232. Washington, D.C.: Textile Museum and Dumbarton Oaks, Trustees for Harvard University.

Gasparini, Graziano, and Luise Margolies
1980   *Inca Architecture.* Translated from *Arquitectura Inka,* by Patricia J. Lyon. Bloomington: Indiana University Press.

Gayton, Anna H.
1973   "The Cultural Significance of Peruvian Textiles: Production, Function, Aesthetics." In *Peruvian Archaeology,* edited by John H. Rowe and Dorothy Menzel, pp. 275–292. Palo Alto: Peek Publications.

Goldwater, Robert
1986   *Primitivism in Modern Art.* Reprint of 1938. Cambridge: Harvard University Press.

Guaman Poma de Ayala, Felipe
1980a   *Nueva corónica y buen gobierno.* 2 vols. Transcripción , prologo, notas y cronología de Franklin Pease. Biblioteca Ayacucho, vols. 75–76. Caracas: Biblioteca Ayacucho. [Originally written about 1615.]
1980b   *El primer nueva corónica y buen gobierno.* 3 vols. Edición crítica de John V. Murra y Rolena Adorno. Mexico, D.F.: Siglo XXI Editores. [Originally written about 1615.]

Haberland, Wolfgang
1971   *American Indian Art: A Descriptive Catalogue.* (Collection of the Museum Rietberg.) Zurich: Atlantis Verlag.

Hagino, Jane Parker, and Karen E. Stothert
1983   "Weaving a Cotton Saddlebag on the Santa Elena Peninsula of Ecuador." *Textile Museum Journal* 22, pp. 19–32.

Harcourt, Raoul d'
1962   *Textiles of Ancient Peru and Their Techniques.* Edited by Grace G. Denny and Carolyn M. Osborne. Translated by Sadie Brown.

Seattle: University of WashingtonPress. [Revision and translation of *Les Textiles anciens du Pérou et leurs techniques.* Paris,1934.]

Helms, Mary W.
1981   "Precious Metals and Politics: Style and Ideology in the Intermediate Area and Peru." *Journal of Latin American Lore* 7, no. 2, pp. 215–238.

Herscher, Ellen
1983   "Stolen Treasures, Missing Links." *Archaeology* 36, no. 5, pp. 58–61.

Iten-Maritz, Johann
1977   *Turkish Carpets.* Tokyo: Kodansha; New York: Distributed by Harper & Row.

Jablonski, Edith
1976   "Peru." *American Fabrics and Fashions,* no. 108.

Jones, Julie
1964   *Art of Empire: The Inca of Peru.* New York: Museum of Primitive Art. Distributed by the New York Graphic Society, Greenwich, Conn.

Joyce, T.A.
1913   "A Peruvian Tapestry, Probably of the 17th Century." *Burlington Magazine* 23 (April–September), pp. 146–150.

Kajitani, Nobuko
1982   "The Textiles of the Andes." *Senshoku no bi (Textile Arts),* no. 20.

Kauffmann Doig, Federico
1980   *Manual de arqueologia peruana.* Lima: Ediciones Peisa.

Keatinge, Richard W.
1978   "The Pacatnamú Textiles." *Archaeology* 31, no. 2, pp. 30–41.

Kelemen, Pál
1943   *Medieval American Art.* 2 vols. New York: Macmillan Co.
1951   *Baroque and Rococo in Latin America.* New York: Macmillan Co.
1961   "Preliminary Study of Spanish Colonial Textiles." *Workshop Notes,* Paper no. 23, pp. 1–4. Washington, D.C.: Textile Museum.
1971   *Peruvian Colonial Painting.* Exhibition Catalogue. Brooklyn: Brooklyn Museum.

Kendrick, Albert Frank
1925   "A Peruvian Tapestry." *Burlington Magazine* 47 (December), pp. 292–297.
1927   "Textiles." In *Spanish Art.* Burlington Magazine Monograph II, pp. 59–70.
1928   "Art Treasures at the Grafton Galleries: Textiles." *Old Furniture* 4, no. 13, pp. 79–84.
1943   "Carpets and Tapestries from South America." *Burlington Magazine* 82 (February), pp. 41–42.

King, Mary Elizabeth
1968   "Some New Paracas Textile Techniques from Ocucaje, Peru." In *Verhandlungen des XXXVI-II Internationalen Amerikanistenkongresses, Stuttgart-Munich, 1968*, vol.1, pp. 369–377. Munich: K. Renner, 1969.

Kosok, Paul
1965   *Life, Land and Water in Ancient Peru.* New York: Long Island University Press.

Kubler, George
1946   "The Quechua in the Colonial World." In *Handbook of South American Indians*, vol. 2, edited by Julian H. Steward, pp. 331–410. Smithsonian Institution, Bureau of American Ethnology, Bulletin 143. Washington D.C.

1962   *The Shape of Time: Remarks on the History of Things.* New Haven: Yale University Press.

1984   *Art and Architecture of Ancient America: The Mexican, Maya and Andean Peoples.* 3rd ed. New York: Penguin Books.

Kubler, George, and Martin Soria
1959   *Art and Architecture in Spain and Portugal and Their American Dominions, 1500 to 1800.* Baltimore: Penguin Books.

Kühnel, Ernst, and Louise Bellinger
1953   *The Textile Museum Catalogue of Spanish Rugs: 12th century to 19th century.* Washington, D.C.: National Publishing Co. for the Textile Museum.

Lapiner, Alan
1976   *Pre-Columbian Art of South America.* New York: Harry N. Abrams.

Larsen, Jack Lenor
1986   *Interlacing: The Elemental Fabric.* Tokyo: Kodansha.

Lavalle, José A., and Werner Lang
1980   *Arte y tesoros del Peru: Tercera parte: Arte textil y adornos.* Lima: Banco de Crédito.

Lavalle, José A., and José Alejandro García Gonzalez
1988   *Arte Textil del Peru.* Lima: Industria Textil Piura.

Lechtman, Heather
1984   "Andean Value Systems and the Development of Prehistoric Metallurgy." *Technology and Culture* 25, no. 1, pp. 1–36.

Lehmann, Walter
1924   *The Art of Old Peru.* New York: E. Weyhe.

Lommel, Andreas
1977   *Altamerikanische Kunst Mexico-Peru: Katalog zur Ausstellung des Staatlichen Museums für Völkerkunde, München.* Munich: Staatliches Museum für Völkerkunde.

Lothrop, Samuel K., and Joy Mahler
1957   *A Chancay-Style Grave at Zapallan, Peru: An Analysis of Its Textiles, Pottery and Other Furnishings.* Papers of the Peabody Museum of Archaeology and Ethnology, Harvard University, vol. 50, no. 1. Cambridge: Peabody Museum of Archaeology and Ethnology.

Lothrop, Samuel K., W.F. Foshag, and Joy Mahler
1957   *Pre-Columbian Art: Robert Woods Bliss Collection.* New York: Phaidon Publishers.

Lumbreras, Luis Guillermo
1974   *The Peoples and Cultures of Ancient Peru.* Translated by Betty J. Meggers. Washington D.C.: Smithsonian Institution Press.

[1979?]   *Pre-Hispanic Textiles.* Translated from *Textiles Prehispánicos.* Lima: Librería ABC.

Maeyama, Sumiko
1976   *Pure Inka no orimono moyo (Pre-Inca Textile Patterns).* Tokyo: Gurafuikkusha.

Marcos, Jorge G.
1979   "Woven Textiles in a Late Valdivia Context (Ecuador)." In *The Junius B. Bird Pre-Columbian Textile Conference, 1973*, edited by Ann Pollard Rowe, Elizabeth P. Benson, and Anne-Louise Schaffer, pp. 19–26. Washington, D.C.: Textile Museum.

May, Florence Lewis
1939   *Hispanic Lace and Lace Making.* New York: Hispanic Society of America.

McIntyre, Loren
1973   "Lost Empire of the Incas." *National Geographic* 144, no. 6. pp. 729–787.

Means, Philip Ainsworth
1932   *A Study of Peruvian Textiles Illustrated by Representative Examples in the Museum of Fine Arts Boston.* Boston: Museum of Fine Arts.

Medlin, Mary Ann
1986   "Learning to Weave in Calcha, Bolivia." In *The Junius B. Bird Conference on Andean Textiles, 1984*, edited by Ann Pollard Rowe, pp. 275–288. Washington, D.C.: Textile Museum.

Menzel, Dorothy
1976   *Pottery Style and Society in Ancient Peru.* Berkeley: University of California Press.

Montell, Gösta
1929   *Dress and Ornaments in Ancient Peru.* Göteborg: Elanders Boktryckeri Aktiebolag.

Morris, Craig, and Donald E. Thompson
1985   *Huánuco Pampa, an Inca City and Its Hinterlands.* London: Thames and Hudson.

Morrison, Phylis
1979   *Spiders Games: A Book for Beginning Weavers.* Seattle: University of Washington Press.

Moseley, Michael
1975   *The Maritime Foundations of Andean Civilization.* Menlo Park, Calif.: Cummings Publishing Co.

Murra, John V.
1962   "Cloth and Its Function in the Inca State." *American Anthropologist* 64, no. 4, pp. 710–728.

1980   *The Economic Organization of the Inca State.* Research in Economic Anthropology, Supplement 1. Greenwich, Conn.: JAI Press.

1989   "Cloth and Its Function in the Inka State." In *Cloth and Human Experience*, edited by Annette B. Weiner and Jane Schneider, pp. 275–302. Washington D.C.: Smithsonian Institution Press.

Murúa, Martín de
1962–1964   *Historia general del Perú: Origen y descendencia de los Incas.* 2 vols. Madrid: Bibliotheca Americana Vetus. [Originally published 1611–1615].

Musées Royaux d'Art et d'Histoire, Brussels
1990   *Inca-Peru: 3000 ans d'histoire.* Brussels: Musées Royaux d'Art et d'Histoire.

Museum of Fine Arts, Boston
1907   *Handbook of the Museum of Fine Arts, Boston.*
1908   *Handbook of the Museum of Fine Arts, Boston.*
1911   *Handbook of the Museum of Fine Arts, Boston.*
1913   *Handbook of the Museum of Fine Arts, Boston.*
1914   *Handbook of the Museum of Fine Arts, Boston.*
1915   *Handbook of the Museum of Fine Arts, Boston.*
1916   *Handbook of the Museum of Fine Arts, Boston.*
1919   *Handbook of the Museum of Fine Arts, Boston.*
1920   *Handbook of the Museum of Fine Arts, Boston.*
1922   *Handbook of the Museum of Fine Arts, Boston.*
1961   *Twenty-five Centuries of Peruvian Art, 700B.C.–1800 A.D.* [Exhibition at] Peabody Museum, Harvard University, and Museum of Fine Arts, Boston. Boston: Museum of Fine Arts.
1964   *Illustrated Handbook of the Museum of Fine Arts, Boston.*
1965a   *Calendar of Events: April.* Museum of Fine Arts, Boston.
1965b   *1965—The Museum Year. The Ninetieth Annual Report of the Museum of Fine Arts, Boston.*
1976   *Illustrated Handbook of the Museum of Fine Arts, Boston.*
1980   *The Museum Year: 1979–80. The One Hundred Fourth Annual Report of the Museum of Fine Arts, Boston.*
1984   *Illustrated Handbook of the Museum of Fine Arts, Boston.*
1987   *Art for Boston: A Decade of Acquisitions under the Directorship of Jan Fontein.* Boston: Museum of Fine Arts.

1989   *Textile Masterpieces* (Exhibition Brochure). Boston: Museum of Fine Arts.

New York Times
1949   "Pre-Inca Mummy Cloth is 87 Feet in Length." *New York Times,* September 23, 1949, p. 26.

Niles, Susan A.
1987   "Niched Walls in Inca Design." *Journal of the Society of Architectural Historians* 46, no. 3, pp. 277–285.

O'Neale, Lila, and Bonnie Jean Clark
1948   *Textile Periods in Ancient Peru. III: The Gauze Weaves.* In American Archaeology and Ethnology, vol. 40, no. 4, pp. 143–222. Berkeley: University of California Press.

O'Neill, John P.
1984   "Featherwork: Introduction: Feather Identification." In *Costumes and Featherwork of the Lords of Chimor: Textiles from Peru's North Coast,* by Ann Pollard Rowe, pp. 144–150, Washington, D.C.: Textile Museum.

Paul, Anne
1985a   "The Stitching of Paracas Embroidered Images: Procedural Variations and Differences in Meaning." *Res: Anthropology and Aesthetics* 6, pp. 91–100.
1985b   "Pre-Hispanic Textiles of Peru." In *Peruvian Antiquities: A Manual for United States Customs,* pp. 23–34, Washington D.C.: Department of Cultural Affairs of the Organization of American States.
1986   "Un Manto de Paracas: La Coloración de sus figuras." *Boletín de Lima* 8, no. 48. pp. 19–33.
1988   "Color Repeats in Paracas Necropolis Embroideries." Paper presented at the 46th International Congress of Americanists, 1988. Amsterdam.
1990a   *Paracas Ritual Attire: Symbols of Authority in Ancient Peru.* Norman: University of Oklahoma Press.
1990b   "The Use of Color in Paracas Necrópolis Fabrics: What Does it Reveal about the Organization of Dyeing and Designing?" *National Geographic Research* 6, no. 2, pp. 7–21.
1991   "Paracas: An Ancient Cultural Tradition on the South Coast of Peru." In *Paracas Art and Architecture: Object and Context in South Coastal Peru,* edited by Anne Paul, pp. 1–34. Iowa City: University of Iowa Press.

Paul, Anne, and Susan A. Niles
1985   "Identifying Hands at Work on a Paracas Mantle." *Textile Museum Journal* 23, pp. 5–15.

Paul, Anne, and Solveig A. Turpin
1986   "The Ecstatic Shaman Theme of Paracas Textiles." *Archaeology* 39 (September–October), pp. 20–27.

Polakoff, Claire
1980   *Into Indigo: African Textiles and Dyeing Techniques.* Garden City, N. J.: Anchor Books.

Posnansky, Arthur
1933   *Precursores de Colón: Las Perlas Agri y la representaciones sobre tejidos artísticos, como prueba del descubrimiento de America antes de Colón.* Publicaciones de la Sociedad de Historia Argentina 1.
1945   *Tihuanacu: The Cradle of American Man.* Vol. 1. Translated by James F. Shearer. New York: J. J. Augustin.

Protzen, Jean-Pierre
1985   "Inca Quarrying and Stonecutting." *Journal of the Society of Architectural Historians* 44, pp. 161–182.

Prown, Jules D.
1980   "Style as Evidence." *Winterthur Portfolio* 15, no. 3, pp. 197–210.
1982   "Mind in Matter: An Introduction to Material Culture Theory and Method." *Winterthur Portfolio* 17, no. 1, pp. 1–19.

Reeves, Ruth
1949   "Pre-Columbian Fabrics of Peru." *Magazine of Art* 42, no. 2, pp. 103–107.

Reid, James W.
1985   *Huari.* Lima: Banco del Crédito del Perú.
1986   *Textile Masterpieces of Ancient Peru.* New York: Dover Press.

Reiss, Wilhelm, and Anton Stübel
1880–1887   *The Necropolis of Ancon in Peru: A Contribution to Our Knowledge of the Culture and Industries of the Empire of the Incas...* Translated by A.H. Keane. 3 vols. Berlin: A. Asher and Co.

Ross, Gary N.
1988   "Threads of Tradition." *Américas* 40, no. 4, pp. 16–21.

Rowe, Ann Pollard
1972   "Interlocking Warp and Weft in the Nasca 2 Style." *Textile Museum Journal* 3, no. 3, pp. 67–78.
1977   *Warp-Patterned Weaves of the Andes.* Washington D.C.: Textile Museum.
1978   "Technical Features of Inca Tapestry Tunics." *Textile Museum Journal* 17, pp. 5–28.
1979   "Seriation of an Ica-Style Garment Type." In *The Junius B. Bird Pre-Columbian Textile Conference, 1973,* edited by Ann Pollard Rowe, Elizabeth P. Benson, and Anne-Louise Schaffer, pp. 185–218. Washington, D.C.: Textile Museum and Dumbarton Oaks, Trustees for Harvard University.

1980   "Textiles from the Burial Platform of Las Avispas at Chan Chan." *Ñawpa Pacha* 18, pp. 81–148.
1984   *Costumes and Featherwork of the Lords of Chimor: Textiles from Peru's North Coast.* Washington, D.C.: Textile Museum.

Rowe, John H.
1946   "Inca Culture at the Time of the Spanish Conquest." In *Handbook of South American Indians,* edited by Julian H. Steward. Smithsonian Institution, Bureau of American Ethnology, Bulletin no. 143, vol. 2, pp. 183–330. Washington, D.C.
1948   "The Kingdom of Chimor." *Acta Americana* 6, pp. 26–59.
1957   "The Incas under Spanish Colonial Institutions." *Hispanic American Historical Review* 37, no. 2, pp. 155–199.
1962a   *Chavín Art: An Inquiry into its Form and Meaning.* New York: Museum of Primitive Art.
1962b   "Stages and Periods in Archaeological Interpretation." *Southwestern Journal of Anthropology* 18, no. 1, pp. 40–54.
1979   "Standardization in Inca Tapestry Tunics." In *The Junius B. Bird Pre-Columbian Textile Conference, 1973,* edited by Ann Pollard Rowe, Elizabeth P. Benson, and Anne-Louise Schaffer, pp. 239–264. Washington, D.C.: Textile Museum and Dumbarton Oaks, Trustees for Harvard University.

Salmon, Larry
1972   "Tapestry-woven Carpet." *Boston Museum Bulletin* 70, nos. 361–362, pp. 142–143.
1976   "The Bible in Peru." *Boston Museum Bulletin* 74, no. 370, pp. 87–93.

Salmon, Larry, Catherine Kvaraceus, and Matthew X. Kiernan
1980   *From Fiber to Fine Art.* Boston: Museum of Fine Arts.

Sarmiento de Gamboa, Pedro de
1960   *Historia de los Incas.* Biblioteca de Autores Españoles, vol. 135, pp. 195–279. Madrid: Edicions Atlas [Originally written in 1572].

Sawyer, Alan R.
1961   *Catalogue List: An Exhibition of Peruvian Spanish-Colonial Textiles.* Washington D.C.: Textile Museum.
1968a   *Master Craftsmen of Ancient Peru.* New York: Solomon R. Guggenheim Foundation.
1968b   *Catalogue List: An Exhibition of Tapestries of Colonial Peru.* Washington D.C.: Textile Museum.

1979   "Painted Nasca Textiles." In *The Junius B. Bird Pre-Columbian Textile Conference,* 1973, edited by Ann Pollard Rowe, Elizabeth P. Benson, and Anne-Louise Schaffer, pp. 129–150. Washington, D.C.: Textile Museum and Dumbarton Oaks, Trustees for Harvard University.

1988   "An Inca-Colonial Tapestry Shroud." Research Report. Department of Textiles, Museum of Fine Arts, Boston.

Schele, Linda, and Mary Ellen Miller
1986   *The Blood of Kings: Dynasty and Ritual in Maya Art.* Photographs by Justin Kerr. New York: Braziller, in association with Kimball Art Museum, Fort Worth.

Schmidt, Max
1929   *Kunst und Kultur von Peru.* Berlin: Propylaen-Verlag.

Schuler-Schömig, Immina von
1984   "Puppen oder Substitute?: Gedanken zur Bedeutung einer Gruppe von Grabbeigaben aus Peru." *Tribus: Jahrbuch des Linden Museums,* Stuttgart, Nr. 33.

Shimada, Izumi
1991   "Pachacamac Archaeology: Retrospect and Prospect." Introduction to *Pachacamac: A Reprint of the 1903 edition by Max Uhle.* Philadelphia: University Museum of Archaeology and Anthropology, University of Pennsylvania.

in press "The Regional States of the Coast during the Late Intermediate Period: Archaeological Evidence, Ethnohistorical Record and Art Outline." In *Pre-Inca States and Inca Kingdoms.* Milan: Jaca Book.

Skinner, Milica D.
1975   "Archaeological Looms from Peru in the American Museum of Natural History." *Irene Emery Roundtable on Museum Textiles,* 1974, *Proceedings: Archaeological Textiles,* edited by Patricia L. Fiske. Washington, D.C.: Textile Museum.

Smith, Leslie Melville
1985   "A Look at Painted Textiles from Peru in the Boston Museum of Fine Arts Collection." Harvard University Extension, Term paper. Photocopy in Department of Textiles and Costumes, Museum of Fine Arts.

1986   "When Textiles are Paintings." In *Symposium '86: The Care and Preservation of Ethnological Materials,* edited by R. Barclay, M. Gilbert, J.C. McCawley, and P. Stone. Ottawa: Canadian Conservation Institute.

Sotheby's, New York
1988   *Pre-Columbian Art.* Sale Catalogue, November 21.

Stafford, Cora
1941   *Paracas Embroideries: A Study of Repeated Pattern.* New York: J. J. Augustin.

Stone, Rebecca
1983   "Possible Uses, Roles, and Meanings of Chavín-style Painted Textiles of South Coast Peru." In *Investigations of the Andean Past: Papers from the First Annual Northeast Conference on Andean Archaeology and Ethnohistory,* pp. 57–74. Ithaca, N.Y.: Latin American Studies Program, Cornell University.

1986   "Color Patterning and the Huari Artist: The 'Lima Tapestry' Revisited." In *The Junius B. Bird Conference on Andean Textiles,* 1984, edited by Ann Pollard Rowe, pp. 137–149. Washington D.C.: Textile Museum.

1987   *Technique and Form in Huari-style Tapestry Tunics: The Andean Artist, A.D. 500–800.* Ph.D. dissertation, Yale University. 4 vols. Ann Arbor: University Microfilms.

Stone-Miller, Rebecca
1992   "Camelids and Chaos in Wari and Tiwanaku Textiles." In *The Ancient Americas: Art from Sacred Landscapes,* edited by Richard Townsend, pp. 334–345. Chicago: Art Institute of Chicago.

Stone-Miller, Rebecca, and Gordon F. McEwan
1990   "The Representation of the Wari State in Stone and Thread: A Comparison of Architecture and Tapestry Tunics." *Res: Anthropology and Aesthetics* 19–20, pp. 53–80.

Stothert, Karen
1979a   "Preparing a Mummy Bundle: Note on a Late Burial from Ancon, Peru." *Ñawpa Pacha* 16, pp. 13–24.

1979b   "Unwrapping an Inca Mummy Bundle." *Archaeology* 32 July–August.

1981   "Corrections for the Published Descriptions of a Late Horizon Mummy Bundle from Ancon." *Ñawpa Pacha* 19, pp. 177–188.

Taullard, Alfredo
1949   *Tejidos y ponchos indígenas de Sudamérica.* Buenos Aires: G. Kraft.

Tello, Julio C., and Toribio Mejía Xesspe
1979   *Paracas. Segunda parte: Cavernas y Necrópolis.* Publicación Antropológica del Archivo "Julio C. Tello." Lima: Universidad Nacional Mayor de San Marcos, and The Institute of Andean Research of New York.

Topic, John R., Jr.
1982   "Lower Class Social and Economic Organization at Chan Chan." In *Chan Chan: Andean Desert City,* edited by Michael E. Moseley and Kent C. Day. Albuquerque: School of American Research, University of New Mexico.

Townsend, Gertrude
1932   "Color in Peruvian Embroideries." *Bulletin of the Museum of Fine Arts, Boston* 30, no. 180, pp. 61–64.

1933   "The Coat of Arms on a Piece of Peruvian Tapesty." *Bulletin of the Museum of Fine Arts, Boston* 31, no. 185, pp. 47–48.

Tsunoyama, Yukitiro
1977   *Textiles of the Pre-Incaic Period: Catalogue of Amano Collection.* Kyoto: Dohosha.

Tuchscherer, Jean-Michel
1988   "Mantle." In *The Museum Year 1987–88: The One Hundred Twelfth Annual Report of the Museum of Fine Arts, Boston,* p. 37.

Tushingham, A. D.
1976   *Gold for the Gods.* Toronto: Royal Ontario Museum.

Uhle, Max
1903   *Pachacamac: Report of the William Pepper, M.D., LL.D., Peruvian Expedition of 1896.* Philadelphia: Department of Archaeology, University of Pennsylvania.

Van de Put, Albert, and A. F. Kendrick
1928   "A Peruvian Tapestry and Some Spanish Weavings." *Burlington Magazine* 53, pp. 24–30.

VanStan, Ina
1961   "Miniature Peruvian Shirts with Horizontal Openings." *American Antiquity* 26, no. 4, pp. 524–531.

1966   *Fabrics of Peru.* Leigh-on-Sea, Eng.: F. Lewis.

1967   *Textiles from Beneath the Temple of Pachacamac, Peru: A Part of the Uhle Collection.* Philadelphia: University Museum of Archaeology and Anthropology, University of Pennsylvania.

1979   "Did Inca Weavers Use an Upright Loom?" In *The Junius B. Bird Pre-Columbian Textile Conference,* 1973, edited by Ann Pollard Rowe, Elizabeth P. Benson, and Anne-Louise Schaffer, pp. 233–238. Washington, D.C.: Textile Museum, Trustees for Harvard University.

Victoria and Albert Museum
1926   *Brief Guide to the Peruvian Textiles.* Department of Textiles. London: Published under the authority of the Board of Education.

Villanueva Urteaga, Horacio
1982   *Cuzco 1689: Economía y sociedad en el sur andino.* Cuzco: Centro de Estudios Rurales Andinos "Bartolomé de las Casas."

von Hagen, Victor W.
1976   *The Incas of Pedro de Cieza de León.*
          Translated by Harriet de Onis. Norman:
          University of Oklahoma Press. [Originally
          written in 1550–1553.]

Wardle, H. Newell
1944   "Triple Cloth: New Types of Ancient Peruvian
          Technique." *American Anthropology* 46, no. 3.
          pp. 416–418.

Washburn, Dorothy K., and Donald W. Crowe
1988   *Symmetries of Culture, Theory and Practice of
          Plane Pattern Analysis.* Seattle: University of
          Washington Press.

Weibel, Adele Coulin
1936   "Fabrics from Old Peru." *Bulletin of the Detroit
          Institute of Arts* 16, no. 1, pp.13–14.
1939   "'Creolerie,' a Peruvian Tapestry of the
          Spanish-Colonial Period." *Art Quarterly* 2, no.
          3, pp. 197–206.

Young, Margaret
1985   "The Chancay Textile Tradition: Textiles from
          Lauri in the Collection of the Amano
          Museum." Master's thesis, Columbia
          University.

Zevallos Quiñones, Jorge
1973   "La ropa tributo de las encomiendas trujil-
          lanas en el siglo XVI." *Historia y Cultura* 7,
          pp. 107–127.

Zick, Gisela
1976   "Callot in Peru: Notes on a Tapestry and Its
          Graphic Sources." *Boston Museum Bulletin* 74,
          no. 370, pp. 72-85.

Zimmern, Nathalie H.
1944   "The Tapestries of Colonial Peru." *Brooklyn
          Museum Journal, 1943–1944*, pp. 25–52.

Zuidema, Reiner Tom
1977   "The Inca Calendar." In *Native American
          Astronomy*, edited by A. F. Aveni, pp. 219–259.
          Austin: University of Texas Press.